T0096108

I HAVE CONTROL

A PILOT'S VIEW OF CHANGING
AIRLINER TECHNOLOGY

Related titles from Airlife

Emergency – Crisis on the Flight Deck
Flying the Big Jets
Flying the Airbus A380
Flying the Boeing 787
The Naked Pilot – The Human Factor in Aircraft Accidents
To be an Airline Pilot

I HAVE CONTROL

A PILOT'S VIEW OF CHANGING AIRLINER TECHNOLOGY

KEITH SPRAGG

Airlife

First published in 2018 by
Airlife Publishing, an imprint of
The Crowood Press Ltd
Ramsbury, Marlborough
Wiltshire SN8 2HR

www.crowood.com

© Keith Spragg 2018

British Library Cataloguing-in-Publication Data
A catalogue record for this book is available from the British Library.

ISBN 978 1 78500 397 4

Front cover images:
ABOVE: Three hundred and forty Souls On Board. The largest aircraft
Keith flew, the Boeing 767-300ER with a maximum weight of over
185 metric tonnes and a range in excess of 6,000 miles.
DEAN MORLEY VIA FOTER.COM

BELOW: Keith's first airliner and the end of an era. A Vickers VC1
Viking of Autair International Airways about to depart from Luton
airport in the late 1960s. KURT LANG

Typeset by Jean Cussons Typesetting, Diss, Norfolk

Printed and bound in India by Parksons Graphics

Contents

Introduction

There is something special about flying. In previous times, people turned to the sea if they yearned for adventure and those who found it sometimes wrote accounts of their experiences that inspired countless others to follow in their wake. As a boy I read the books of Arthur Ransome and dreamt of going to sea myself, but this idea was gradually overpowered by the flying stories I read later. The early aviation pioneers, the record breakers in the 1930s and the British test pilots who, in the 1950s, were pushing the boundaries of speed, altitude and distance, described something that was, to me, even more exciting.

By my eleventh birthday it was decided: I was going to be a pilot. Of course, at that age one does not consider the difficulties that might be encountered when one attempts to follow one's dream. I belonged to a normal, working-class family. My father was a printer, a seven-year apprenticeship, hot-metal man, who wanted a safe, reliable trade for his two sons. While we enjoyed a good standard of living, it was hard-earned and there was little money to spare. My mother was widely read and had more sympathy for our aspirations, but we were really not the sort of people who flew. Worse, I was not academically gifted. I hated school and it was not until I was fourteen that I even began to understand the connection between examinations and employment.

The conventional answer to my problem was to join the Royal Air Force, a route many young men like me had taken with success. For a long time it seemed that I had no alternative. I joined my local Air Training Corps squadron, made some good friends, learnt a lot and enjoyed a variety of sports, but my heart was not in the military. The RAF wanted officers to lead and to fight; flying was incidental to the task. I just wanted to fly and the conviction was growing in me that the life of an airline pilot would be the ultimate expression of my desire.

Turning my back on the RAF delivered a strong dose of reality. There followed a frustrating period where I worked at various jobs while searching all the time for some way into civilian flying. A Commercial Pilot's Licence is the basic requirement for being paid to fly and at the time, in addition to passing the exams and tests, the experience requirement was 150 flying hours. It seemed not an insurmountable total, given the availability and relatively low cost of ex-wartime Austers and Tiger Moths at local flying clubs. But I wanted the best possible training, so I sold my car, scraped together my savings and embarked on a course of training for my Private Pilot's Licence with the Oxford Air Training School's centre at Elmdon Airport, Birmingham.

Just as I received my Private Pilot's Licence and started to build my hours, a Government Committee on Pilot Training changed the rules. The experience requirement for a Commercial Licence was raised to 700 hours. It looked hopeless, but my determination had been noticed and some people had faith in me. Principal among these was Gordon 'Ginger' Bedggood, Chief Flying Instructor at Birmingham who offered me a contract to work as a general dogsbody at his new school with minimal payment, but with training to become an assistant flying instructor. At that time, a flying instructor did not need a Commercial Pilot's Licence, provided that he and his students belonged to a registered club. Four years later, in 1967 I had the licences I needed to fly for an airline.

I joined Autair International Airways as a co-pilot on the Viking Freighter at its base in Berlin, later moving to Luton on the Handley Page Dart-Herald and then the BAC1-11. I got my command on the BAC1-11 in April 1971. Autair became Court Line Aviation and expanded rapidly, until it went bust in 1974. After a brief spell of unemployment, I joined Monarch Airlines, again on the BAC1-11, then, in 1975, Royal Brunei Airlines, which was just starting a new operation in Brunei with Boeing 737-200 aircraft.

Four years later, I joined Cathay Pacific Airlines as a first officer on the Boeing 707 aircraft, but returned to the UK to join the new Orion Airways, again initially on the Boeing 737-200. I qualified as an instructor and examiner with Orion (IRE/TRE) on the Boeing 737-200, 737-300 and Airbus A300B4. When Orion was taken over by Britannia, I joined TEA – Trans European Airways – as a trainer on the Boeing 737 until that company too folded.

My last employment was with Airtours International (since renamed as MyTravel and now merged with Thomas Cook), first as a captain on the MD83, then as a trainer on the Boeing 767, Boeing 757 and the Airbus A320/321, serving briefly as Long-Haul Fleet Manager. I retired in 2001, having accumulated a total of 17,200 flying hours, including over 12,000 hours in command on jet transport aircraft and a further 2,500 hours in flight simulators.

This book contains my reflections on those thirty years. Many airline pilots stay with one airline throughout their careers. They are discouraged from changing employers by the seniority system that ensures, should they decide to switch, they will have to start again as the most junior co-pilot in the fleet. It is only when new airlines are formed, or during periods of unusually rapid expansion, that direct-entry captains are accepted. Had Court Line survived, I would probably have stayed with them until I retired. But they went bust during the fuel crisis of 1974 and I was launched onto a more varied path.

It was all great fun. Some of the changes that followed were enforced by financial failures or takeovers, some through my own efforts, but throughout I was extraordinarily fortunate. I remain forever grateful to my family, friends and colleagues who helped me along the way. The flying always lived up to its promise and I never once regretted the course I had taken. Even when I eventually encountered medical problems and lost my licence, I was conscious more of how lucky I had been than of any disappointment at no longer being able to fly.

It is natural to want to share some of that experience with others, but I had read enough self-indulgent autobiographies and didn't want to inflict another one of those on anyone who might be interested in what I had to say. So I thought long and hard to determine what was unique about my experience. I tried to see my career in context, to understand what was happening to society during that period and what I had learnt that would be relevant to other people's lives.

It was not difficult to see that changing technology has had, and continues to have, great influence on people's lives. In many ways, aviation is at the forefront of the introduction of technology and I realized I had witnessed a broad spectrum of change through the aeroplane types I had flown. Just as my father's trade was to be superseded by computer layout and printing techniques, and the pens and pencils of my brother's days as an engineering draughtsman were to be overtaken by computer-aided design, so the basic flying and airmanship skills I had learnt during my training were being threatened by sophisticated digital autopilots and Flight Management Systems (FMS). The days of 'a job for life' are long gone and the idea of 'taking up a trade' is antiquated. What I came to understand while writing this book is that opposition to technological progress is futile, but that is certainly no cause for despair. Technology can make life safer, more productive and more rewarding. It can relieve us of boring, repetitive jobs and allow more of us to enjoy creative and interesting work. The Luddites are wrong. Young men and women will encounter great changes over the course of their adult lives, but they must still follow their dreams. Their focus may initially be narrow, but they must learn to broaden their interests and to explore new opportunities so that they can be flexible in the knowledge, skills and attitudes they acquire. As a society, we should pay more attention to ensuring that technology is developed in accordance with human needs and aspirations, helping to satisfy them, and to make full use of them, not to banish them. With the imminent introduction of computers making use of Artificial Intelligence, these two requirements – keeping an open mind and developing technology that is subservient to human needs – are more important than ever.

CHAPTER 1

As It Was

The light is fading as we drone over featureless stratus cloud towards Wolfsburg at the entrance of the Centre Corridor that leads to Berlin. My captain, known to everyone as Speedy because his reactions are so slow, is tapping his foot in time to the brass band music that I know is playing through his headphones. His bushy eyebrows move randomly. The smoke from his cigarette curls lazily up from his hand on the control wheel before it is drawn away through the open side window.

'Tempelhof is below limits, Speedy,' I say. He doesn't respond, so I wave the weather reports under his nose. He takes them, scanning them without a word.

God, he annoys me! I've got nearly 2,000 hours and reckon I know a bit about flying, but I'm completely ignored. Under the regulations, we are forbidden to enter the corridor unless the cloud base at our destination is at least 300ft and the visibility is more than 600m.

In a few minutes it will be too late; we can't turn round in the corridor.

'Hanover?' I prompt. The ash on his cigarette grows another quarter of an inch. I wait. The foot keeps tapping and, bizarrely, I seem to detect Procol Harum's 'Whiter Shade of Pale' running through the harmonics from the engines and propellers. Why can't the Old B... make a decision?

Eventually, he takes a long drag on his cigarette, holds it nearer the window so that the ash is whisked cleanly away, and speaks. 'We'll just have a look,' he says.

Have a look? What's he talking about? We're not allowed to 'have a look'. But I know he won't listen to anything I say, so I get out the charts for an Instrument Landing System (ILS) approach to runway 27 Left at Tempelhof. I study the go-around procedure and the route we will have to take from there to Hanover. We have enough fuel, but not much extra.

I change frequency to the American controller in Berlin, who identifies us on radar and, when we get nearer to the airfield, starts to give us vectors towards final approach. We descend into cloud and it is immediately darker. There is light turbulence. Ice starts to form on the airframe and round the engine air intakes, but this soon changes to rain, rattling like hail on our cockpit. Water flows in through the windscreen and drips onto our knees. I get an update on the weather – it's worse, but Speedy only grunts.

'You are cleared to descend with the glide path.' The controller sounds bored, near the end of his shift and ready for a drink. 'Contact Tower now gentlemen, Good day!'

The gear is down and locked, checklist completed, we're cleared to land or go-around. Apart from the final extension of flap, which in this aircraft is never made until a landing is assured, I have nothing to do but monitor the instruments and call the heights.

'One hundred above!' I call at exactly 300ft above airfield level. We must have the approach lights in sight at 200ft or apply full power and climb away. It is fully dark now and still turbulent.

'Wipers!' I flick the rotary switch on the overhead panel and the archaic system of rods and cranks whirls into life, though the wipers make absolutely no impression on the water streaming over the screens. I can't see a thing outside.

I am impressed, reluctantly, by the precision of Speedy's flying. The electronic instrument landing beams are very narrow at this level and the lower speed of the aircraft demands larger control movements, but he keeps the needles exactly centred. He makes swift, nervous corrections to the control wheel. His eyebrows are thrashing about now too and his face is twitching.

'Minimums!' I call, moving my hand toward the throttles to make sure they go fully forward.

'Full flap!' Speedy shouts.

What? Full flap means we're landing, but nothing beyond the windscreen has changed. I can't even detect a lightening of the black void to indicate we're over the approach lights.

'Full flap!' Speedy curses, so I select it, feeling the aircraft pitch down as the drag increases, open mouthed in disbelief, amazed at how Speedy keeps the needles centred, despite the change of trim. His movements are now an intense blur.

Outside, we are still in complete blackness and streaming rain. There is a swish of tyres on wet tarmac and then one dim light slides down the right-hand side of the aircraft. There's another, and another, on the left this time, and then a string of runway lights appears to show that we are slowing in the centre of the runway.

We turn off the runway and taxi to the apron in silence. Speedy is a criminal and I'm an accessory. But I'm in awe of the most amazing piece of flying I've ever seen, a display of unbelievable skill.

When the doors are opened everyone is disturbingly normal. The engineers and the customs men are all as courteous and welcoming as ever. Don't they understand that Speedy has got us here by a miracle? He's made a completely blind landing hand-flying an ancient aeroplane with very basic instruments.

He has already packed his stuff away and got his raincoat on while I complete the paperwork. He picks up his briefcase. He never says good morning or goodbye; usually he just stalks off. He's an ignorant, bad-tempered old tyrant. But tonight he pauses to look me in the eye. Could that be the ghost of a smile on his lips? He gives a broad wink, and then he is gone.

CHAPTER 2

To Berlin .

There aren't any characters nowadays, I thought. Not like there used to be. I was browsing through my old logbooks, thinking about the early years of my career as an airline pilot. The pages from 1967 and 1968 contained only the bare facts of each flight:

REGISTRATION: G-AGRW   TYPE: Vickers VC1 Viking
FROM: Schipol   TO: Tempelhof
DEPARTURE: 1400   ARRIVAL: 1630
TOTAL TIME: 2 hours 30 minutes

Here and there, when the captain had graciously allowed me to land the aircraft myself, he had added his signature to authenticate the claim.

When I turned a page, a photograph slipped out. It revealed a youthful version of me sitting at the controls of the piston-engined freighter. My uniform carried a single gold stripe. The windscreen was edged in wood and the profusion of large, strangely shaped levers and mysterious dials had clearly not been influenced by modern ergonomic design.

Memories surfaced quicker than I could organize them: the excitement of living in the divided city of Berlin, the hippy phenomenon and student riots, and how cold it used to be in the unheated aircraft. The flight deck had been noisy and everything vibrated, but, despite its nickname of 'The Pig', the Viking handled beautifully in the air. The flying control surfaces were linked directly by pushrods, cranks and cables to the control column – no power assistance – and the airflow made it come alive. Flying it had felt like stroking a wild animal.

I reached for a drink and suddenly I could smell that cockpit once again. Spilt coffee had made the controls and radio panels sticky. The odours of fuel, leather and hot electrics, mixed with the accumulated dust and grime of the cargoes we carried, came back to me. At once I was slouching again in that comfortable leather co-pilot's seat.

An idea was forming: it seemed to me to have been an extraordinary journey from junior co-pilot on a piston-engined freighter to modern airline captain. Should I write about it? Would anybody want to read what I wrote? The lack of a literary tradition was discouraging. I knew of only two memoirs by airline pilots: *A Million Miles in the Air* by Captain Gordon P. Olley[1] and *Fate is the Hunter* by E.K. Gann.[2] Olley was an

Imperial Airways pilot who wrote his book in 1934. He was an early pioneer who made seventeen forced landings during his first passenger service from London to Paris; his story was obviously justified by its historical significance. Gann was an accomplished professional writer whose record of his airline experiences from the 1930s, through World War II and into the 1950s has become a classic; it is regarded as compulsory reading for anyone who flies.

There was nothing that had been written later, a fact that argued for doing something about it, but alongside these two great books, any effort of my own would be modest indeed. I am just one of many people who did this job. I fought no wars, had no crashes and never got my name in the papers. I would have to concentrate simply on what life was like for an airline pilot during my years in the job. It would be nice to capture some of the magic, but that would involve describing emotions, which is the very antithesis of an airline pilot's creed. Flying may be seen by some to be an exotic way to earn a living, but the truth is, of course, more prosaic and my erstwhile colleagues would be quick to ridicule my efforts if I tried to glamorize it. Pilots are no different to people in any other profession. The slim, grey-haired veteran who commands immense respect, looking elegant in his immaculate uniform, exists; so too does one of the best airline pilots I flew with. He was a short, overweight, unshaven scruff who carried his manuals and night-stop gear in a plastic carrier bag. All I could do would be to aim to keep it simple, to confine myself to my own personal impressions and to be honest. At the very least I might encourage some of my contemporaries, who have more interesting stories to tell, to pick up their pens or settle to their word processors.

It didn't seem enough. I dismissed the idea several times, but further thought made me conscious of another story that ran parallel with my own. During the time I was airline flying, the aircraft changed significantly. From hastily designed post-World War II piston-engined types with low power, poor performance and very basic equipment, we progressed to high-performance, pressurized jets. Then came the sophisticated autopilots, remarkably accurate navigational aids and computerized Flight Management Systems. The progression from simple, manually operated equipment to semi-automatic machines was a story about to be re-enacted in many other fields, not least in the cars we all drive. My own unspectacular participation in the history of aviation had coincided with a revolution in technology. I had first-hand experience of the highs and lows of that revolution.

The accident rate had improved dramatically during my time, too. I couldn't claim any responsibility for that improvement, but I had occupied the best possible seat from which to see it happen. I had taken part in the changes in working practices that were demanded during that revolution. People are still made out of the original model human being, with the same potential for brilliance and incompetence, but the way pilots go about their work is very different now from how it was when I joined an airline and I witnessed that change at first hand. When I reflected on the changes, I saw them as a war between skill and technology. Like all wars, it had destroyed some of the good along with the bad. What was needed for safe, reliable airline operation was a perfect blend of skill and technology. But skill had been annihilated. Technology had won the war against accidents and the depletion of human skill was collateral damage. Now we are seeing the consequences. Perhaps I had a story to tell after all.

*　　*　　*

I joined my first airline in 1967 and flew as an airline pilot continuously, except for two brief periods of unemployment, until 1998. As I get older, I begin to realize just how short a period of time that is. The rate of technical progress during that time seems incredible. Thirty-one years represented about one-third of the total history of aviation up to the time I stopped flying and nearly half of the history of airline flying.

The order for me to proceed to Berlin had arrived by telegram. Today, in the age of email and mobile phones, it is difficult to understand the fear that form of message could generate. The typed strips on the yellow paper, its buff envelope, the uniformed delivery lad on his red bicycle, all these were associated with bad news by my parents who had lived through the war in Coventry, bringing up my brother and myself during the tough years of air raids, rationing and shortages. Even more than twenty years after the war had ended, while they were proud of what I had achieved and pleased that I had got the job I wanted, they still had difficulty seeing aeroplanes as anything other than evil things that crashed or dropped bombs.

But times were changing. The piston-engined airliner was being abandoned as a transport system at just about the same time as the telegraph concluded its role in the world of communications.

It is not just the technology that has changed. The way people go about their jobs has changed, too. Speedy would not survive in an airline today; his uncommunicative arrogance and cavalier attitude to regulations would be unacceptable to management. Although still legally liable for the safety of the aircraft, its crew and its passengers or cargo, a captain today is allowed very little discretion. He is expected to make decisions by consensus, discussing problems with the first officer and cabin crew, and to consult with air traffic controllers, engineers and operations specialists by radio. Above all, the company's Standard Operating Procedures (SOPs) guide his every action. Even Speedy's immense flying skill would atrophy in a fly-by-wire airliner where computers move the controls and the idea of disconnecting the autopilot is frowned upon. To me, even in 1967, Speedy was out of date, a relic.

Of course this happens, to some extent, in every field of human activity. The old generation must give way to the new. But in airline flying, a relatively new industry driven by technological progress, that ancient struggle is accelerated. New technology demands new attitudes. Pilots acquire new knowledge and learn new skills all the time, but attitudes develop more slowly and less consciously. While we can always learn how new technology works and master the techniques of operating it, our understanding of the job itself, our values and priorities, are informed by our previous experience. Attitudes are formed mainly in our teens or twenties and are resistant to change thereafter. So eventually, as the job changes, we get left behind.

No doubt the young pilots I flew with at the end of my career saw me as a dinosaur. It is an odd conceit we perpetuate when we imagine life evolving in a continuum from cavemen to spacemen. Our experience contradicts that model. Children take space travel, genetic modification and nanotechnology for granted and yet, by the time they come to retire, they will have become dinosaurs themselves. As individuals, we travel backwards from the cutting edge of technology to the Stone Age. So be it. The process has been necessary to turn airline flying into a safe, reliable transport system, but something has been lost along the way. When my memory sparks, the world I recall is more sensual and exciting than the sterile atmosphere of a modern airliner flight deck. I hear the rush of the real wind, not the roar of the air-conditioning system. And I remember characters whose skills and attitudes were forged in a more testing environment than the one ruled by Health and Safety regulations today.

In 1967, Europe – the world – was in a state of great change. The women's liberation movement was at its height. Only the year before, *Time* magazine had featured London on its cover and dubbed it 'the swinging city'. The birth-control pill had become available and in sex, art, music, fashion and philosophy, young people were challenging the old order. Berlin itself, the divided city, saw student riots mirroring those in Paris. But in our little world of airline flying, the revolution was more modest; it meant not calling the captain 'Sir'. Our revolution was slower to take off, patchy and less dramatic, but it was there and it was serious.

Speedy didn't seem to notice. I sometimes wondered if he would notice if I didn't turn up for the flight. He was so self-contained that he would probably have done the whole trip without realizing that the right-hand seat was empty.

Toppling hierarchical structures seems to be a side effect of technology, so with the ongoing changes in the airline industry it would be surprising if tensions did not arise from time to time. Of course, new technology does not come into airlines as soon as it is invented; apart from the years of testing and development and the rigorous certification processes, there has to be a clear and pressing need for it. In commercial aviation the rules of survival are brutal. During the good times airlines can generate real money; fill the seats, charge high prices, keep the aircraft flying and all of the financial director's dreams come true. When business is booming, turnover, profit and the all-important cash flow can reach levels that make other businesses seem pedestrian. But the good times do not come very often and they never last long enough. Ever since the first airlines were formed in the 1920s they have struggled with high overhead costs. There are few ways of losing money more quickly than an unprofitable airline.

So while there is a constant spur for more efficient aircraft, the money for new equipment is almost always tight. Older aircraft are rarely updated once they are in service. Unless a real financial benefit can be proved, with a short payback time, it is better to wait until it is possible to borrow against new aircraft. This means that many of the world's airline pilots soldier on with relatively ancient aircraft for much of the time.

That's why my first airline job was on a piston-engined freighter at a time when jets had been in service with some companies for several years. The outfit I joined was an anachronism, a hangover from the Berlin Airlift. The operation depended upon a single contract to carry fresh flowers, which the Berliners valued highly, from Amsterdam every day. Any other work that came along was a boost, but we stayed in business only by virtue of minimal costs and exceptional personal relationships between the principal businessmen involved. The shipper was used to us, knew we were reliable, and had enjoyed a long friendship with Herr Friedrich, the highly respected manager of our Berlin base. The directors of our parent airline back in the UK were more interested in scheduled passenger services, but they tolerated the Berlin operation because they could find no other work for the freighters. The two resident captains were both trainers and it provided an excellent training ground for new co-pilots.

I might have started on a more modern aircraft. A promised job with a UK airline operating Viscounts was withdrawn at the last minute and I had to chase around to find a sponsor for the Instrument Rating course I had booked with Tony Mack's training school at Gatwick. I was offered an interview in Luton and dashed down the M1 in my old Ford Anglia, uncomfortably attired in my best suit.

Five minutes: that's how long the interview lasted. I couldn't believe what my watch was telling me. After all the years of dreaming, sacrificing and scheming, after all that studying, the written examinations, flying tests, raised hopes and hopes dashed, I got the job. The office, built on a gallery against the end wall of a hangar, had been tiny. The Chief Pilot and the Flight Operations Director had been squashed together at a little table. I had to squirm round the door and shuffle awkwardly into the chair facing them. And then I was standing outside again, five minutes later, looking down from the gallery on to the hangar floor where engineers were working on a piston-engined airliner. Not only did I now work for the same company as them, I was being paid to do my Instrument Rating training. The motherly secretary in the next tiny office promised to write to confirm the arrangements and wished me luck. It seemed too easy.

Of course, it hadn't been easy. What was remarkable was that I had finally got through to people who made decisions, people who knew what they wanted and had the knowledge and confidence – and the cash – to make it happen, quickly. With the financial burden lifted the Instrument Rating training was a delight. Then came Berlin and real airline flying. I knew I was immensely fortunate to get into the business and, as the years have gone by, I've come to realize more and more just how lucky I was to start where I did on the Viking in Berlin. I was twenty-seven years of age and hungry for every scrap of knowledge I could glean about my new job.

CHAPTER 3

The Viking

The Vickers Viking had been developed from the wartime Wellington, mainstay of RAF Bomber Command, and many of the captains I flew with had learnt their trade on the original bomber. The changes were extensive; most of Barnes Wallis's geodetic structure had been replaced by a more conventional stressed-skin construction, but, if you climbed up inside the engine nacelles and looked at the interior of the wing centre section, you could still see some of the diamond-shaped geodetic links. A stressed-skin shell of considerably wider proportions had replaced the bomber's fuselage. The engines, wing planform, flight controls and systems had been retained, together with the undercarriage that was of the tail-wheel type. But the aircraft's heart was in its engines; wonderful double-row, sleeve-valve radials giving 1,690 horsepower each and driving elegant, four-bladed, 12ft diameter constant speed propellers. It could cruise at 200mph, a high speed for its day, though its plump appearance led some people to suggest it was a fat version of the Douglas DC-3 and caused others to nickname it 'The Pig'.

It is often said that the Americans took advantage of Britain's preoccupation with the war in Europe to develop superior commercial aircraft ready for when the war ended. There is some truth in that, but in fact Britain had been neglecting airliner development in the years between the wars too, clinging to biplanes for far too long and then concentrating on flying boats. The Viking was one of several attempts during the later stages of the war to catch up and to have the Viking in service by 1946 was a considerable achievement. If it wasn't exactly pretty, it was quick and though it was twenty years old by the time I got my hands on it, I found it delightful to fly.

We had two of these aircraft: G-AGRW and G-AHPB, both full of character and rejoicing in the names of 'Vagabond' and 'Variety'. In addition to these names painted in fading letters on the nose, there was a smaller legend that the engineers had added above the crew hatch that we sometimes used to gain access to the flight deck when the fuselage was full of freight. It referred vaguely to livestock we sometimes carried and obliquely to the great esteem in which aircrew are held by engineers. It read: 'Pigs in other end'.

Out of respect for their age and in order to keep fuel costs down, we cruised at a much reduced speed, but the Vikings were ideal for the job, carrying over 3 tons of cut flowers in cardboard boxes and bulking out at just about maximum take-off weight. On the ground, their handling was unpredictable due to the odd undercarriage layout and the fact that the fat fuselage shielded the fin, but in the air they were superb.

Flight instruments were basic, but in addition to the trusty old Automatic Direction Finder (ADF), or radio compass, we had VHF Omnidirectional Range (VOR) and ILS, which was the standard navigation equipment for all western airliners from the end of World War II until the 1980s and is still in use today. We could operate to weather limits of 200ft and 600m, the same as everyone else, until the fancy autopilots capable of autoland came along.

We had an autopilot too. An early Sperry affair, which could do a fair job of holding height and heading, providing the aircraft was set up properly in trim before the great lever was pulled back to engage it. It had to be disengaged whenever a change of heading was required; the aircraft would be hand-flown through the turn, an estimate made for drift on the new track and, when all was set, the autopilot zeroed and re-engaged. A Vernier knob, provided to allow small adjustments to rudder trim, could be turned to make small corrections to heading, but if this was overdone, the aircraft ended up out of balance. Speedy made great use of this feature. Apparently absorbed in his *Daily Express*, which he had purchased in Amsterdam, and wreathed in smoke from his cigarette, he would suddenly and apparently randomly lunge forward and spin the knob violently. It would not be long before the aircraft was flying sideways, one wing low, in a crabbing motion. This would become most uncomfortable for his luckless co-pilot. When I could not stand it any longer I would boldly take the autopilot out, set everything back to zero and re-engage it, while Speedy looked up from his newspaper and curled his lip in disgust.

The aircraft was unpressurized and we did not carry oxygen, so we were limited to 10,000ft altitude, though occasionally we would go higher for a short time to get over cloud build-ups. We did have a quite effective de-icing system that supplied liquid to the leading edges of the flying surfaces through porous metal strips, but there was no weather radar.

There was plenty to learn. It was technical and operational at first. The Viking was so much more complicated than the aircraft I had flown up until then. The routines for starting and operating the engines, for instance, understanding the fuel system and engine cooling system and coming to terms with the importance of the weight and balance limitations; all these tasks took my knowledge to a new level. The route we flew to Amsterdam and return was simple enough, but it involved procedures that were new to me. I learnt more about the air itself, too, such as how to negotiate cloud and turbulence, as well as ice and strong winds.

I was also learning the lore that pilots had built up for themselves over forty years of airline flying. Anyone who joins an airline will have a reasonable amount of flying experience and will therefore have accumulated his own ideas about how things should be done. It is natural that he will tend to resort to those methods in moments of doubt, but an airline pilot is paid to do things the airline's way. It takes time and not a little effort to change, particularly if the previous experience has been in single-pilot aircraft, or if it involved an independent, quick-reaction, culture.

I learnt to ensure that any figures I wrote down were clear and legible. My handwriting was awful and has deteriorated since, but even today I cross my sevens and my Zs. I never operate two switches at the same time either – find out if you have operated the right switch on one engine, that it has the effect you anticipated, before risking the same error on the other engine.

We encounter checklists as a way of conducting safe and reliable procedures in many disciplines today, but few who either use them or merely pay lip service to them, understand the complications. I had resisted the trend of introducing printed checklists into the basic flight training world. It had seemed a distraction with no practical benefit and I still believe it is better for the pilot of a simple aircraft to rely on memory and mnemonics. But on the Viking I began to see that, not only are they essential, but that, if they are to be effective, there is a whole philosophy of reading and responding to checklists that must be mastered.

First, you need to be aware of the errors that can be made when using a checklist. Lines can be skipped, or incorrect responses can be given because the position of a switch or control is not where the responder thinks it is. Resuming the reading of a checklist after an interruption is a particularly fertile area for mistakes. You can even pick up the wrong checklist, or one that is out of date. All of these potential traps must be borne in mind as you go through the list so that your concentration is maintained. A checklist is useless if it ever becomes a thoughtless routine, a litany chanted so often that it loses its power.

Unusually, I had always dreamt of airline flying as the ultimate job for a pilot. The airline pilot's attitude to flying is more like that of a member of the string section in a classical orchestra than that of a soloist in a jazz band. He is a member of a team following the conductor's interpretation of the composer's vision. It is not that there is no room for innovation or flare, but that any inspired improvement must be worked out collaboratively and integrated with the whole. If an airline pilot thinks he knows a better way to fly, he must not experiment with it. Instead, he should explain it to his Chief Pilot so that it can be analysed and discussed, trialled and developed. If the management and training staff determine that the idea is a good one, it will be introduced over the whole fleet in such a way that all the crews can make use of it. That's the theory, anyway.

It seemed to me that the airline pilot enjoyed a more complete aerial life than pilots in other forms of flying. Not only did he have to concern himself with his crew, the passengers or freight and the navigation, he also had to fly accurately and safely as a matter of routine, every day. He had to be ready to handle an instrument approach to precise limits in any weather, day or night, with an engine failure or any other malfunction, whether he felt tired, had toothache or even if he was in the middle of a divorce.

Inevitably, learning a lot of new things means learning about oneself. I struggled at first with my position as the lowliest pilot in the fleet. I had been used to the exalted status of a Deputy Chief Flying Instructor – a big fish in a small pond, perhaps – and felt resentment when my ideas were ignored and my experience dismissed. It wasn't the practical jokes that bothered me – my sense of humour was well up to coping with those. It was the assumption that I knew nothing which hurt. It took quite a long time for me to realize that this assumption was perfectly reasonable.

The pleasures were worth the effort. The cloud of blue smoke whipped away in the propeller's slipstream when the Hercules started up at Tempelhof in the morning often began an enchanted day. The long taxi to backtrack the runway for a westerly take-off allowed the oil temperatures to rise into the correct range and I could experiment with steering the aircraft using only the adverse drag from the ailerons. That was a skill, incidentally, that I did not find useful again on any aircraft until twenty-five years later when I flew a Piper Cub on floats.

Rumbling low over the green German countryside produced new delights on every trip. In the centre corridor, Alex, our other resident Training captain, often asked for the lowest available level because it meant we were out of radio contact for twenty minutes or so and he liked the peace and quiet.

On arrival at Amsterdam, the shipper's agent always presented us with the load details for the return trip to Berlin. Before we could slope off to the canteen, the captain had to determine the take-off weight and order the appropriate fuel uplift. I waited with some impatience for Alex to do this one day. I was hungry and his calculations seemed even slower and more deliberate than usual. He muttered to himself and licked his stub of pencil, marking heavy black figures on the back of his cigarette packet, while a cold north wind snatched the last remnants of warmth from my uniform.

At last he spoke. 'Maximum payload,' he said. 'We can't carry any excess weight. Spragg! Drain the de-icing fluid; that will save a hundred kilos.' It seemed a reasonable decision. The skies were clear over our route and we were unlikely to encounter airframe icing. He pointed to an empty drum in the rear of the fuselage. 'Don't spill any, it's expensive.'

I had never performed this task before, but fortunately I remembered that the drain was situated in the port engine nacelle and set to work. Or rather, I tried to. The neck of the drum was narrow and it was impossible to get the top of the drum really close to the drain. The wind blew mercilessly and the clear, oily de-icing fluid sprayed everywhere with very little actually getting into the drum. In a few minutes my uniform was soaked and my hair plastered to my head. I struggled and cursed, but the task got more difficult as the drum got heavier and my fingers grew colder. Alex's shouted criticism didn't help.

At last, with the drum half full and the pressure of the draining fluid beginning to reduce, Alex called a halt. 'That'll do, Spragg. You'll flood half of Amsterdam.' And indeed, a wide stain of the oil was spreading over the freight apron.

I turned off the cock and screwed the top back on to the drum. 'Where do we leave it?' I asked.

'Leave it?' retorted an incredulous Alex. 'You can't leave it! Someone will steal it. Put it in the hold and we'll take it back to Berlin.'

I realized I'd been had. My misery was complete, but not for long. Practical jokes like this would not be tolerated in today's society. There would be accusations of bullying and harassment and perhaps that's a good thing. I don't believe they did much real harm though and they had the benefit of getting rid of any precious airs and graces in short order. My uniform was never quite the same, but before we had finished lunch in the canteen I was laughing about it, though not perhaps as heartily as Alex.

That uniform aged quickly. The Berlin pigeon fanciers' club was refused permission to take its birds through East Germany by truck or train due to some obscure livestock regulation, so we undertook to fly the birds to Hanover sometimes, when we were routing empty towards Amsterdam. They were loaded in the cool of early morning, but if our take-off was delayed the temperature in the fuselage crept up and the smell and dust created a real health hazard. We were issued at first with painters' dust masks and later with more sophisticated masks incorporating a microphone. Speedy hated those masks and would fume, his curses muffled, as clouds of dust and the occasional feather drifted through the cockpit. Hans, our mechanic, was always the last to leave the aircraft before departure, collecting in his hat any pigeon eggs he could find for his breakfast.

While the birds were unloaded at Hanover and released to race back to Berlin, Alex suggested one day that we grab a quick cup of coffee. We walked to the passenger terminal where there was a very smart espresso kiosk, but unfortunately it was surrounded, three deep, by German businessmen in smart suits and overcoats, clamouring to be served. I hesitated. 'This is going to take ages,' I said. 'We haven't got time.'

'Nonsense! Follow me!' Alex strode officiously up to the throng and stood close behind the last group of travellers. I followed and was surprised when the businessmen began to make way for us. We got some strange looks, but in no time at all we were being served at the counter and enjoying a little oasis of space. I thought at first that this was an extreme example of how polite the Germans were, or perhaps it demonstrated their respect for uniforms, but Alex's chuckle alerted me to the real reason for our priority. 'You don't notice it now,' he told me. 'But next time you go to put your uniform on, try smelling it.'

Aircraft operations today are not as susceptible to the weather as they used to be: autoland, better anti-icing systems, greater power and the ability to cruise at high altitude have seen to that. And this invulnerability distances the pilots from intimate interaction with the excesses of their medium. I learnt more about flying in weather during my short stint on the Viking than in the rest of my thirty-year airline career. Plying between Berlin and Amsterdam in winter in an unpressurized, unheated piston freighter, we endured conditions that are hardly credible today. The cold was unbelievable. The heating system had been stripped out of the airframe to save weight, as well as to remove the temptation for us to turn it on and so damage the cut flowers we carried.

We dressed in heavyweight winter uniforms all the year round and flew wearing thick, military-style raincoats. We were expected to record the weather we encountered on route, drawing and annotating a cross-section of the frontal cloud on a piece of paper attached to our flight logs, which we handed to the forecasters at our destination. But in cloud the old windscreen leaked, dribbling water onto our knees and soaking the log, so large sheets of clear polythene salvaged from packages delivered to the maintenance hangar were prized as protection to be draped over our laps. If we could get hold of a couple of tough polythene bags they were pulled over our shoes to keep our feet dry.

In freezing cloud the drips from the screen were transformed into fine sprays of ice crystals. After a few minutes of this, we began to look like those pictures of Antarctic explorers we've all seen with snow coating their clothes and ice ringing their mouths and noses. Speedy kept a roll of black sticky tape in his bag and would, from time to time, tear off a piece and stick it over any hole producing a particularly annoying spray of ice. It did not last long and new sprays kept appearing, but it gave temporary relief. Dick, a senior first officer under training to become captain, did the same, but on one very cold trip found he had forgotten his roll of tape.

'Can I borrow some of your tape, Speedy?' he asked politely. And waited while Speedy considered this request at some length. He replied eventually with a phrase that was added to his legend: 'Get yer own tape!'

Airframe icing did not seem to be as big a problem then as it is now.

We had any snow and ice brushed off the aircraft with yard brooms before take-off and the fluid de-icing system was supposed to prevent any ice build-up in-flight. As aircraft were developed and wing-section design became more critical, even small accumulations of ice produced a dramatic reduction in performance. A research programme in the 1970s proved that a coating equivalent to the thickness of rough sandpaper on the leading edge of a swept wing could make the aircraft uncontrollable at low speeds.

Our problem was ice on the engine intakes. There were mesh screens in front of the ducts that carried air to the carburettors. When ice built up on these, the power available from the engines was reduced. We could compensate to some extent by opening the throttle wider, then reducing the pitch of the propellers to increase their revs, but unless we could descend into warmer air or climb clear of the cloud, the airspeed would begin to fall. Sometimes the linkages from the control quadrant out to the carburettors and propellers would freeze solid, leaving us with no further control.

In these conditions conversation tended to falter. As co-pilot, I would be on the radio, badgering Air Traffic for clearance to a different flight level. Lumps of ice flung off the propellers would be crashing into the fuselage behind our heads, while, through the sprays of ice crystals from the windscreen, we would watch the needle of the airspeed indicator slowly drop. Eventually, before the inevitable uncontrolled descent, the captain would be forced to take drastic action. With a long sigh, followed by the sharp intake of breath that preceded a brave decision, Alex would grasp the fuel cock of the most badly affected engine and slam it shut, then open it again a second later.

With luck, this would produce a great backfire from the engine, expelling hot air and fuel forward through the air intake to clear the ice and the engine would roar back up to full power again. Sometimes it took more than one attempt before we could try it again on the other engine. But it was never done unless absolutely necessary, because, as well as cutting off the fuel, the cock cut off the oil supply to the engine. There was always a possibility that, if the cock stuck in the closed position, we would have a fast-rotating mass of engine and propeller out there without lubrication, meaning that fire and destruction would surely follow.

Passengers today probably notice turbulence more than any other feature of the weather and fear it most. But except for sudden encounters in clear air, where people can get thrown about and hurt because there is no warning, it rarely poses serious problems today. The ability to fly at high altitude and the availability of weather radar enable modern jets to avoid most cloud that might be turbulent. In the Viking, approaching a squall line near Osnabrück, where the thunderstorms seemed to gather, we would cruise along the towering wall of cloud trying to find a place to penetrate, for all the world like a small boat following a line of cliffs while seeking a cove in which to shelter.

Then we would lower our seats, turn the flight deck lighting up full, set the power and trim for the turbulence penetration speed and make sure everything loose was secured. Turning at right angles to the wall, we would head for the likeliest spot. The old aeroplane would buck and sway and groan. There would be ice and hail and sometimes surprising vertical excursions, but I would never feel there was any real danger. In more extreme conditions, Alex might reduce his workload by getting me to look after roll control with the ailerons while he concentrated on the more important pitch control. It could be alarming, but I was always confident we could keep her on an even keel and trusted that, despite her age, she would hold together during the beating she took.

Before taking off in a large piston-engined aircraft, the pilots must exercise the variable pitch propellers. The pitch is variable because, for maximum efficiency, the angle at which the propeller blades meet the air must be kept within a narrow range. An additional function ensures that, should an engine fail, the blades can be 'feathered' like the oars in a rowing boat, that is, turned in line with the airflow to offer minimum resistance. An hydraulic mechanism uses oil to accomplish these tasks and exercising it ensures that the oil is warm and the mechanism is operating properly.

We did the engine run-up with the aircraft stationary on the ground, facing into wind if possible. The throttle was set so that the engine was running smoothly, with the propeller spinning freely. Then the pitch lever was moved smartly into the feathering range of its operating quadrant. This action caused the blades to rotate towards their coarsest setting, but, because the aircraft was not moving forward through the air, they stalled and the air that had been flowing so easily over them broke away, swirling and thrashing in noisy chaos. The noise was like the angry growl of a big animal. What gave me such particular pleasure was that it provided the first convincing indication since boarding the aircraft of the substance of air. I was suddenly reassured that air, such an insubstantial gas in everyday experience, really does have the power and strength to lift this great machine. It is a noise we do not get much opportunity to hear today. Modern light twin-engined aircraft still use the procedure, however, and it is worth going out of your way to listen for it.

Of course, the noise of the engines themselves used to convey a great deal of information to pilots. Piston engines must be treated delicately and they were fussed over and cosseted by the engineers on the ground. Any unusual noise was a cause for concern and investigation at the earliest possible moment, though fortunately by the time I was involved with them they were so reliable that the irregularities were usually imagined. Equalizing the pressure in our ears as we climbed would alter the sounds we heard and the engines always changed their note unaccountably whenever we crossed the coast to head out over the sea.

All piston engines with propellers provide evocative sounds. I will still rush outside and look up when I hear big piston engines droning over my house today. Living near Derby, we are quite often treated to the best sound in aviation: the Rolls-Royce Merlin engine in a Spitfire, Hurricane or Lancaster. Someone connected with the RAF Memorial Flight must realize that there are still a lot of elderly engineers and craftsmen living here who worked at 'Royce's' on the engines that played such a vital part in World War II, and so route the aircraft over the city whenever possible. Almost everyone in Derby looks up when they hear the deep, sonorous note of the great V12 cylinder engine with its accompanying low whistle.

In airliners, propellers have gone the way of open cockpits and there are fewer distinctive noises by which the pilot may sense his environment. Modern airline pilots can still hear – just – the roar of heavy rain on the aluminium skin of their flight deck, or be startled by the sudden ferocity of hail. But they are no longer disconcerted by lumps of ice being flung off the props and hitting the fuselage behind their heads.

The Berlin flower flights provided other, unique treats. We normally had time during the turn-round in Amsterdam to visit the KLM canteen for lunch. The food was excellent, the building comfortable, the people friendly and the prices amazingly low. Of course, it was subsidized by KLM and I don't think we were entitled to go there at all, but our crews had been taking lunch there every day for so long no one thought to question the arrangement.

If the shipper had an extra consignment for Berlin, one of the aircraft would make a second journey. It meant a long day for the pilots, but I never once heard a complaint. We loved the flying and would have flown double trips every day if asked. Before we left Berlin for the second time, Herr Friedrich, our base manager, would arrange for our supper to be loaded aboard in a big cardboard box. The memories of such flights are stored in a special part of my mind, the part reserved for moments of pure bliss. Cruising in the cool, smooth air above the neat fields of Germany in our beloved Viking, we would open the box and tuck into the goodies we found there. Chicken, beef, fruit, fresh milk, pies and cakes: there seemed no end to the profusion. The image of a co-pilot, seat pushed back, feet up on the instrument panel, gnawing away on delicious chicken and throwing the bones out of the open window at his side is one of complete contentment. The controls would get a bit more sticky and the chicken bones would sometimes get caught by the propeller and ricochet off the fuselage with a clang, incurring a disapproving frown from the captain, but we didn't care. The years of struggle and the sacrifices we had made to get a licence had at last paid off.

To round off a perfect day, Herr Friedrich himself would marshal us onto our stand under the eastern end of Tempelhof's enormous art-deco terminal canopy. The diminutive figure stood erect, a broad grin on his old face, and waved his arms with more enthusiasm than accuracy. It didn't matter; we knew where to park. And as we grew closer we could see that he wasn't holding the traditional marshaller's bats, he was holding two bottles of cognac that the whole team would be expected to finish before we retired to Heidi's place across the road for beers and more food if we could manage it.

We were a self-contained little band with rarely any contact with head office in the UK. Occasionally other pilots would join us to cover for holidays or sickness. They provided variety and more opportunity to learn. The resident captains were trusted to run the operation as they saw fit and the company regulations were seen by everyone more as a guide than a constraint. In such a small group, it was obvious how much we depended on each other. Pilots, engineers, office staff and administrators respected the skill and integrity of their colleagues. Skill was pretty much all we had; that and the accumulated wisdom of those who had done the job before us. Gradually I earnt some of that respect too, and my confidence grew in line with my ability. I began to feel I belonged.

Attitudes to alcohol were different then. I had been scheduled to operate the second flower flight out of Berlin one morning, to take off an hour after the first machine. When I arrived at the hangar office, Dick, who was to be co-pilot on the first flight, was nowhere to be seen. In case he had met with an accident, I rushed to the met office to pick up the weather reports and to file flight plans for both aircraft, racing back in order to take over the first flight myself if necessary.

Speedy was already on board and was starting the engines. The engineers were flapping and telling me to hurry up and join him.

'He'll be in a foul mood if he's delayed,' they reminded me. I left the second flight's paperwork for whoever followed and was just about to run out onto the apron when Dick appeared. His uniform was immaculate, as always, but it was his languid stroll and relaxed smile that amazed us.

'Where the Hell have you been? Speedy's waiting!' we chorused.

He took the paperwork I offered with a polite 'Thank you,' and placed his flight bag on the desk. While we urged all haste, he took out a half-full bottle of champagne and a cut-glass flute. Calmly and slowly he filled the flute and drank it down, relishing every drop. Then he smiled again, dropped both bottle and flute into the bin, put the paperwork into his bag and strolled leisurely out to the aircraft, whistling nonchalantly.

He would not have survived much longer than Speedy in an airline today, but he did have style.

CHAPTER 4

Turboprop Schedules

The Handley Page Dart Herald boasted many of the features of modern aircraft design, but it did not represent the epitome of progress. It offered pressurized, air-conditioned comfort and turbine smoothness, but the cockpit design was retrograde. After the space and light of the Viking, the cramped pilots' quarters were awkward to get into and the view from the tiny windows was disappointing. The seats could not compare with the Viking's voluminous leather affairs and in winter our feet got every bit as cold. Electrically heated floor panels were fitted in an effort to coax circulation back into the modern pilot's toes, but they never seemed to work very well.

Worst of all, the performance was disappointing. On a long leg, say Jersey to Hull, with anything near a full passenger load, its range was marginal and its altitude capability risible. Handling was safe, with adequate control, but did not inspire any eulogies. These airframe features no doubt owed something to the fact that it had originally been designed as a four-engined, piston-powered aircraft and only later redesigned as twin-engined turboprop.

Those Rolls-Royce Darts were its finest feature. They gave smooth, consistent, reliable power all the time under any conditions, producing enough electrical power and hot air to provide a reasonable de-icing capability at the same time.

Navigation equipment consisted of the same VOR and ILS sets that I was used to in the Viking, but now with the provision of an early zero-reader form of flight director. This clever device was a separate instrument that looked similar to the ILS display, but which was supposed to remove the need for mental calculations. Just fly to centre the needles and, regardless of crosswinds, it would hold you on track and glide slope. It was an interesting asset, but few of us trusted it fully or made great use of it. Thus the introduction of technology had a light touch at first. It did not change our job much from what we had done in the Viking and we hardly noticed that the challenge to our skill had started. Perhaps we were aware of a slight distancing from our environment. We flew higher without the need for protective clothing and, apart from keeping an eye on the pressurization system, we did not have to worry about the oxygen level. But these changes were soon forgotten in the business of the day.

The layout of the basic flying instruments was bizarre. Contrary to normal British practice, they seemed to have been positioned randomly on the panel. We didn't complain about it though. The Handley Page test pilot who had shepherded the type through its development and certification had joined our company as a line captain. He was such a charming chap we didn't like to risk offending him. But, when I heard him tell an amusing story at dinner, involving old men on a bowling green complete with exaggerated actions, I wondered if that was how they had positioned the instruments: bowled them down the fuselage and bolted them in where they stopped.

A brand-new toy was the weather radar. Instead of cruising along the edge of a cloud front and then plunging into the least threatening bit, we could actually see the heaviest rainfall, and therefore the most likely areas of turbulence, from miles away. For the first time in my experience it was possible to plan a smooth route, rather than just accepting whatever nature chose to throw at us. The tiny screen was an analogue, monochrome affair that took some time to master, but, when we had learnt its ways, it was an excellent tool.

Along with the new aeroplane, I was introduced to formal, planned pilot training. Until this time, only the large, long-established airlines and the military ran any sort of formal course and there was no requirement for airlines to provide such training. Anyone who wanted to become an airline pilot had to learn to fly at a club or commercial centre, build up his experience to 200 flying hours, sit the Ministry of Aviation written examinations for a Commercial Licence and undertake the flying tests. The final qualification involved passing the demanding Instrument Rating flight test, a short procedural flight including airways and approach procedures in an aircraft equipped with screens so that the applicant had to rely entirely on his flight instruments. Armed with these qualifications, if there were jobs available, he was in.

But times were changing. The Government had set up an inquiry into pilot training under Lord Hamilton, which recommended a more structured system. Soon after I had got my Private Pilot's Licence, the number of flying hours required for the Commercial Licence was increased from 200 to 700. Naturally, I regarded this as a typically pointless piece of legislation because the examinations remained the same, making the process longer and more expensive with no improvement in standards. Still, new attitudes were needed with the introduction of more complex aircraft and airlines were being forced to take training seriously.

Once employed, issued with a copy of the company manual and a uniform, I had been sent away to study on my own for the Air Registration Board's examination for the Viking. Having passed the multi-choice written examination, flying training consisted of sitting in the jump seat on a few commercial flights, then a couple of hours' circuit flying with a Training Captain until he considered me competent to take off, land and cope with an engine failure.

Standards were not high: new pilots flew as co-pilots, after all. The Training Captains usually had no qualifications in training; they had done the Type and Instrument Rating examiner's course, which involved learning the standard acceptable limits for checking purposes, but involved no consideration of training techniques. Line Training Captains had not done any sort of course. New recruits simply flew with them, accompanied by an experienced co-pilot initially, until they were considered good enough to be cleared to fly with the other line captains. The new boys were usually forbidden to take off or land the aircraft for a few months, allowing time for their handling skills to deteriorate before they were permitted to do a landing with passengers on board. I was exceptionally fortunate to be posted to Berlin on the Viking, where we were allowed to fly the empty legs right from the start.

This sounds now like a hit-and-miss procedure and in some ways it was. The help the recruits received varied enormously, depending on with whom they flew, and the resultant standards they achieved varied, too. But the regulatory authorities saw safety as primarily the responsibility of the airlines and they in turn relied entirely on the judgement of their most experienced captains.

For the Herald, I was treated to the luxury of a manufacturer's ground school and even a week at Rolls-Royce in Derby, learning the intricacies of the Dart engine. I did the course on the Avro 748 first, but in accordance with the arcane practices of crew scheduling, I was transferred to the Herald fleet before I had a chance to fly it. This was a mixed blessing. The 748 was considered by the pilots to be the superior aircraft, but the Herald was used by the airline for scheduled passenger flights around the UK and the continental seaboard, which appealed to me more than the charter flights that were the staple of the Avro.

Turbine engines produce a constant, monotonous whine at almost any stage of the flight. I was trained to fly the Herald by a delightful old gentleman from a previous age called Bill. He was short and slight and his blue eyes, wreathed in wrinkles from years of staring into the sun, rarely seemed to blink. He spoke softly, with an old-world courtesy, and his movements were never hurried. He loved flying with a quiet passion and the fund of flying stories he had to tell was topped only by the legends about him that circulated among the co-pilots. It was said he was the model for a character in one of Neville Shute's novels and that, when his seat collapsed on a training flight, pitching him back into the galley area, he resumed his place at the controls, cigarette still drooping from his lip. His trainee offered to do the landing from his conventional position in a still-secure seat, but Bill replied, 'Oh no, I've wanted to do this for years.'

He flew the aeroplane to an excellent landing while standing erect like the captain on the bridge of an ocean-going liner.

Bill never lost his love for piston engines. When I praised the reliability and power of the turbines, he looked doubtful. 'Yes,' he said. 'But,' and here he rubbed his thumb and fingers together as if trying to identify an elusive element in the air, 'they don't talk to me.'

Many of the pilots I flew with in the early part of my airline career were World War II veterans. They had a maturity and a quiet wisdom that is rarely encountered today. Their flying skills varied and some were better captains than others, but every one of them commanded respect. With few exceptions, they were gentlemen, with genuine concern for individuals and charming manners. They seemed to carry with them a calm detachment and a sense of proportion that enabled them to face unreasonably frenetic commercial pressure with an indulgent smile. They knew how to relax and enjoy themselves and they were not about to be told how the job should be done.

The other captains in my early years were mostly a later generation of ex-RAF pilots and a few, like myself, who had made their own way into commercial aviation via a number of different routes.

Our little co-pilots' revolution – refusing to call the captain 'Sir' – was more obvious on the scheduled passenger service fleet where more crews were involved. Traditionally, probably dating back to the pre-war days of Imperial Airways or certainly to the early post-war Atlantic Barons of BOAC, the co-pilot would attach a respectful 'Sir!' to every response. The captain might call, 'Flap One!' and the co-pilot was expected to answer, 'Flap one, Sir!' Then again, when the flap had run out and had reached position one, 'Flap one set, Sir!'

This tradition seemed outdated to us. We did not lack respect for our captains, nor did we intend to undermine their authority. But we had worked hard for our licences and they were the same as those held by the captains. We lacked experience, but we were required members of the operating crew doing an important job and there was a new philosophy abroad that saw airline pilots working together as a team, rather than as a man and his boy. So we dropped the 'Sir!'

Some captains, like Speedy, hardly noticed; either they agreed with our stance or didn't care. Others gave us pompous lectures about discipline, respect and etiquette. A third group adopted the interesting tactic of giving us a leg, allowing us to fly the aircraft, then responding to our calls with an emphatic 'Sir!' We assumed they were endeavouring to teach by example. It didn't work. We abandoned the 'Sir!' and we looked to carry the fight into other areas.

Not every captain allowed the co-pilot to fly the aircraft. Few bothered to justify this stance; some pointed out that training was not part of their job description. If a co-pilot damaged an aircraft or frightened the passengers, the captain would be held responsible. Why take the risk? And given the cursory training given to most co-pilots in those days, the position of these captains was not unreasonable. But after a spate of jet accidents around the world, airlines were beginning to see the need for a highly trained and competent co-pilot playing his full part in the operation of the aircraft. They were beginning to understand that it took two to do the job safely. We couldn't wait. In the liberated spirit of the 1960s, we pressed for more democracy.

It was different flying passengers. The schedule was all-important and my already well-developed respect for punctuality began to develop towards an obsession. It is epitomized in a gesture I remember a number of captains making in those days. After the passengers had boarded, the doors had been closed, the engines started and the systems reconfigured for power from the main generators, the ground crew would disconnect the tug and the start-truck. We would read the checklist and I would call the tower for taxi clearance. Sometimes, when the clearance was given, nothing would happen. I would look across to see why the captain had not released the brakes to see him holding a thumb out towards the clock, which was ticking the seconds up to departure time. We might wait thirty seconds until the sweep second hand reached the magic number, then move off, exactly on schedule.

Carrying passengers also, of course, meant flying with a cabin crew. There were no stewards in the airline and consequently the cabin crew were always referred to as 'The Girls', something else that would not be acceptable today. Instead of the battered old thermos flasks we carried on the Viking, these delightful 'girls' now made coffee for us. Many of the senior ones were paid rather more than I was myself. Eating was still a problem. When we could, we would try to get something to eat in the airport terminal during turn-rounds. Often there wasn't time. I came to dread the frequent order of the day: 'Don't rush it – leave it!'

Interspersed amongst the thousands of boring, bland, tasteless, rushed meals I have suffered during thirty years of airline flying, there are a few memorable exceptions. The services operated with the Dart Herald out of Teesside served only cold sandwiches or rolls to the passengers. But if one of the girls had been shopping the day before the crew might get a treat for breakfast. There were no ovens, but a large hot cup, used for boiling water for drinks, could be pressed into service to heat up 'boil in the bag' meals. Kippers were our favourite and the aroma released when they were opened must have driven the starving passengers mad as it drifted through the whole aeroplane.

John was a typical captain of the time. He was tall and imposing, with a natural air of authority, which he seemed reluctant to dilute by indulging in unnecessary communication. He flew well and it was possible to learn a lot simply by observing how he went about the job. Co-pilots, however, would go to great lengths to avoid flying with him because he would never, ever, let them touch the controls of his aeroplane.

Innocently unaware of this, I found myself scheduled to fly with him for several days on the Dart Herald. The first day wasn't so bad; two sectors flown in silence save for a terse ticking off for some minor transgression he deemed me to have made. I began the next day, involving four sectors, with little enthusiasm. Sure enough, he silently assumed the handling pilot's role outbound and again, on the return to base. I followed him round with the checklist, made the radio calls and filled in the paperwork. On arrival back at Luton there was no sign that things would improve, so, while he was occupied with the load sheet, I decided to raise my spirits by dashing off to the canteen. I was back in a couple of minutes with hot bacon sandwiches, dripping in fat and HP Sauce, enough for the cabin crew and myself. Just before the passengers boarded, I squirmed back into my seat, still munching on the sandwich, no doubt filling the confined space of the flight deck with a mouth-watering aroma.

John watched me eat for a moment and then he spoke. 'Did you get a bacon sandwich for me?' he asked.

Slowly, I finished chewing and considered carefully what my reply should be. I thought of Speedy. Eventually I said quietly, 'Get your own bacon sandwiches.'

There was another longish pause, then, 'Okay! You can fly the next leg.' I flew with him many times after that and he always gave me half of the flying. We got along fine and the other co-pilots could not understand why I was so happy to be rostered with him.

Once or twice a year now we read in our newspapers that an airline pilot has been arrested, somewhere in the world, breathalysed and perhaps jailed for reporting for a flight with alcohol in his system. It is tempting for me to retort that, when I started, it was compulsory to fly in that state, but on reflection that is not quite true. We drank a lot. We worked hard for long hours and at irregular times so that a conventional social life was difficult to arrange. The reduced humidity in an aircraft cabin makes you thirsty; we frequently felt the need to relax after a hard day and looked forward to easing the tensions with a few beers. More than that, we enjoyed what we were doing and we enjoyed the companionship of our fellows; there was a strong desire to preserve that fellowship, to carry it through to the informal atmosphere of a bar, to swap stories and to laugh a lot. Sometimes the fun got a bit boisterous and high spirits got out of hand. But on the whole pilots were remarkably responsible about drinking and flying. For one thing, we enjoyed our job so much that we didn't want to dull the pleasure of flying by carrying a hangover.

Of course, there were infringements, but attitudes were different in those days. Rather than condemn alcohol outright and introduce mechanical testing by policemen, individuals were trusted to be sensible.

No one really cared what the crew got up to in the period before the flight providing they were in a fit condition to do the job when they reported for duty. And what exactly constituted 'a fit condition' was left up to the individual.

On the Herald fleet we did not get many night stops away from base. When we did, it was an event. We looked forward to going out for a meal as a crew and seeing something of a foreign city. But on one occasion, in Geneva, we arrived too late for socializing and went straight to our rooms to sleep. The next morning I was ready early and looking forward to the return flight. While I was waiting for the crew to assemble in the hotel lobby, the senior stewardess appeared and spoke to me in a confidential whisper. She was a lot more experienced than me in the ways of airline flying, so I took what she said seriously. The captain had apparently asked her for a bottle of brandy before she closed the bar on the previous day's flight.

'He doesn't seem to have it with him this morning,' she said. 'Keep a very close eye on him!'

You can be sure that I did. I watched him check out at the reception desk. I watched him walk across the lobby to the door and I watched him intently as he negotiated the steps down to the waiting transport. He didn't speak to anyone, but then he rarely did. He moved hesitantly and slowly, but that wasn't unusual either. On the drive out to the airport he sat stiffly erect and rather grey-faced, but I could detect nothing in his behaviour to suggest he was anything other than fit to fly.

There was the usual rush and bustle at the airport: finding the agent's office, getting the weather forecast, writing the flight plan and calculating the fuel uplift, getting out to the aircraft and doing the checks. I was too busy to watch the captain closely, but I was becoming increasingly aware that time was running out. If anything needed to be done – if I was going to accuse him of being unfit to fly – it had to be done before we took off.

At last the passengers were boarded and the doors were closed. We started the engines and taxied out to join the queue for take-off. Still he did not speak. I got no briefing from him and his responses to my checklist calls were grunts. Again, this was nothing unusual. So we took off and climbed into a cold blue sky, the captain hand-flying the whole way. His flying was smooth and accurate and his eyes seemed to show a little more life; they didn't exactly shine, but they were not quite as dull as they had been. The trip proceeded exactly as planned and when we arrived at our destination in the UK he flew an immaculate instrument approach. I was impressed. It was quite a lot better than I could have achieved myself.

On the ground, he signed the paperwork I had completed and walked off to his car. He did not speak to anyone, nor say goodbye. The two stewardesses joined me for a drink in the Flying Club bar and were eager to know how things had gone. What could I tell them? Considering all the evidence in a relaxed atmosphere after the event, we concluded that he had almost certainly drunk that bottle of brandy overnight before the flight, but, since he had shown no signs of incapacity of any sort and had done his job perfectly, there was nothing any of us could have done about it. Perhaps he always flew like that. I never saw him again. I believe he retired not long after that flight.

There are many watering holes adopted by aircrews close to airports around the world. In the UK there were still then private flying clubs sharing many of the airfields we operated from and we were welcomed into a number of their clubhouses. Luton had a disreputable establishment within yards of our airline's offices. Teesside had a more elegant place just a hundred yards from the terminal building where the private pilots were always glad to see us – or was it the stewardesses we brought with us? Friday night was Club Night. The flight up from London was always full of businessmen returning home to the North East after a hard week in the city. They used to put in requests to the company that it be crewed by the liveliest girls. Passengers and crew would meet up in the Flying Club bar after landing and a riotous evening was guaranteed.

We got to know each other quite well. Cruising north on one occasion, a passenger who had been shown up to the flight deck peered over my shoulder and asked which aircraft we were flying. I had to look at the placard – they were all the same to me. 'Whisky Bravo,' I told him.

'Thought so,' he replied. 'The exhaust gas temperature is always a bit high on the port engine, isn't it?'

Popular myth has the airline pilot at the heart of a mid-air drama, saving his ship and all his passengers by his icy cool temperament and superhuman skill. It will be no surprise to discover that real-life airline flying is not like that. The age of adventure in airline flying was over before I qualified as a pilot. Aeroplanes had been developed to the point where they had plenty of performance and a high degree of reliability. Operationally, enough had been learnt to determine best practice and for most pilots to avoid situations that would require exceptional responses from them.

With the introduction of turbine engines, the philosophy of design and management had been refined to make the whole operation fail-safe wherever possible. Redundancy was built into every system. Airliners had a minimum of two engines, two sets of flight instruments and two pilots. Anything that might fail or break was at least duplicated; often there were three or four back-ups. So airline flying had become routine.

Of course, things still went wrong, as they do even today. Usually that means a raised eyebrow on the flight deck, a short discussion, a call for a checklist and an entry in the technical log for a part to be replaced at the next stop. But the nature of flying, the imperative of speed through the air to support the mass of an aircraft, means that when the unexpected happens, it happens quickly. And a sudden, unexpected threat can induce fright.

Fear is quite different to fright. Fear needs time to develop. It grows slowly from a vague apprehension through a nagging worry to an awful dread, until it is a cold, paralysing dead weight carried in the pit of the stomach. There is rarely time for that in an aeroplane. Disaster threatens, there is a shot of adrenaline and a brief shock of fright. Then it is over, quickly suppressed by action based on training and rational thinking. It is usually followed by a period of silence on the flight deck, then by an outburst of giggling.

It is rarely a single event that leads to an incident. What the great aviation writer E.K. Gann called 'complication'[3] has to take place. A simple error is made, it is given significance by some other minor event and the combination of the two aberrations leads to another, unforeseen condition. Thus, unless corrective action is taken quickly, the snowball starts to roll, gets bigger and faster and gains energy until an avalanche is inevitable.

Any sudden noise in the air is unwelcome. One of the Heralds in our fleet had a faulty catch on the galley table, which was situated just behind the flight deck. It was the responsibility of the cabin crew to ensure that everything was secure for take-off, which included stowing the table vertically, but the retaining catch was faulty. We snagged it on every trip, but for some reason the engineers took a week or two to fix it properly. Every time we rotated for take-off it would fall free, landing with an almighty crash just as we left the ground. I don't know how the passengers felt about it, but it frightened the pilots. Several of the more ambitious co-pilots expressed a hope that it wouldn't be repaired before it gave one of our older captains a heart attack so that we could all move up one on the seniority list.

A more general source of fright is the presence of conflicting traffic. Again, technology has changed, but it has not entirely eliminated the problem. One of the pilot's first lines of defence against getting too close to another aircraft used to be by listening to the radio chatter and paying close attention to the position and intentions of other aircraft. That is still a sensible thing to do, but the volume of traffic today reduces its value. Blocks of busy airspace are divided up between controllers, each working a different frequency, so that it is often difficult for a pilot to fathom the overall picture and the conflict may not be heard.

I was given an early lesson when an Air France Caravelle overtook our Dart Herald over the Channel one day. My captain, John, remarked how beautiful she looked in the morning sun as she slid effortlessly overhead. The London controller cleared us to change frequency to the French and while I busied myself with the radio, John craned his neck to keep the sleek machine in sight just 1,000ft above us.

There was chatter in French on the frequency and I had to wait for it to stop before I could transmit our position. When the break came, I moved my hand back to the transmit button on the control wheel, but found it wasn't there. With a loud oath, John had put the wheel hard over to the left and our aircraft was rolling into a steep bank.

'He's cleared that b***** through our level!' he shouted. Sure enough, when he rolled the aircraft level again, we watched the graceful jet ease down past us, through the airspace we had been occupying only seconds before.

It was just good fortune that John spoke French fluently. Most pilots don't need to do so because English is the international language of the air. It is not practicable to learn the language of every country we fly over, though knowing the numbers one to nine in a few different languages can be useful.

The weather too can bring surprises. Crossing the North Sea in the Herald, in solid cloud one winter's day, we began to accumulate a lot of ice. The controller could not give us clearance to descend until he could be sure traffic below us was clear. Jimmy, my captain that day, was new to the type. He had just returned to the UK after several years of flying in clear skies over the hot sands of Arabia and was nervous about ice. He started to twitch while we held altitude in the cloud and the ice continued to build up around the windscreens, on the engines and wings and, we assumed, elsewhere on the airframe. Even with maximum continuous power from the engines, the airspeed was falling. The lower speed dictated a higher nose attitude to maintain height and this increased the rate of ice accumulation. Jimmy squirmed in his seat, nagging me to hurry up with the clearance. When at last the controller freed us for descent, he grasped the throttles and pulled the power off. Now I suppose that was an understandable action by a pilot eager to descend, but in an aircraft laden with ice and the delicate aerodynamics of its airfoils misshapen and spoilt by great ridges of the stuff, it would have been more prudent just to lower the nose gently and let the speed increase slowly, leaving the power as it was.

I was too late to stop him. My cry of, 'Don't do tha ...' was stifled as the aircraft plummeted. It set off for the grey waves of the North Sea below at a rate I felt sure would be very difficult to arrest. Jimmy could fly; I'll give him that, although some said he needed to be good to get out of the situations in which he put himself. Somehow he regained control of the machine and when we broke out of cloud he was able to stabilize the aircraft in the cruise. The air was warmer here and the coast was in sight. We sat in silence for a while, listening to the ice flying off the propellers and hitting the fuselage, feeling the aircraft lighten and gain speed while we learnt how to breathe again. Jimmy's irrepressible smile returned and he giggled. 'Sorry!' he said. 'I won't do that next time.'

Economics and technical progress had dictated the change from four piston engines to two Rolls-Royce Dart turboprops for the Handley Page Herald. These were very fine, reliable engines and the Herald was well built, but the combination of the two left something to be desired from a performance point of view, at least over the routes on which we operated it.

Inbound to Jersey one fine afternoon, my captain, Jimmy again, was anxiously studying the take-off charts for the easterly runway. He was concerned that we would be weight-limited and may not be able to load enough fuel for our next leg, against the wind, to Hull.

When I contacted our agent on the company frequency, they gave an expected passenger load outbound of, I thought, fourteen. Jimmy was delighted. 'No problem!' he announced. 'We can take plenty of fuel.'

On the ground, after the passengers had disembarked and the fuel was already being pumped into the tanks, the agent arrived with the final load figures showing a passenger load of not fourteen, but forty, plus a few items of freight. There followed a moment of frantic activity. While I rushed to stop the refuelling, Jimmy reworked his calculations to find, by great good fortune, that our actual take-off would now exactly match the maximum allowed off the runway in the prevailing conditions.

There were relaxed smiles all round. It was a great relief to find that the awkward, slow and unpopular process of defuelling would not be necessary. So we sauntered over to the office to enjoy a cup of coffee while the cabin cleaning was completed and the new passengers boarded.

Just as we were about to go back on board, the dispatcher, who was responsible for producing the load sheet, arrived to point out that the aircraft's centre of gravity would be well aft. Again, I rushed to check the actual position of the passengers and freight while Jimmy checked the load sheet carefully.

We found the loading was correct and the centre of gravity was exactly on the rearmost permitted limit and therefore acceptable. Again, relaxed smiles broke out. All was well, we thought. But that was probably the point at which we should have called a halt to proceedings and reviewed the situation in detail. Nothing was wrong and nothing was unacceptable, but with the weight at maximum and the centre of gravity on the aft limit, it might have been wise to reflect at some length upon the possible consequences of this condition.

Engine start and taxi proceeded as usual, except that another aircraft appeared on final approach and we needed to expedite our line-up and take-off quickly. Jimmy got a move on and we completed the take-off checks in good order. As I checked the application of full power I was aware that the latest surface wind passed to us by the tower gave slightly less of a headwind component than previously, but it seemed insignificant at the time.

For higher take-off weights, the Herald used a reduced flap setting and a higher rotation speed. Halfway down the runway we began to realize that acceleration was slow. Jimmy was muttering and wriggling about in his seat. I decided not to look at the runway end rushing towards us, but to concentrate on calling out the airspeed indicator reading as accurately as I could. At last the magic figure appeared and, coincident with my call, Jimmy hauled back on the control column.

A lot of things happened in the next couple of seconds. In retrospect it was obvious that with such an aft centre of gravity, only the gentlest pressure was needed on the control column to raise the nose into the flying attitude. Jimmy's great heave resulted in an over-rotation that must have come close to banging the tail of the fuselage on the runway. The sudden increase in angle of attack caused a great surge of lift from the starboard wing, but the port wing stalled and the aircraft rolled violently to the left.

Jimmy's reactions were swift and brave. He pushed the control column hard forward again, which settled the aircraft back on the runway and also revealed the meagre few yards left to us. Still he waited until the last possible moment before delicately, oh, so delicately, easing the column back again. We skated into the air from the very end of the tarmac. It was touch and go; we waited, expecting to hear the approach lights ripping through the lower fuselage, but we must have cleared them by inches. I had the gear retracted in record time but neither of us breathed for a long time until the speed increased enough to allow flap retraction and we could start our turn onto a northerly track.

We sat in stunned silence while the aircraft settled into the climb. Neither of us could speak. I was acutely aware of the beauty of the scene below – the patchwork green of Jersey's fields and sunlight sparkling on the white surf contrasting with the intense blue sea. It seemed we had been spared from disaster and a spectacularly violent end and yet still, we were witnessing heaven.

The mood was broken by the appearance of a vivacious stewardess between our seats. 'Coffee or tea, chaps?' she asked brightly and then she looked puzzled as we rolled our eyes and puffed out our cheeks and started to giggle.

Sometimes, in any aeroplane, things just happen very quickly. I didn't fly the Herald for very long, but it provided a disproportionate number of memorable events. Landing at Luton with my old friend Jimmy in heavy rain, everything seemed to be going well. He flew a good approach and put the aircraft on the required touchdown point at the correct speed. The standard procedure was then to brake firmly and, as the speed reduced, to pull back a lever on the throttle quadrant that would put the propellers into ground fine pitch. This gave two benefits: first, it caused an increase in drag from the discing propellers, which helped with the breaking process; second, it reduced the load on the engine at low speeds, preventing the turbine temperatures from going too high.

There must have been some instances of pilots failing to select ground fine pitch during the landing roll because a notice had been issued by the Chief Pilot reminding captains of the need for this action and warning of dire consequences for those who failed to do so. In the worst case, high temperatures could wreck an engine completely and upset the accountants. Jimmy had obviously read the notice and was keen to comply; too keen, as it turned out. The moment the wheels touched the runway, Jimmy snatched the lever back and the propellers snapped to the ground fine pitch position. The braking effect was impressive, but as with any two independent mechanical systems, the two propellers did not react at exactly the same time. The left propeller achieved its full discing effect about half a second before the right hand one, which was enough to yaw the aircraft smartly to the left.

Sliding sideways at high speed down a flooded runway in a 20-ton aircraft with forty passengers on board was a new experience for me. I have no doubt my eyes were as wide open as my mouth and I expect my hair was standing on end too. But, once again, I was able to relax and to marvel as I watched a true master, in a flurry of rapid arm and leg movements accompanied by a colourful string of oaths, bring the machine back under full control.

There was a trip into Teesside where the captain I was with, after considerable time with his head down trying to make sense of the radar returns, pronounced it useless and resorted to the old method of just pressing on into the weather. I found time to fiddle with the radar too and decided that it did not make sense to me either. However I adjusted the gain or the tilt, the whole screen seemed to light up with a solid return. We made an approach and landing in dark cloud, light rain and moderate turbulence, to find the visibility very poor when we broke out of cloud close to our minimums. We landed and taxied to the gate in the gloom and then, just as the doors were opened, there were several brilliant lightning flashes with simultaneous thunderclaps and the heavens opened in a torrential deluge. For twenty minutes no one was able to disembark because the rain was so heavy. The wind shook and swung the aircraft, threatening to move it bodily off its chocks, and the apron was flooded. Gradually it dawned upon us that there had been nothing wrong with the radar; it had been accurately showing us the full extent of a massive thunderstorm.

A very useful feature on that early weather radar set, which I have never seen on any other model, was its ability to function as a drift indicator. By tilting the scanner fully down so that it was showing only ground returns and adjusting the gain, the most prominent area of return could be read off against a scale to show drift to left or right in degrees. We already had airspeed and compass heading information from our instruments and it was easy enough to measure or estimate ground speed, so, with drift, it was possible to navigate reasonably accurately anywhere. It would be a superfluous feature today when aircraft have Inertial and Global Positioning System (GPS) navigation, but there were many occasions on the earlier jets when it would have been worth its weight in gold. I guess the idea just went out of fashion, like the visual drift indicators fitted to aircraft such as the DH Dragon Rapide between the wars. It is just another really useful, simple, cheap, reliable device forgotten on the march towards technological Nirvana.

Flying scheduled services on the Herald taught me about punctuality, safety, passenger care, crew management and a dozen other facets of professional airline operation. But it also reinforced my suspicion that nothing, absolutely nothing in the real world can be brought under total control.

I was quite pleased to be called early while on standby duty one murky November day. At least I would be flying. Early morning fog had disrupted all the schedules and none of the aircraft or crews were where they needed to be. Crewing wanted me to operate the London to Edinburgh service, which should have left Heathrow at 8:30am, but now was planned to leave Luton at 2:15pm.

The flight was so late that only one passenger could be found. At least he had the undivided attention of two pretty stewardesses and the choice of where he would like to sit. The moist, warm-sector weather system that had produced the fog and drizzle was being swept away by a ferocious cold front as we prepared for departure. The torrential rain and fierce, gusting winds delayed everything further. When we did eventually get airborne, the strong north-easterly airflow cut our ground speed significantly and embedded showers and troughs provided unrelieved turbulence.

The weather reports soon showed that Edinburgh was out of the question and the company asked us to divert to Glasgow. The captain I was crewed with, a big, amiable Canadian, was philosophical, but, as I got re-clearance from Air Traffic Control and we changed course into the teeth of the gale, he did complain about the lack of coffee.

Pressing the crew call-bell for such things was usually bad form, but, after all, there was only one passenger – the girls couldn't be too busy – so he stabbed a thick finger into the button. The face that appeared between us a few minutes later bore no relationship to either of the pretty young things who had been so chirpy before take-off. It was a pale visage with a touch of green about it and the once frivolous blonde fringe was plastered to a moist forehead. Both of our stewardesses had apparently succumbed to airsickness soon after take-off and were really of little use to anyone thereafter.

Glasgow, of course, was busy. Air Traffic promised to sequence us for an approach as soon as they could, but asked us initially to hold at a non-directional radio beacon a few miles south of the airfield. By now it was dark, the wind was probably even stronger and the turbulence had certainly not reduced. Flying a precise, four-minute racetrack pattern, designed to hold the aircraft within a defined, safe area, without any other navigation aids, is a skill that involves accurate instrument flying and some mathematical calculation, but my captain set to the task with quiet competence. I was impressed by the large amount of time for which he held a steady heading into wind and surprised when he then continued the turn all the way onto the inbound heading, having allowed no outbound track at all. With the aircraft bucking and swaying and the radio compass needle twitching and drifting over the dial, it was difficult to be sure but we seemed to be somewhere near the correct inbound track. We both focused on the stopwatch. Four minutes came and went. Then five. Then six. The wind speed must almost have matched our airspeed. It was as if we were held stationary in a turbulent bucket of black air. The big Canadian started to chuckle. His great frame shook and humour finally exposed the ridiculous situation in which we found ourselves.

'We started from the wrong place, at the wrong time and we're going to the wrong destination,' he said. 'The flight has taken twice as long as it should have done already. It's as rough as a bear's arse and if this controller sends us round the hold again we might be up here all night. Reckon our passenger will want to fly with us again?'

Eventually, we made our approach, landed, taxied to the gate and the doors were opened. Remembering that the cabin crew were not at peak efficiency, the amiable Canadian left me to complete the shutdown checks while he went aft to assist the passenger and perhaps commiserate with him on the unfortunate lapse in our airline's normally high standards on this particular trip. He soon returned, laughing more heartily than ever.

'How did he take it?' I asked.

'Oh, he's fine,' he replied. 'A bit confused, perhaps, but he wasn't even upset when he found out we'd left his baggage behind.'

CHAPTER 5

The Jet

Jet aeroplanes did not represent just another step on the evolutionary ladder – they transformed the airline business completely. Pilots and engineers have always thought of their times as the peak of technological achievement, only to discover very quickly that there was more to come. In his book, written in 1934, Imperial Airways Captain Gordon Olley points out that he had '... lived through a remarkable period of aerial progress'. He compares his early days when, 'We had none of the scientific aids to navigation – in the shape of organised wireless, meteorology and guiding beacons – which we find at our disposal at the present time,' to the perfection he saw in 1934: '... when the dependability of our big multi-engined airliners is such that the latest British figures for all-the-year-round reliability stand at just on 100%.'[4]

In just the same way, the jet seemed to us to provide true mastery of our element for the first time. It was not just the speed, though that transformed the way in which pilots, commercial planners and passengers perceived distances. It was the power to soar to great altitude effortlessly, to banish ice, to carry duplicated systems for every conceivable eventuality and to cruise in vibrationless comfort.

The triumph of technology in those times seemed to suggest that anything was possible. During my first year on a jet, Neil Armstrong and Buzz Aldrin walked on the moon. The chatter on the radio and in every airline crew room that day was about the progress of Apollo 11. I raced home from my flight eager to watch the television coverage, but fell asleep on the sofa during the long wait while the crew prepared for their 'extra vehicular activity'. When I awoke, it was to the pictures of the century and the famous phrase, 'One small step for man ...', I was elated. Driving to the airport for my flight the following day I felt buoyed by an unquenchable optimism: if human beings can do this, they can do anything. Later that year, we went to see the musical *Hair* and we danced on the stage and we sang, 'It is the dawning of the age of Aquarius ...'. We had no idea what that meant, but we had no doubt that it was good. The old ways had been swept away and replaced by a better world in which technology solved all our problems.

The jet handled magnificently. The BAC 1-11, which provided my introduction to jet flying, had a power-assisted elevator and rudder with conventional, unpowered ailerons. The controls were rather heavy;

perhaps the designers or test pilots were worried that we might be carried away by the aircraft's performance and be tempted to try aerobatics if the controls were too light. But, apart from a slight dynamic instability in pitch, which was only noticeable when attempting to fly level, very accurately at 250 knots (probably introduced with the change from a manual to a powered elevator), the aircraft was easy to fly throughout its operating envelope. Unlike propeller aircraft, where the pitch attitude varied very little, you had to point a jet where you wanted to go. This, together with the inertia and clean aerodynamic form, meant new flying techniques had to be developed. Not all pilots were able to make the transition, but those who did had no wish ever to return to propellers. We fell in love with it. So did the passengers and business boomed.

Progress always comes at a cost. Perhaps the biggest loss in the case of the jet was related to the altitude at which it flew. It is a clean, wide, beautiful world up there, but you can't see the ground very well. I missed the long summer days spent rumbling gently over the German country-side, admiring the neat fields and the wooded hills with the sun glinting on the rivers. Then, flying was a more natural part of life. I was able to observe that the countryside, the mountains, the wide cold seas and the winds that swept them were the world, not cities. Even the Herald spent most of its time down in the weather at an altitude that enabled me to feel part of the natural world. But the jet operated in its own, pristine atmosphere. During the short times we were at low level we were too busy to spend much time admiring the view. We took off in one place, rushed up to the stratosphere and descended a few hours later at some other place. I missed being close to the countryside, but even this was compensated for, in no small measure, by the big picture. There were days when, flying back from the continent, we could see the south coast of England stretching away beyond the Isle of Wight on the left and the coast of Norfolk to the Wash on the right, with the whole wide expanse of South-East England in-between.

These feelings were strong, but since I was young and ambitious, they did not trouble me much. I suppose every pilot regards the aircraft on which he got his first command with affection, but my respect for the BAC 1-11 went beyond that. For the first time I had a machine that did everything I asked. It had plenty of power to do the job properly and it had reserves of power for hydraulics, electrics, pneumatics and pressurization. It had a ground power unit and its own retractable steps, so that it could be operated independently of ground services. The navigation equipment was not much different from previous aircraft, but it was presented in a far more user-friendly fashion. Aircraft designers had discovered ergonomics; we felt that a real, practising pilot had been involved in the cockpit layout and that information was being provided in a useful, coordinated way. We still had round-faced mechanical instruments, but now we could select the information we wanted displayed on them, so that VOR or Automatic Direction Finder (ADF) bearings could be shown on the same compass card.

Distance Measuring Equipment (DME) gave us another tool to work with, but demonstrated yet again the principle, discovered by navigators over centuries of voyaging, that no navigational system should be relied on in isolation. The readout was mechanical and it was possible to see the wrong mileage displayed, still turning over at the correct rate, but possibly tens of miles in error. Then, while we looked at it and tried to make sense of it, it would suddenly spin to a more believable figure.

The provision of a modern flight director was perhaps the most significant instrument advance. In essence, the zero reader had been cleverly combined with the artificial horizon to provide each pilot with one Attitude Director. It made accurate instrument flying possible, easily, under all circumstances, reducing the high level of concentration that had been demanded up until now.

Even the management of systems such as fuel and electrics was made straight-forward by simple, graphical presentation. Switches and indicators were arranged on the panels in a logical layout matched by the diagrams in the aircraft manuals. Many of the systems were automated and now we had a real autopilot through which we could manoeuvre the aircraft in any axis. Later models even had provision for auto-throttle.

With hindsight, it is easy to see the direction in which these improvements were leading us. The days when raw flying ability was paramount and everything else was secondary were over. Flying – making the aircraft do what you wanted it to do – was now easier and, if we wished, semi-automated. We were being distanced from our flying environment, but we weren't thinking ahead. We were seduced by the jet. We revelled in the freedom the new designs offered us. We embraced the technology, but we continued to hand-fly the aircraft a lot, because it was fun.

On a BAC 1-11 that first year I was surprised to be given the leg by a rather dry old Training Captain who never gave much away. Viv didn't speak much at all unless it was to criticize with rather heavy sarcasm. We were descending to Pisa, tracking towards their Non-Directional Beacon (NDB) near the coast, when the controller cleared us to make the approach. We were flying in and out of towering cumulus cloud with occasional glimpses of the sea below when I levelled off at our safety height. Taking care to do everything by the book, I reduced speed with the intention of descending further when we crossed the beacon, while turning outbound in the instrument procedure for the approach.

A few seconds before we reached the beacon, Viv suggested in his dry, slow way, that I might care to start the descent now. I was surprised. The rules were quite clear: we should not leave our en-route safety height until crossing the beacon to start the published procedure.

But it was safe; I had caught a glimpse of the coast and knew there was no high ground below us. And he was the boss, so I eased into a 500ft per minute descent. Just as the needle on the radio compass started to drift, indicating we were reaching the overhead, we emerged from the cloud into clear air and were confronted by an enormous American Air Force four-engined jet freighter, head on, opposite direction, maybe 300ft above. Then we were swallowed up in the cloud again and, somewhat shaken, I tried to concentrate on flying the descending turn accurately. When I had a moment I looked across at Viv. He was nodding his head slowly.

'Thought that might happen,' he said. He didn't really speak Italian, but had recognized enough of the numerals in the conversation between the controller and the Italian-speaking American to guess that he had been cleared down to our level.

Back in the days when I was a flying instructor at Birmingham Airport, students, qualified private pilots and instructors all experienced some difficulty in using their brains for navigational calculations or decisions while hand-flying the aircraft.

'Yeah, you can fly. And you can think. But can you do both at the same time?' was a question that often cropped up. We were either so preoccupied with the flying that we could not think clearly, or, while we turned our minds to other things, our handling skills deteriorated. Usually both tasks suffered. Experience had eased the problem for me a bit. Just by spending hours in the air and becoming more at home in my environment the problem had lost some of its urgency. But it was clearly still of major importance and I began to realize that the time had come, if not to solve it completely, to move up to the next level of competence.

Airlines in the UK had started to expand rapidly with the introduction of the jet and a pilot shortage developed. These were exciting times. Jets had transformed the holiday charter business. The public was clamouring for cheap, sun-filled holidays in Spain, Italy and Greece and the airlines were fighting for market share. Several of my colleagues were promoted. I looked up my position on the seniority list and realized it could be my turn soon. Only captains were expected to do the thinking in those days, so I decided I had to get serious about improving my command skills. Within days I was treated to a perfect illustration of how it should be done.

It happened on the return to the UK after an overnight charter flight to Spain. Our BAC 1-11 was descending at last over continuous stratus cloud above the Channel. Long-haul crews will tell you that they are the only ones who know about fatigue and jet lag. Don't believe it; you don't need to cross any time zones. A random roster, mixing night and day duties of ten or twelve hours, will do it. And when the crewing department throws in the odd twenty-four-hour rest period, thinking they're doing you a favour, you soon become an expert in the exquisite effects of sleep deprivation.

So, in the early hours of that morning with the sun reflecting off the cloud sheet, stinging like sand in my eyes, and my mouth dry from countless cups of tasteless coffee, my thoughts, incoherent as they were, centred on how long it would take to get onto the ground, into my car and home to my bed.

We were last in a stream of at least six aircraft inbound to Luton where the weather was deteriorating, but still above limits for landing. Stansted's weather was similar, but the cloud base was higher. In the left-hand seat was Freddie, a cheery, 20,000-hour, World War II veteran who never seemed to take anything seriously. He showed more interest in his crew's love life than he did in flying.

'I think,' he said, speaking slowly, 'we should ask for diversion to Stansted.'

I was appalled. What's the matter with Luton? I would have to call London Airways to arrange a diversion and then contact the company to tell them what we were doing. They would have to organize coaches to get our passengers and us back to Luton and to position the next crew with their passengers over to Stansted. It would cost a fortune, cause endless delays and – much more serious – I wouldn't get to my bed for hours.

Freddie was unusual in that he would explain his decisions. His logic proved compelling. The weather at Luton was deteriorating. There were several aircraft ahead of us and by the time we got our turn to make an approach it would probably be below our limits. If we didn't land, we would have to go to Stansted with a lot less fuel than we had now and might well be put into a queue there as well. I did the calculations and realized that if we did not do something soon, fuel could get very tight.

The London air traffic controllers were as helpful as ever; nothing ever ruffles them. I got out the charts while Freddie took up the new routing and we were soon being handed over to Stansted Approach. Everything was set up and we were told to expect no delay. Perhaps I would get home before lunchtime. Unreasonably, I began to feel pleased with myself. We were being smart, ahead of the game. Then, along with the latest Stansted weather, which was also getting worse, the controller gave us the news that their ILS was unserviceable. Now we were faced with an NDB approach with only a fifty–fifty chance of getting in. Fail here and, with Luton out and our fuel low, we would have to declare an emergency and hope we had enough fuel to get into Heathrow.

Freddie began to smile. He was enjoying this! The NDB approach was an anachronism even then. It was devised for an older, slower generation of aircraft and not many jet pilots could guarantee to fly one really accurately, first time, when it was sprung upon them like this. But Freddie was able, not just to demonstrate some real precision instrument flying, but to give a master class. He provided me with a running commentary while he hand-flew the approach, pointing out the discrepancies between the needles on the radio compass as they wavered uncertainly over the dial. Averaging their readings carefully, we appeared to be, as accurately as it was possible to tell, exactly on the track published on the charts.

'But the charts are wrong,' Freddie claimed. 'They're two degrees out. If they were correct we would see the runway there,' and he leant across the cockpit to point to a spot on my windscreen. 'But we won't. It will be there,' and he moved his finger to another position on the screen.

Three things happened at once. I called, 'Minima', the clouds parted and the runway appeared through the gloom exactly under Freddie's finger.

'See!' he said.

When we had landed and the passengers had disembarked, I received a radio message from our company.

'All the other aircraft have landed successfully at Luton, Freddie,' I told him.

He shrugged his shoulders. 'Why were you so keen to get home?' he asked. 'Who are you going out with now?' He was completely at ease with his decisions and knew better than to dwell on them.

What had impressed me most, apart from Freddie's flying, was how relaxed he was and how much time he had. He never seemed rushed. Realizing he was a bit special, a friend and I took him out for a beer some time later and asked for his advice to prospective new captains. We wanted the benefit of his experience, but he refused to be serious at first, showing much more interest in how we entertained the new steward-esses. Eventually he relented.

His advice did not flatter us co-pilots of the day, but it showed how advanced his thinking was for the time. 'When everything is going wrong,' he told us, 'trust your instincts.' He paused and we looked at each other doubtfully. 'On that dark and stormy night when you're short of fuel, all the airports are below limits, you have an engine failure and the galley's on fire, just make up your mind what you most want to do. Then, before you do it, ask your co-pilot what he would do. There's no pressure on him; his answer will be quick and uninhibited. It is just possible that he may have thought of something you have missed, but it is more likely that his suggestion will be nonsense and you will be able to reject it out of hand. In this way your faith in your own decision will be greatly enhanced, and you will be able to carry it out with confidence.'

I tried to learn from every captain I flew with and I was gaining experi-ence all the time, but some things just could not be predicted. Approach-ing the island of Menorca one morning, we found the normally peaceful place ravaged by the Mistral. The infamous wind that channels down the Rhone Valley had built up to gale force and was sweeping on unchecked over the Mediterranean to the low-lying island.

Fortunately, or more probably by design, the runway aligned perfectly with the wind so that aircraft could still land, although crossing the low cliffs between the southern coast and the runway threshold meant facing significant wind shear and gusts. The controller was giving frequent reports of the wind direction and speed to the aircraft ahead of us.

'Zero one zero, fifty knots,' he intoned. 'Zero two zero at fifty eight knots.' The information was welcome and useful on the latter stages of the approach and we listened with interest as we flew overhead and turned back to line up with the runway ourselves. Even though we turned early, the wind carried us further south than we would have liked and, as we settled into a slow drag back towards the island, our windscreen gradually coated with salt from the white and angry sea below.

The previous aircraft landed uneventfully and taxied clear. We were cleared to land with the wind 'Zero one zero sixty knots.' The tension had begun to rise in the cockpit because it was obvious that if we did not land on this approach, another layer of salt from a second attempt would mean we would not be able to see forward at all. As we crossed the cliffs, peering with difficulty through our nearly opaque windscreen, we realized the controller had been silent for some time.

'What's the wind now?' I asked.

'I don't know, sir,' he shouted. 'My anemometer just blew off the roof!'

Air Traffic delays were a feature of flying between the UK and Spain in those days. The rapid increase in traffic threatened to overwhelm the system and controllers in France and Spain were overworked and underpaid. When they worked to rule or went on strike, it was not unusual for aircraft to be held on the ground with passengers on board, doors closed and ready to go, for several hours. We had to be ready to be airborne within minutes of a clearance coming through; if we were not able to take off in time, we lost the slot and went to the back of the queue again.

Pilots who were determined to beat the system showed plenty of initiative. We filed for different routes, avoiding the bottlenecks but often creating jams elsewhere. Longer flight times meant a much higher fuel burn, but that was not nearly as important as getting the aircraft to where it was supposed to be. We tried flying west out of Spanish airspace and routing up over the Atlantic outside of French airspace, even though this was of doubtful legality because we did not carry suitable navigational equipment for flight out of range of fixed, ground-based radio aids. Sometimes we could get clearance at a much lower flight level, again having to accept a considerable fuel penalty.

Preparing to leave the UK for Spain one day, I asked the co-pilot from an inbound crew what the restrictions were like.

'We didn't have any,' he said. 'The French have gone on strike and won't speak to anybody. It's much better that way.' He seemed happy with the situation, but the idea of dozens of airliners criss-crossing French airspace without any form of separation was alarming.

The controllers themselves were highly professional and responsible and I never heard any acrimonious exchanges between them and the flight crews. On occasion, they showed compassion. Having got airborne after three hours' delay from Alicante with Mike, another World War II veteran, we were told that we would not be allowed to cross into French airspace and must enter a holding pattern at the border. While I tried all the usual tricks to negotiate a better clearance, Mike reduced speed to conserve fuel and spoke to the cabin crew and passengers to let them know what was going on. We had just about accepted that we would have to hold for forty-five minutes and calculated that we would have just enough fuel to do that when the cabin crew reported a problem. We were carrying a passenger, a twelve-year old girl, with a broken leg. She had been given pain-killing injections to make her comfortable for the duration of the flight, but the effects were now wearing off and she was in some distress.

Mike, whose language skills were far superior to mine, immediately conveyed this information to the Spanish controller, who consulted his French colleague and within a minute cleared us direct, a straight line at maximum speed to Luton Airport. All the controllers we spoke to thereafter, Spanish, French or British, were waiting for us and did everything they could to expedite our flight. We must have broken the record for a flight from northern Spain to the UK and were able to arrange for a medical team to meet us when we arrived on stand.

At destinations where there was no convenient pub, and often when there was, it was usual for the crew to treat themselves to a drink from the aircraft's bar. On the last sector, we would give our orders before the bar was sealed and enjoy a snifter as soon as the engines were shut down on stand. When the jets came in, this civilized custom became known as a 'reverse thrust cocktail'. Like so many customs, it could get out of hand. It became a challenge for the cabin crew to see how strong they could make the drinks. Swigging them back too quickly after a long duty day in an oxygen-reduced environment, the dehydrated pilots found these drinks had a powerful effect. If they stumbled negotiating the steps down to the tarmac, the girls thought it was hilarious.

My progress up the first officers' seniority list had brought new responsibilities. Flying as a supernumerary crew member to monitor and assist a new co-pilot was not a popular duty. It meant we did not get to fly the aircraft ourselves and had to ride in the jump seat. This cramped and uncomfortable folding contraption behind the centre console was awkward to rig, tricky to stow away and had minimal upholstery. On the descent at the end of one such trip, I was dismayed to learn we would be diverting to Stansted. We would probably have to hang around there for ages and then endure a long taxi ride. Anticipating going to the Flying Club, I had declined a reverse thrust cocktail before the bars were sealed. It now looked as though I wouldn't get a drink at all because the club would be shut by the time we got back to Luton.

We landed at Stansted and taxied in. The skipper shut down the engines, the passengers disembarked and the number one stewardess delivered stiff gins to him and the new co-pilot. They drank them with extra relish because I didn't have one, but their mock commiserations were cut short when the agent came on board.

'Luton's weather has improved,' he announced gaily. 'The company want you to fly the aircraft back there empty.' The captain and the new co-pilot looked at each other, aghast. How could they fly after a stiff gin? And how could they explain having a drink before leaving the aircraft?

There are moments when justice seems a natural part of life. 'My leg I think, gentlemen,' I said. So I got to fly the aircraft that day after all and arrived back in time for a drink in the club as well – several, in fact.

Down to fly with a captain I had not met before, but had heard of by reputation as a test pilot with a lot of jet experience, I was looking forward to the meeting. Pete was pointed out to me when I reported for duty, a shortish figure with rather bandy legs. He was hunched over the briefing table, his head, covered in black curly hair, bent low over the meteorological chart. I went and stood next to him and introduced myself. There was no reaction. He continued to stare at the chart for a while then stood up straight, turned to look me in the eye and said, 'Bum!' Then he turned on his heel and made his way out to the aircraft.

Not an auspicious start. I collected the briefing material together, picked up the navigation bag, collected the cabin crew and we followed him out to the aircraft. Checklist drills were more formal on the jet and my surly captain was obliged to call the items and acknowledge my responses, though he did this in a croaking monotone with no apparent enthusiasm or even interest. But my goodness, he could fly. It was apparent the moment the wheels left the ground. I had never seen anyone on the jet fly with such smooth, effortless precision. It was as if he and the aeroplane were made for each other. He seemed to change into a machine, while the aeroplane came alive. The power of the jet, its lack of vibration and its soaring performance had transformed the idea of flying for all of us. It realized our dreams: the simple, graceful silence of a sailplane empowered as if by magic to soar through its element, the complete master of its heights.

We flew in silence to Faro on the southern coast of Portugal in perfect weather. As soon as we could identify the airfield, still over 100 miles away, Pete croaked out an order, 'Tell 'em we're visual!'

Most of the pilots I flew with were a little in awe of the jet. They were generally competent and safe, but they were still coming to terms with its speed and inertia and they were uncomfortably aware of its rumoured vices. They had accustomed themselves to the feel and the sounds of propeller aircraft over many years and, as yet, the jet did not speak to them. But Pete had no such inhibitions. When he started the descent I was puzzled. He seemed to me to have left it a bit late. We continued straight to the airfield and passed overhead in a wide descending turn, speed bleeding off, but still carrying a lot of energy. After a short outbound leg, Pete rolled early into the final turn, calling for flap in stages as the speed allowed and then the gear as we straightened up smoothly in perfect alignment with the runway. It had been a stylish, even flamboyant approach executed with dashing confidence. Unfortunately, we were far too high to land from it.

I heard a long, despairing sigh from Pete. His pale blue eyes regarded me sadly from his wrinkled, swarthy face. 'Why didn't you say something?' he asked.

'You're the big ace,' I replied. 'I thought you had something up your sleeve.'

'But how ...?' He sighed again and set about recovering the situation as best he could. The landing, when eventually it came, was as smooth as butter sliding into a hot pan.

Pete turned out to be intelligent and articulate, though he was often moody, especially when he had a hangover. His sense of humour was never far from the surface. He relished the company of young people and would be ready in an instant for wild, partying excess. We became firm friends and he taught me a lot about flying jets.

The only reason for being a co-pilot was to become, eventually, a Captain. There were one or two so-called 'professional first officers' who had failed command training or put up some dreadful black that meant they would never be promoted within the company. They might have lost the confidence or energy to try a different airline, but for the rest of us, the prospect of a command dominated our every waking thought. And dreams too. It was rumoured that some co-pilots had four rings sewn onto the sleeves of their pyjamas. We devoured the pages of *Flight* magazine, studying the market for pilots, and schemed continuously to achieve our goal. We would have gone anywhere at a moment's notice, flown anything and accepted the most atrocious pay and conditions in order to write our names in the column of our logbooks headed, 'Pilot in Command'.

Slowly, we learnt that patience and diplomacy provided the surest route to success. We studied the aircraft manuals and the company operation manuals and every paragraph of every regulation. We knew and practised every aspect of the SOPs and we studied the Captains we flew with. Many of them were still entirely autocratic; they had never heard of Crew Resource Management. They thought that communication was something that happened when they growled out an order.

Even the most surly, incommunicative and frankly objectionable Captains were analysed and discussed in order to glean knowledge from them. Their operation may not have been in accordance with the company model, their aircraft handling may have been rough and their brains a little slow, but they had somehow obtained a command and had not yet killed themselves, so they must know something.

Most difficult of all, we learnt to curb our tongues. We were tactful. We asked our Captains questions in deferential terms and flattered them if necessary. We made sure we had the answer to every question they might ask of us and that we had all the information they might need even before they knew they would need it. And gradually we gained the knowledge, the wisdom even, of Captains ourselves.

Training for command, to promote a co-pilot to Captain, was something of a lottery in those days. Many of today's co-pilots will tell you it still is. Co-pilots were supposed to be promoted in accordance with the seniority list, based on length of service with the airline, providing that they had obtained the full Airline Transport Pilot's Licence (ATPL). In fact, it was at the whim of the Chief Pilot, who looked at each pilot's training records and might ask the opinion of his Line Trainers. Once selected, the candidates flew a competency check in the left-hand seat and went on to fly the line as an Acting Captain, with a Line Training Captain as co-pilot, who retained legal command. A final line check, with a different trainer if one was available, sealed his fate. Unless the trainer deigned to offer any useful advice, there was none. There was no formal syllabus. The new Captain was expected to know, somehow, what was required and to learn from criticism during the debriefings.

My own command course benefited from a new innovation. Benefited? Well, the simulator had arrived and a working relationship began that was going to play an increasing part in my career. At first, we all thought of it as a bit of a joke. It was obviously safer – and cheaper – to practise certain procedures in this device on the ground than in the aircraft and we were impressed by the realism, but it wasn't flying. From the inside, the flight deck was real; all the seats, equipment, controls and instruments were exactly the same as in the aircraft. The view through the windows was artificial. At first, a miniature TV camera reproduced the scene below cloud by moving over an enormous model that covered one wall of the building. There was supposed to be an electronic cut-out to prevent the camera hitting the model, but it didn't always work. The engineers got fed up of replacing broken trees and houses and the jokers had fun trying to position spiders on the end of the runway.

Later models had electronic visual displays. The early ones could only provide a monochrome night scene that played its part in associating the simulator forever in the minds of many of its victims with a place of dark depression, like a torture chamber in a medieval dungeon. Even the modern, full-colour daylight visuals rely on a reduced light level inside the flight deck and are not cheerful places.

The flight deck was mounted on a six-axis hydraulic platform that moved to provide motion clues. When accelerating along the runway, for instance, the whole machine would tip backwards smoothly so that the pilots felt themselves pushed back into their seats. In-flight, the system would wheeze and squeal and bang, occasionally providing physical jolts to the whole machine.

The stories of pilots becoming so engrossed in the exercise they were performing that they forgot they were in a simulator are apocryphal. Simulators were simply not that good. They could, however, produce genuine ill effects when the hydraulics failed and the machine came crashing down onto its stops. When that happened, the motion detected by the pilot's body was so far divorced from the movement his brain was assuming from the instrument indications that it could make him feel seriously ill.

When the novelty wore off, most of us found we heartily disliked the device. But we could not avoid the fact that it was going to decide the outcome of our careers. We had to overcome our distaste and learn to master it. If we wanted to survive and prosper as airline pilots, we had to be able to perform well in the simulator.

Modern simulator manufacturers will claim that their products are much more faithful to the real experience of flight today. They will point to the superb computer-generated visual systems, the smooth, silent and reliable hydraulic platform and the accurate control responses derived from actual test-flight data provided by the aircraft manufacturer. They will claim that the simulator has evolved to provide an experience very similar to flying the real aircraft. I think they are wrong: it is the aircraft that have evolved to handle more like simulators.

Once again, technology had moved on, but attitudes were slow to change. After passing our final command line checks, Kurt and I – we had gone through the process together – were summoned to the Chief Pilot's office. Another World War II veteran, this grand gentleman greeted us cordially. His advice was brief, but we were left in no doubt about what was expected of us. Stressing the need to trust our own judgement he said, 'If every other airline in the world lands here while you are refus-ing to leave Spain because you don't think the weather is good enough, you will never hear a word of criticism from me. But bend one of my aeroplanes and I'll come down on you so hard you'll wonder what has hit you!' At that, he reached into a drawer in his desk, pulled the rings on three cans of beer and we drank to our success.

The learning curve took a new upward slant with command. It was a shock, collecting the pre-flight briefing material at flight despatch, to find that when I suggested something, people jumped to do it. While I had not always been totally ignored as a first officer, it often felt as if I had.

I made mistakes, of course. Fortunately the co-pilots I flew with were quite capable of looking after me and the whole system of European airline operation existed to help me. Air traffic controllers were, as ever, extremely helpful and my own airline's management was tolerant.

I was assured that, having been considering the worst possible scenarios during training, I would find actual line flying as a captain something of an anticlimax. In fact, the minimum altitude to which pilots were authorized to descend on approaching an airport without seeing the approach lights was higher for a new captain. As a result, I had to go-around from my minima and divert to another airport three times in my first five weeks. There was also an early lesson to learn when, due to unexpectedly bad weather, failure of ground-based navigational equipment, poor communications and my own poor decision-making, I found myself approaching Lisbon, an airfield with which I was not familiar, with very little fuel in the tanks. I remember the cockpit became unnaturally quiet. Mentally I was rehearsing the same calculations over and over again in my head. Yes, the answer was the same each time: we would have enough fuel to reach the airport and to land safely. But not much more and I could not stop recalculating the figures. The only sounds on the flight deck came from me biting my nails and Mitch, the laconic co-pilot, reaching forward every few seconds to tap the fuel gauges.

Cleared for an ILS approach, I concentrated on accurate flying while Mitch, who probably thought he should have got a command before me, read out the details from the airport approach chart.

'Maintain 2,000ft until intercepting the glide slope,' he intoned. 'Cross the outer marker at 1,500ft … the minima is 200ft and the go-around …'. Here he stopped reading and threw the charts over his shoulder. 'You don't want to know about the go-around,' he said.

Not all of my mistakes could be attributed to the novelty of command. Most pilots see themselves as expert weather forecasters. They like to gaze up at the sky, their eyes sharpened by thousands of hours of experience, their souls mystically in tune with the elements, and make sagacious predictions. At no time is this truer than towards the end of the English holiday charter season. There is something about those quiet autumn days that makes us philosophical. We see the mist penetrated by a weak but benevolent sun. We eagerly embrace the cold mornings after the heat of summer. The scent of resinous sap where the farmers have cut the hedges provides a refreshing, more mature aroma on the drive to work than the mown hay of August. And the sight of golden leaves on the dew-frosted grass is satisfying and reassuring, somehow.

I taxied out for take-off from Luton at dusk on one of those days in a BAC 1-11 jet. The darkening sky contained only a few high strands of cirrus cloud and the wind had dropped. The air was clear and soft, but there was a halo of mist showing just above the grass around the runway lights.

'Could be fog in the morning,' I pronounced, as if I knew.

We were operating a big programme of holiday flights to and from the Spanish resorts and, in an effort to cope more efficiently with weather problems encountered earlier in the season, the company had issued its captains with specific guidance. 'If there is fog in the UK, don't take off from Spain,' it said. 'Wait for a better weather report. If you are already airborne when you learn of it, don't delay or hold. Make an early decision to divert and tell Operations about it.' The plan was intended to provide time for suitable surface transport arrangements to be made so that delays would be reduced and inconvenience to the passengers minimized.

Well, I was right about the fog, but that was the last thing I got right that night. The weather reports we received in Spain showed visibility down to 200m in Luton.

'It will be shallow,' I said. 'Gone by the time we get there.' So I ignored the guidance and took off. By the time we reached northern France the reports were showing no change, so I got clearance to reduce speed, saving fuel while drifting slowly towards our destination. When we reached the overhead position we could see the airfield through thin sheets of fog, but the visibility reported was still not enough for us to make an approach. So I entered a holding pattern. I was doing exactly what I had been asked not to do, but I was convinced we would soon be able to land and everyone would be grateful to me. Eventually, forced by dwindling fuel, I diverted to the East Midlands airport.

It was midday when, tired and bedraggled, our sorry crew straggled back into the company offices at Luton. I tried to tiptoe past the open door of the Operations Manager's office, but his eagle eye had spotted me.

'Spragg!' he bellowed. I stopped and turned to face him through the door.

'Prat!' he shouted.

'Yes, sir,' I said, and crept off home to my bed.

My previous flying experience did sometimes make a positive contribution to the operation, like when I had rashly accepted an altitude restriction in the BAC 1-11 that I soon began to realize I would not be able to make. The Spanish controller in Barcelona had offered us a choice: cross the boundary into France above flight level 330 (33,000ft), or hold for half an hour. There was no choice really, as holding would be a complete waste of time and fuel; accepting, even if we found later that we could not meet the restriction, gave time for the situation to change.

On modern aircraft the Flight Management Computer would give a very accurate prediction of exactly where it was possible to reach the desired flight level. On the 1-11 things were less certain. Our own, very subjective, estimates were always subject to error, but this time I was clearly going to be way out. While the rate of climb reduced to less than 100ft per minute, I contemplated the scene outside and wondered how long I could wait before admitting our predicament to the controller. The snow covering the mountains of the Pyrenees glistened in the sunlight; above us, long thin strands of cloud marched in a line to the north-north-west. The rate of climb would rise, taking my spirits with it for a few moments: 200, 300ft per minute, then fall back to 100, or even zero.

The penny dropped eventually. My sluggish brain suddenly made the connection between the images it was registering: the snow-covered mountains, the cloud and our varying rate of climb. The clouds were lenticulars, which generally occurred in standing-wave conditions. A stable air stream was flowing over the mountains and forming waves downwind in the area where we were flying. On the upside of the wave we were being carried up at a splendid rate, while in sinking air on the other side the 1-11 could not climb at all. It required only a moment's thought to estimate when to turn. As luck would have it, I got it right first time. Turning 45 degrees right put us firmly in the upside of a wave and we soared up at 400ft per minute. I held this course as long as I could, then turned 90 degrees left, quickly cutting across the sinking air before turning into the next uplift. Zigzagging like this, we went up like a lift, stopping briefly at every floor, until we reached our target with time to spare. Not for the first time, the co-pilot had to suffer my rendition of the 5th Dimension's 'Up, up and away in my beautiful, my beautiful, balloon!' Then I stopped singing and tried to keep the triumphalism out of my voice as I made the position report. The snow-covered mountains smiled on me. I wondered what the radar controller had made of our manoeuvres and if he had made a bet with his colleagues on whether we would make it.

There was plenty of competition among the pilots on the BAC 1-11 to achieve a really good landing. Most people know that, statistically, approach and landing are the most dangerous times for aeroplanes. I was to fly sometime later with a colourful character in another airline who liked to use this fact to satisfy his odd sense of humour. Stan would delight in addressing his passengers over the PA as he approached the south coast of England with the reassuring phrase, 'Ladies and Gentlemen you are now about to commence the most dangerous part of your journey.' And he would leave a distinct pause before completing the sentence, 'your drive home from the airport'.

Pilots are taught at a very early stage in their careers that the secret of a good landing lies in a good approach and that for a good approach, the aircraft must be well positioned, in the correct configuration, at the correct speed, right at the start. It is true of small aeroplanes and it is even truer with faster, heavier machines. The aim is to have plenty of time in the final stages of the approach with the aircraft fully stabilized so that the pilot is relaxed and needs to make only minute corrections to the flight path. It is no exaggeration that while watching pilots start their descent from 35,000ft I have said to myself, 'This will result in an untidy arrival.' And no doubt many of them have said it about me.

But popular definitions of a good landing do not often describe what the pilot is trying to achieve. A very smooth landing is usually undesirable in a jet transport aircraft. What is needed is to be accurate, touching down in exactly the right place at exactly the right speed. A firm arrival improves the chances of achieving this and it also reduces the chance of aquaplaning on a wet surface because the wheels break through the water layer and spin up quickly, activating the anti-skid system. It must not be too firm, however, because then the aeroplane will bounce back into the air and, unless the pilot carries out a go-around, the whole process will begin again, further down the runway.

Plenty of things on the pilot's mind then, in the later stages of the approach. He is scanning the instruments to ensure that he is exactly on speed and that the other flight parameters are stable. And he is scanning the outside scene to ensure that he is exactly on the centre line at the correct angle of approach. He does this by comparing the apparent shape of the runway with an ideal mental picture. Even with the many electronic and visual aids available nowadays, it requires concentration and it is necessary to guard against tunnel vision.

Landing a BAC 1-11 at Strasbourg one misty morning, the first time I had visited the airfield, my concentration on achieving the correct profile on final approach and an accurate touchdown obscured the bigger picture. It was not until the aircraft was rolling down the runway under braking that I became aware of the maintenance work in progress. Men and machines, trucks and heavy rollers were aligned along the runway edges. Why the airport was accepting traffic in these conditions, without issuing warning notices, I never discovered. I did insist, however, that they were all removed to a safe distance before I took off again.

Amid the new excitement and challenges that flying the jet brought, the old enemy, fatigue, flourished. Working irregular hours, starting duty in the early hours of the morning or in the evening, is difficult enough. Switching from 'earlies' to 'lates', or suffering some sort of delay that means the current programme is disrupted, is worse. Even excessive rest periods can break the cycle of work and sleep. Worst of all is the dreaded 'twenty-four-hour slip'. It sounds fine at first; finish duty at 4:00pm and come back on duty at 4:00pm tomorrow. But assuming you are able to manage a full eight hours of sleep, when should you take it? Go to bed in a couple of hours' time and be awake for fourteen hours before the next duty starts? Or try to stay awake for sixteen hours before sleeping? Most, if their body rhythms are not too far adrift from local time, will try for as normal a night's sleep as possible, say from 11pm to 7am, but that still leaves nine hours awake before starting the next duty, which may not finish until four the next morning.

The effects of sleep disruption are, of course, cumulative. And you can't store up sleep in advance of when it might be needed. So airline pilots become intimately acquainted with fatigue in all its stages. It is normal to get tired after a hard day. Work a regular twelve hours every day and sleep eight hours overnight and, providing you get plenty of fresh air, good food and exercise, you can stay fit indefinitely. Work a disruptive roster for five days a week – even with regular days off – for more than a few weeks and you will begin to feel weary all the time. Keep going for several months and you will enter the realms of long-term fatigue.

There are various ways of coping with this state and some of them are socially unacceptable. There were a number of complaints from the airline's office staff about rowdy parties in progress in the crew room when they came in to work at 9am. Our Chief Pilot, however, knew how hard his crews were working and was reluctant to criticize what he considered harmless relaxation. He posted a couple of notices politely asking for some restraint and consideration for others, but they had no effect whatsoever. He was finally forced to come down more severely when, on a particularly boisterous occasion, someone set fire to his notice; the fire engulfed the noticeboard and damn near burnt the place down. After that, we limited ourselves to a couple of beers in the crew room and went off somewhere else if we wanted to continue the party.

The flight-time limitations in the UK are better now, though constantly under threat from commercial and ill-informed political interests. Even so, many of today's pilots will be familiar with long-term fatigue. It is a half-state of life. Pale, unshaven pilots with hollow cheeks wander round their homes in a daze. Their families are strangers and nothing can hold their interest. Reporting on time for the next flight and following the Standard Operating Procedures through the duty period becomes their only goal. They become tetchy, impatient and intolerant, or they are suddenly bored with no energy for anything. Keep this up long enough and serious long-term damage to the nervous system can result.

But winters at that time were slack. Flying once a week meant we soon recovered and started to pester the crewing manager to find us more flights to do. We even took leave. Pan American Airways had just introduced the Boeing 747 Jumbo Jet on its round the world services and even though the planes were fitted with only 250 seats, the company still couldn't fill them. With a fellow pilot I travelled to New Zealand via Hong Kong and came back via Tahiti and San Francisco. We didn't follow the advice offered by singer Scott McKenzie to 'wear some flowers in your hair', but we felt we were at the heart of things and that the world was getting smaller.

Back in the UK, companies in the holiday business were always searching for winter work and a keen bachelor captain who was prepared to go anywhere, for as long as necessary, at a moment's notice, was offered some exciting postings. I was to do spells in Central America and in the Caribbean. I was doing what I had always wanted to do, thoroughly enjoying it and being paid well for it. I was on top of the world.

CHAPTER 6

Caribbean Contrasts

Whatever the altitude, there are occasionally spectacular views from the jet's flight deck. Passengers, if they had the chance, would pay extra for the pilots' seats. From there they could see everything the world has to offer from the Grand Canyon to the Himalayas to the bustling centre of Hong Kong.

Pilots rarely mention this priceless extra to their remuneration package. I don't think it is because they fear they might be taxed on it, or that it could be used as a bargaining chip during the next round of pay negotiations. No, they don't even speak about it at the time, between themselves on the flight deck. I think that is because the really special sights are a very personal experience.

Oh, they might draw each other's attention to some specific item of interest: Mount Fuji clearly visible out of the starboard window, or the Humber Bridge rising out of the mist, say. But the sights they remember, the memories that stay with them for the rest of their lives, often have an importance only to themselves. And often these especially memorable sights are not what you might expect. They are not necessarily the famous or the spectacular features of our planet. They can just as easily be a certain pattern of light and shadow across an empty expanse of ocean, or a cluster of lights on an otherwise shapeless black coastline.

In good weather, the Greenland ice cap can sometimes be seen from over 300 miles away. It looms so clear in the windscreen, in such dazzling detail, that it appears much nearer than it really is, so that pilots new to the experience have to check their position and their ground speed to confirm that they are still moving at the same rate towards the mountains. Then, crossing the landmass itself, there are very few pilots who have their eyes inside the cockpit for much of the time. From the most southerly point, the evocatively named Cape Farewell, to the massive mountains and ice sheets of the interior, the grandeur of this remote wilderness will silence the most talkative of co-pilots.

The air in these latitudes is so cold and dense that aeroplanes perform much better than normal. Landing at Søndre Strømfjord in the BAC 1-11, I found that, on the approach, with gear and full flap extended, the engines gave ample power even with the throttles almost closed. When we came to take off again, we proved that the configuration warning horn, designed to warn the crew if they try to take off with an unsuitable flap or trim setting, did not work because the throttles never went far enough forward to trigger it.

My first experience of Greenland occurred on a ferry flight bound for the Caribbean, an area about which I knew very little. Islands? Pirates? Rum? Pete had spent a lot of time there. Whiling away the long hours of a night flight we had sometimes debated what the ideal job would be, if we couldn't fly that is. I had favoured being a bargee on the Danube; I imagined it would be a relaxing life and full of variety. But after due consideration, Pete had decided that being Water Sports Manager at the Barbados Hilton would be better.

Hopping between the islands in the Caribbean was to provide some of the most satisfying flying I experienced in the BAC 1-11. The facilities provided at many of the airfields we visited were basic to say the least. At Pearls, Grenada, there was a commercial radio station from which we could get bearing information as we approached the island, but the approach was strictly visual. The runway was built at right angles to the coastline, sloping up steeply towards the first of a series of ever higher, thickly wooded ridges. If we had approached from the sea and lost an engine before touchdown, the aircraft would not have had the performance to clear the hills on the climb out in the event of a go-around.

Wiser and more experienced heads than mine had considered the problem and decided the answer was to fly inland and make the landing towards the coast. While this meant flying close to the hills and demanded an accurate touchdown on the short runway, it had the advantage that, should an engine failure occur at any point, the aircraft could be turned to fly over lower ground towards the sea. An extremely capable and experienced West Indian pilot developed a safe technique and reduced it to a procedure, almost flying by numbers, that was so straightforward that even we city boys from Europe could follow it.

I could do it now, forty years later, without further training and without hesitation. We crossed the coast at 1,100ft, at 150 knots, gear down, flaps 25, parallel to the runway on our right. This meant we were heading towards a hospital building – white with a red roof – two-thirds of the way up a dark green hill about three or four miles from the coast. There was no specific turning point; we just kept going towards the building until it felt uncomfortable. Then we banked right and began our turn to line up with the runway. Halfway round the turn, we took landing flap and set 88 per cent N1 on the engines. This produced a rate of descent that would bring us very close to a ridge running parallel to the runway. Through the trees on the crest of the ridge we could see a white shack with a cross on its roof. Crossing it with the altimeter showing 650ft was okay, though it looked very close; that is 650ft above sea level, goodness knows the height of the shack. Even better would be 600ft. We sometimes wondered whether the people who lived there had put the cross up before we started flying over them or afterwards.

If everything was going to plan, this would leave us lined up with the runway, coming down onto a good glide slope, with the speed reducing nicely to our landing reference speed. There was one more wooded ridge to cross, the lower the better. The engines were spooled up all the way and needed only fine adjustment at this stage for the aircraft to be perfectly positioned to touch down early on the runway at exactly the correct speed. Just to make sure, there was a yellow line painted across the runway a few hundred feet from the threshold. If we were not firmly on the ground before that line we must open up the power and go-around to try again. The runway sloped down, of course; it was short and only a few rocks and a narrow sandy beach separated its far end from the Caribbean breakers.

I don't recall anyone going around for a second attempt. It was a matter of pride to get it right first time. I do remember removing branches from the undercarriage after one impressive approach and landing flown by my friend, Colin. It was a safe procedure, but it demanded skill, discipline and confidence and was a source of great satisfaction to us all. After a few weeks, we had no difficulty achieving the required precision time after time, even in heavy rain with the visibility reduced to less than a mile.

We were based in Antigua and I shared a large old house on a hill overlooking a beach with Colin and two other pilots. It was a sociable place. The doors and windows were always open and the trade wind blew continuously through the house along with a stream of visitors. A party of variable intensity ebbed and flowed continually. When I left to go flying in the morning, couples might be swaying to the soft rhythms of Caribbean music on the patio and when I returned in the evening, the same couples, or others, would be jumping up and down to steel band music while smoke from the barbecue scented the air. Even on the rare occasions when the house was empty, it was rarely quiet. We had inherited an old eight-track stereo on which Elton John seemed always to be asking: 'I hope you don't mind, I hope you don't mind that I put down in words, how wonderful life is while you're in the world.'

It doesn't matter how many times you do it, a take-off in any aeroplane is a thrill. Sometimes it can provide more of a thrill than you expect. Getting airborne from San Juan, Puerto Rico, was always exciting. There was an amazing amount of traffic – airliners, private and executive aircraft of all shapes and sizes, and military fast jets – controlled, more or less, by excitable, gung-ho Americans who rattled out their instructions in an accent that would be a Southern drawl if it was slowed down a dozen times. The mix of US Federal Aviation Regulations and Caribbean style came as a shock to those of us who had gained our experience in the more restrained, more formal, European environment. Aircraft would be cleared to land while there were still two or three aircraft ahead of them on final approach. Others, in the take-off queue, would be cleared for take-off long before they reached the runway, so that it became a free for all; if you've got your clearance and you can see a gap in the traffic, go for it! Jet fighters that seemed to operate by their own rules added spice to enliven the mixture. So when you thought it safe to land and were just lining up on short finals, a couple of fighters would streak underneath and land in front of you.

On one particular day, as usual, we had been delayed on the turn-round and were trying to make up time. We had been given our take-off clearance and were positioned number two at the runway threshold, but the landing traffic was heavy. Eventually the American Airlines Boeing 707 in front of us saw a gap and taxied into position for take-off. We heard the rumble and saw the smoke billow out from its four engines as the plane started to lumber forward and I realized that the next aircraft on finals had gone around. If we were quick, we could take off behind the Boeing. The tyres weren't actually squealing on our BAC 1-11 as we lined up, but I wasn't hanging about. Soon we were up to take-off speed and I could rotate into flight at last. With the gear retracted I settled the machine at the precise climb-out speed and trimmed. The difficult part was over, now we could relax.

Suddenly we hit moderate turbulence. The speed fluctuated and the aircraft rolled quickly right, hesitated and rolled quickly left. It was over before I could make much of a correction, but it was sufficiently strong and close enough to the ground to give us a fright. I recalled that the 707 was bound for a Canadian destination and so would be heavy with fuel. We had encountered its wake turbulence and had been lucky to escape so lightly. Exchanging a relieved glance with the co-pilot, I eased the aircraft back into climbing attitude. Then, at about 500ft above ground, we hit the vortex again.

The left roll was more violent this time and the speed decayed rapidly. I could not lower the nose much to conserve speed because we were too low, so I aimed for a level attitude while opposing the roll with aileron. Then the roll reversed. Still with a dangerously low and fluctu-ating airspeed, the whole aircraft shaking in the turbulence, we rolled rapidly right, so that, in opposing it, I hit the stops on left aileron. As the roll increased through 45 degrees I cautiously added left rudder to assist in opposing the roll, but it did not seem to make much differ-ence. This was not a comfortable condition in which to find ourselves: low down, low airspeed, full left roll controls and still rolling quickly to the right. I resolved that, if the rate of roll had not reduced by the time we went through the vertical, I would reverse my control input and go with the vortex, in an attempt to complete the full 360-degree roll before hitting the ground. Fortunately it was not necessary. The roll stopped at, I believe, something over 60 degrees. We hung there momentarily, while the shaking eased and the speed slowly increased and eventually we rolled back level so that I could continue our climb.

We didn't giggle much that day. In fact, we were very quiet and thoughtful as we continued our schedule through the sleepier islands of the Caribbean. Back in Antigua we stopped off at the Sugar Mill bar on the way home and, forgoing the rum punch, sipped several cold beers in silence as the sun went down and the trade wind cooled our brows.

There were occasions when it appeared doubtful whether we would get airborne at all. The runway at Vigie on the island of St Lucia was short and bumpy and crossed by a public road. Sometimes aircraft had to abandon their take-off run because a vehicle, or a group of islanders, had chosen that moment to wander across the runway.

Just off one end of the strip, the ground fell away in a low cliff to the sea at the entrance to the harbour. Occasionally, take-off would coincide with the arrival or departure of a cruising yacht with a tall mast, the avoidance of which called for fine judgement and an improvised departure procedure.

At the other end of the runway the ground was flat for a short distance, then rose steeply to the summit of a substantial hill. Performance calculations showed that, should the BAC 1-11 suffer an engine failure on take-off, it would be unable to clear the hill. So a standard early turn was adopted. The procedure called for a 15-degree left bank as soon as the gear was up, to track to the left of the hill out to safety over the sea. We did this on all occasions, engine failure or not, so that we were practised and ready. But it was the only place on our routes where we did this, so we briefed for it before each departure.

The schedule allowed us only a ten-minute turn-round time in Vigie. Ten minutes to get departing passengers off, joining passengers on, unload and load baggage and freight and to check and sign the load sheet. It was always tight. The take-off checks were completed and the brief delivered as we back-tracked the runway and when we rolled down the runway at full power my mind was naturally occupied with the turn procedure.

The first standard call made by the non-handling pilot on take-off is 'V1!', which is the calculated decision speed. At any time before the aircraft reaches this speed, it can be brought to a stop safely on the remaining runway available. After V1, we must fly. Any attempt to stop after V1 will mean running off the end of the runway into whatever lies in wait for us. The second standard call is 'Rotate!', which means that the aircraft has reached a speed where a gentle back pressure on the control column will raise her nose, allow her wings to develop lift and cause her to soar effortlessly into her element.

Running through my mind were the actions to follow this sequence: check for a positive rate of climb; call for gear up; and then roll on smoothly 15 degrees of left bank.

'V1!' came the call and all was well.

'Rotate!' was called, but when I applied the usual back pressure on the wheel, nothing happened. I increased the back pressure, but the attitude did not change. The nose wheel stayed firmly in contact with the runway. An extra effort brought the control column all the way back to its stop with a clunk, but still nothing happened. I found myself accelerating through about 130 knots with the control column in my lap and the windscreen filling with the hill beyond the rapidly approaching runway end.

The feeling was one of great disappointment and sadness, a profound sinking feeling. But something had to be done. Even as I reached for the trim wheel, thinking I might help the elevator by adjusting the angle of the tail plane, the nose began to rise enough to extend the oleo of the nose wheel. The fractional increase in the wing's angle of attack produced a little lift, which, at the increasing speed, allowed the nose to rise further until, very slowly, painfully slowly, we crawled into the air in the last few yards of the runway. The co-pilot had the gear retracted in a flash and I eased the machine into its left turn. I lost sight of the hill, but remained uncomfortably aware of its presence. I'll never know by how much we cleared its scrub-covered rocks and I don't want to know. It is enough that we did clear them, and could settle to the routine task of continuing our flight to Barbados.

On the ground there I discovered 2 tons of freight at the forward end of the front hold that was not accounted for on the manifest or on the load sheet. Of course, it should not have been there. Neither I, nor any of the other pilots on the fleet, would have accepted it. But that would have meant that the consignment would have remained in Vigie forever. It very nearly did anyway.

The daily flight direct from Antigua to Barbados – the earliest departure on our schedule – took off before sunrise and supplied me with sights I still treasure. Setting out from the house was enchanting. Apart from any remaining dancers or the body asleep on the sofa, the whole island might have been deserted. There was just the black sea sighing under the trade wind and the ghostly coastline showing faintly in the light from the moon and stars. The tree frogs' rhythmic piping was subdued and the smell of the limes was strong.

At that hour even the bustle of the airport was muted. It was as if no one wanted to disturb the peace. No doubt the roar of our take-off changed that brutally, but in the aircraft it was still silent. We climbed to the south-east through a monochrome world of silhouettes: a black land mass, phosphorescent surf and pale grey clouds edged with silver. Then suddenly, the transformation compressed in time by the speed at which our aircraft was rushing towards it, the sun rose and instantly our world was full of colour. The brilliant blue of the sea, the golden edges on the clouds, the dark green of the trees and a multitude of bright and busy hues dazzled our eyes. The full glory of a Caribbean day was delivered so quickly it took the breath away.

I don't know where it comes from, perhaps it is a legacy of the region's history, or perhaps it is something in the rum, but there is a dark mystery beneath the surface brilliance and vitality of the Caribbean. I felt it at odd moments, fleetingly. It was an elusive, sad and fearful emotion that did not relate to any particular place or person or event. It was particularly strong when we struck unexpected turbulence in clear air over Mont Pelée in Martinique and it was often present during a night approach to Tobago.

The airfield on Tobago when I was flying there was equipped only basically. Today it is a fully equipped international airport that regularly accepts Boeing 747 Jumbo Jets. Then, the runway was short and sloping and for night operations there were a few dim runway lights on either side of the strip. Does my memory play tricks, or were they really goose-neck flares and oil cans with long spouts holding flaming wicks? Anyway, bright they were not. We let down over the sea from a non-directional radio beacon on the island, heading out into the blackness, reliant totally on our instruments. At the completion of the turn inbound, heading back towards the field at an angle to the runway, there was a moment when we had to resist the temptation to look up. Still turning, still descending, low over the water and only just emerging from the base of the scattered cloud, we could become prey to strange disorientating illusions. The runway lights were indistinguishable from the other scattered lights on the island and they all sloped down irregularly with the land. In conditions like this, the pilot's eyes quickly try to latch on to any horizon for reference, but here there was none, or if you thought you had found one, it was in dizzying conflict with your instruments. Recognizing and dealing with phenomena such as this is all part of a pilot's training of course and we learnt to concentrate on our instruments exclusively until the non-handling pilot reported that he had a clear view of the runway. But for some reason here, the urge to look up was unusually powerful, as if some primeval force on the island was trying to lure us into danger. There was a sense of trespass, of a time warp between our modern jet transport and the spirits of Carib Indians and pirates from another age. All nonsense, of course, but I still see those lights in my mind's eye sometimes, and shiver.

We flew the BAC 1-11 on schedules round the Caribbean while the local pilots were training in England. Island hopping in the sun from San Juan to Trinidad and partying in Antigua every night, it was one of the airline business's most desirable jobs. The cabin crew were all female, all complexions and all beautiful. With their varied West Indian accents and spirited, outspoken character, they brought a riot of colour to an already colourful operation. The uniform they wore – a micro-mini, slinky, close-fitting affair in purple with matching hot pants – fitted them and the region perfectly.

We were often late and trying to make up time, so we had to prepare well to make full use of the eight or nine minutes we might have on the ground in Trinidad. The youngest stewardess, the one who was most fleet of foot, was given the order and a pile of money. As soon as the door was opened and the steps hit the ground, she was off, across the apron, out of the gate and down the street to the hot-food seller's barrow. Then she would scamper back, struggling with a big bag that threatened to split and spill its precious contents, and she'd squeeze back on board just as the steps were retracted and the door slammed shut. Within minutes of getting airborne and raising the gear and flaps, we would be tucking into delicious, steaming samosas, the hot grease dribbling down our fingers and chins.

When one of the local co-pilots returned from training in the UK and flew with me on the line, I was impressed. He did not have much experience but he had flown the Avro 748 turboprop on the same routes before so he knew all the islands and their airfields. Nevertheless, the move to the jet was a big jump for him. He was both keen and nervous and, when I offered him the leg into Martinique, was anxious to do a good job. He was doing well enough, too. He judged the descent reasonably well and got the speed under control, but he was trying a bit too hard for precision on final approach. He was tense, overcontrolling and not very smooth. Perspiration appeared on his brow, but I was reluctant to interfere, hoping his confidence would return and that he would relax.

Alas, the West Indian female does not have such patience. At 700ft on finals, the cabin door burst open and a tall vision of Caribbean loveliness stamped onto the flight deck full of righteous fury. She swung a massive punch at the co-pilot's shoulder, pointed at the control column and shouted, 'Listen man, when you move dat t'ing do it gently – we bouncin' back dere!'

I don't remember what the landing was like because I was helpless with laughter, tears rolling down my cheeks. The co-pilot took longer to recover.

It was a wrench to leave the islands and the colourful, generous friends I had made there. For me, the technology associated with the jet had been put in abeyance while I enjoyed the opportunity to hand-fly visually in good weather and so thoroughly acquaint myself with the basic physics of jet flying. For a brief spell I had been back in the world of skill, autonomy and respect for my colleagues. I would return, but the work was again in Europe. The first challenge was a simulator check followed by a line check to prove that I could still meet the exacting instrument flying standards and could adhere to the procedures demanded in that environment.

So it was back to Europe, its industrial cities, its busy airports and its mountains. Familiarity might be expected to dull the impression of the Alps for European pilots, but they still provide memorable scenes. Mont Blanc can be seen from great distances and it is not unusual to hear an air-traffic controller clear an aircraft, 'Direct to The Mountain.' The whole mountain range demands the respect of pilots operating into any of the airfields that lie close to it. A thunderstorm that would promise serious turbulence, strong vertical currents, icing and hail anywhere else, can be particularly vicious in the Alpine region.

The weather was glorious, however, on that late autumn day. The first of the skiing holiday schedules to Germany and Switzerland were just beginning as the summer sun faded on the Spanish beaches, so we were to take passengers to Munich, then position empty to Barcelona to carry passengers from there back to the UK.

I was looking forward to the trip, but my expectation was tempered when I learnt which Training Captain had been scheduled to carry out my line check. He was a serious chap with a reputation for being a bit tense and irascible. Short in stature, his round face shone, polished with zeal, above his shiny buttons and his row of medal ribbons. Still, he seemed affable enough when he installed himself on the jump seat and all went well on the first leg to Munich. I had begun to feel at home as a captain; my confidence had grown and I had learnt in the West Indies how to extract maximum enjoyment from my flying. While we were taxiing out at Munich, the controller asked what flight level we would like for our empty leg to Barcelona and I requested 220, that is, 22,000ft. As I anticipated, the Training Captain began to protest, spluttering about how much fuel we could save by climbing much higher.

'Mike,' I said, appealing to his softer side, 'it's a lovely day. I thought the girls might like a good view of the mountains.' His eyebrows arched up towards his bald head, but to my relief he said no more.

After take-off, we turned towards the mountains and they filled the windscreen. Soon we could see the whole range from deep into Austria to the South of France. When we levelled off at our reduced cruising height we seemed to be skimming the peaks. I pressed the cabin call bell and got the rest of the crew up front to share the view. For half an hour, we marvelled at the snow-capped peaks. We saw some high-level skiing resorts at close quarters and were treated to glimpses of rivers, like silver ribbons, deep in winding green valleys. Our flight deck resounded to squeals of delight as the girls identified new wonders, pointed out and named by Mike, who was himself bobbing up and down in his seat with excitement.

The descent into Barcelona between the brown Pyrenees and the blue Mediterranean was almost an anti-climax, but our spirits remained buoyed for the rest of the day. The passengers must have wondered at the crew's good humour and, to cap it all, I passed my line check.

The independent airline sector in Britain in the 1960s was a free-for-all. After World War II there had been plenty of companies trying to establish themselves in commercial aviation, but there was no discernible pattern of development. The Berlin Airlift had provided some of the entrepreneurs with an initial boost and the survivors were gradually able to replace their DC-3s, DC-4s, Vikings and Yorks with Avro 748s, Handley Page Heralds and Viscounts. There was little specialization. Everyone seemed to be chasing all the business: freight, scheduled passenger, short haul or long haul, and charter.

A more stable industry struggled to emerge, but the big change came with the jets. The British people wanted to go abroad for their holidays. They wanted sunshine, cheap food and wine, but they didn't want to spend all day in a slow, unpressurized aircraft, bumping through the low-level turbulence to Perpignan and then endure an epic bus journey to the Costa Blanca. The jets could whisk them close to any Spanish destination in a couple of hours and do it in style.

By packaging the flight with hotels and including advice and excursions during the holiday, the entrepreneurs tapped a whole new market. People who had never imagined they might travel, fly, or enjoy the exotic delights of Spain or Italy found they could afford to do it all.

Prices were low primarily because of the remarkable productivity of the jets; the Boeing 737, the BAC 1-11 and some second-hand DH Comets could carry twice as many passengers as the piston-engine types and they could do three return trips a day instead of one. By selling holiday packages nationwide, the airlines could fill the seats on every flight. Some operators achieved an overall load factor of 97 per cent, compared to the 65–70 per cent normal on traditional scheduled airlines. Hoteliers in Spain and Italy were in need of the business and their lower costs meant that they could easily undercut hotels in Britain.

The boom time continued right up to the mid-1970s, when the oil crisis suddenly raised operating costs dramatically. Some operators survived by cautious, prudent management, but the airline I was with had taken on substantial debt in order to expand and was hit by rising inflation. It went to the wall.

The Flight Operations Director rang all of us who had been due to fly, so that we wouldn't turn up in uniform with the fleet grounded. We did not know what to do, so we went to the airport anyway, in civvies, and found that most of the airline's employees had done the same. The sight of 400 cabin crew members in tears was moving enough, but to stand in the Chief Pilot's office looking out over an airfield devoid of our company's aeroplanes was even worse. The office, which was bigger but not much grander than the one in which he had hired me eight years earlier, was strangely silent. The great man who was held in such high regard and awe by his pilots was deflated and a little bitter. His career was over. He was in the process of gathering all of the pilots' personal files to take home with him for safekeeping and over the next week or so he was to provide a hand-written personal reference for every one of us.

The shock of unemployment heralded a traumatic time. My first reaction was that it was another adventure: something unexpected and challenging. It wasn't until I realized that there was no more money coming in, none at all, and that there were no jobs available anywhere else, that the gravity of my situation began to strike home.

I met an old friend while trawling round Birmingham Airport looking for work. I had declined the job he had offered me only a week before the company failed and though he was sympathetic to my plight, he had already filled the vacancy.

The old pilot had only advice. 'Remember, Keith,' he said seriously. 'Whenever one door closes, another one slams in your face.' It seemed harsh, but actually it helped a lot. Over the next few months, when things were looking particularly bleak, I would remember his words and smile.

Sudden unemployment affected people in different ways. Only two pilots, I think, had flying jobs to go to. Others, many of them highly skilled and experienced captains, drifted away from the industry and were never heard of again. Some of us earnt pocket money by delivering cars for the local auction centre and met once a week in a local pub, after queuing up to collect our dole money from the Labour Exchange. We swapped news, commiserated with each other's misfortunes and sucked down half-pints of the cheapest ale. Mike, who had enjoyed the sight of the Alps while conducting my line check, joined us occasionally, radiating confidence, resplendent in a smart suit and tie and drinking expensive gin and tonics, though he was in the same desperate plight as the rest of us. Pete appeared too and we tried our best to see it all as an exciting challenge, without noticeable success. That winter we recalled laughing faces and colourful West Indian parties as if they had been some fantastic dream.

The wives of many of the married pilots found jobs and went out to work for the first time in years. Many of them were back home after a few weeks when they found that their family life was totally disrupted and that financially the family was no better off. A couple of pilots with large houses managed to sell them, pay off their mortgages and rent more modest accommodation. One told me that he had not realized how wasteful and profligate his lifestyle had become and wished he'd done it years earlier.

It was a sustained period of survival that tested our resolve, but we had tasted the flying life and giving it up was simply not an option for many of us. The British people had tasted the jet lifestyle too and wanted more, but they were more cautious now and careful with their money. The airlines began to specialize. By concentrating on their strengths, be it inclusive tour, scheduled passenger or chartered freight, some were able to weather the difficult times and gradually, with some failures and mergers along the way, things improved.

Then suddenly there were more jobs than pilots. The contacts we had maintained without much hope started to involve meaningful exchanges. We had always said to each other, 'If you should ever find two jobs, tell me about the second one.' Now those links – networks we would call them today – were buzzing with intelligence. I was offered, and accepted, a job on the BAC 1-11, then engaged in a furious row with the management when I revealed I was leaving to take up another offer. People had been under a lot of stress and feelings were running high.

In April we watched the Fall of Saigon on television, saw the desperation of people trying to get on the last helicopters to fly out of the city and our own problems seemed minor in comparison. By September, a year after the airline had gone bust, I was on my way to South-East Asia myself, destined for a wealth of new flying adventures.

CHAPTER 7

A Boeing in Borneo

When I travelled to Seattle with some of my colleagues to convert from the BAC 1-11 to the Boeing 737, I was not expecting a great improvement. The two aircraft had been at the centre of a technological debate that was being fought out in the harsh commercial arena of aircraft sales. Boeing was winning the sales and it was generally assumed that it had also won the design competition: two engines under the wing produced a lighter structure than two engines at the tail and the benefits of a clean wing did not compensate for that.

In fact, things were more complicated – they usually are – and the fight was not equal. More significant was the fact that no one had accurately predicted the strength of the market for 100- or 150-seater short- to medium-range jets. Boeing could produce its aircraft more quickly and the configuration allowed plenty of scope for growth in the aircraft's size, weight and power. Even in the mid-1970s, when I flew it for the first time, it had grown considerably from the initial product. Today, still selling like iPhones, the Boeing 737 is the most successful commercial aircraft programme ever.

The BAC 1-11 was a fine technical achievement, a reasonably successful commercial investment and a very good aircraft, but it could not compare to the 737. The difference was obvious the moment I rotated on my first take-off. The American company's confidence was exemplified by the way Don, my instructor pilot, slammed back a throttle, leaving me to climb away on one engine – this was a truly great flying machine.

Handling was even better than the 1-11. It was different, in that the low-slung engines produced a very strong pitch up when power was increased and the slightly more swept wing, with a pronounced dihedral angle, exaggerated what are known as 'the further effects' of the rudder. A small angular displacement of the big rudder, by yawing the aircraft, produced a marked difference in lift between the two wings. In practical terms, this meant that any inappropriate pressure on the rudder pedals – or loss of thrust from an engine – revealed itself in a spirited roll, rather than yaw. The small, unpowered ailerons were augmented by differential deployment of effective spoilers, giving tremendous roll power to balance everything out. These characteristics take some getting used to. Watch an early 737 on approach in anything other than smooth conditions and you can tell how experienced the pilot is. If he is new to type, you will see a small lateral oscillation due to overcontrolling in roll. Correction of this 'pilot-induced oscillation' is easy. All the pilot has to do is release the wheel and take his big feet off the rudder pedals, but that is not an instinctive reaction.

When these peculiarities have been assimilated, the Boeing 737 pilot can rejoice in tremendously effective control in all axes, which gives him immense confidence in absolutely any flying conditions he might encounter. Changes introduced with the -300 series and later models compromised this ideal situation slightly. I am told that the difference in 'feel' is partly due to a different autopilot clutching arrangement. But it is still a magnificent aircraft. Navigational equipment was almost identical to the BAC 1-11. The DME readout was now electronic with an LED display, and had a much greater range, though some of us still did not trust it entirely.

With the new aeroplane came a new country and a new set of people to work with. We were starting a new airline in a tiny Islamic Sultanate in Borneo. The staff were airline professionals from the UK, Australia and many other countries alongside a local team trained by Singapore Airlines as managers, operations officers, maintenance engineers and cabin crew and there was a wonderful atmosphere of excitement and commitment to the new venture. We had our differences, of course, mainly between the UK or Australian management and the British pilots – nothing new there – but the local people made us feel completely at home.

Our main contact naturally was with the cabin crew. During my brief airline career to that date I had learnt that there is far more to their job than passengers generally realize and I had come to respect and admire them. Their real job, the only reason they are legally required on the aircraft, is safety. Their training in the use of the safety equipment on board and in the procedures to be followed in the event of an accident is rigorous.

On the Herald and the BAC 1-11 I had been introduced to smoke drill and I dreaded it. Smoke drill involved crawling through a mock-up aircraft cabin, in the dark, with the seats thrown in chaos to impede our progress. We had to drag a fire extinguisher with us to put out a small fire at the aft end of the cabin. The smoke they pumped into the cabin was said to be non-toxic, but it was thick and unpleasant. Worst of all was the breathing apparatus; it did not matter which type was provided, it never seemed to deliver enough air. I don't normally suffer from claustrophobia, but I always struggled to maintain my equanimity during that exercise. Often, it was only the sight of a young slip of a girl, doing the drill for the first time, hating it, but getting stuck in and doing it quickly and efficiently, that prevented me from backing out.

I was doubtful when I was first introduced to our new cabin crew. Malay or Chinese, the girls were beautiful and the few stewards were smart and intelligent, but I wondered if they would be tough enough for the job. An official order, to ensure that we returned to base every evening at all costs so that they could be safely back home at night, did little to reassure me. The girls wore stylish uniforms with long pencil skirts split to the knee so that they walked with delicate short steps. They gave an overall impression of delicacy, modesty and, at first, provinciality.

I shouldn't have worried. They proved professional and quick to adapt. Some of them were a bit naïve at first, but when at last the schedules won out over protectiveness and the crews started to slip in foreign cities, they were keen to learn the ways of the world. On an early night stop they pleaded to be taken to a disco. The co-pilot and I agreed and arranged to meet them in the hotel lobby. We had a drink while they assembled and after a few minutes, one of the girls looked round the lobby, taking in the piano player and asked me quietly, 'Is this the disco?'

Like anyone else, they were a bit morose in the early morning, but their sense of humour was never far from the surface. Waiting for transport to the aircraft in the passenger terminal at Singapore in the early hours of one morning, I spotted a sole Japanese tourist wandering through the shopping arcade. He wore one of those shiny grey suits with a wide-shouldered jacket and trousers three inches above his ankles and he carried an enormous camera on a strap around his neck.

'Any moment now,' I told them, 'He's going to multiply a hundred-fold.' Sure enough, his fellow tourists appeared, dozens of them, all dressed the same, with the same cameras, making the girls smile. And when the leader of the group arrived, dressed exactly the same, but equipped with a flag on a pole to provide a rallying point, they began to giggle and laugh and we were ensured of another good-humoured flight.

Within weeks it seemed, the splits in the skirts had risen a foot above the regulation knee height; they were at home in the bustling cities of the world and demonstrating a new confidence at work.

The airline was competing in a tough market; the international airlines of South-East Asia are renowned for the highest standards of passenger service in the world. Determined not to be outdone, the food they served, especially to first-class passengers, was superb. On the flight deck we were spoilt. Hardly had the gear come up and the flaps been retracted before one of the cabin crew would appear to put a plate of satay on the centre console for us to share. 'That's for starters,' he or she would say. 'Would you like the steak or the lobster for main course?' Bliss!

We had an evening schedule from Bangkok to Brunei. Cruising over the black expanse of the South China Sea we would turn the cockpit lighting down to its minimum level, press our faces against the windows, and marvel at the millions of stars above. That close to the equator, we could sometimes distinguish the Pole Star on our left and the Southern Cross on our right. Then we would be served a dinner of Thai green fish curry, fresh and delicate of flavour, with finely spiced rice, and watch the moon sail up in front of us like a giant, golden balloon.

Relations with the expatriate management were not always so pleasant. One of my new colleagues, Terry, suffered at first hand on one flight. Though senior and experienced, he had been passed over for command, yet was acting as safety pilot for the successful applicant who was under training by the Australian Chief Pilot. The trainee occupied the captain's left-hand seat for the pre-flight checks and engine start procedure, while Terry performed the co-pilot's duties in his usual right-hand seat. To his surprise, the trainee commenced to taxi while the Chief Pilot remained in the jump seat behind them both.

Knowing that the trainee had not passed a left-hand seat check and could not yet legally act as captain, he had assumed that the Chief Pilot would take command by changing seats with Terry himself. As they neared the runway end and prepared for take-off, Terry felt increasingly uncomfortable. This was a public transport flight with fare-paying passengers; surely the Chief Pilot had forgotten that the trainee was not qualified. If he did not say anything, Terry would be in breach of the regulations himself. Even given his own Australian birth, he could not have anticipated the violence of the antipodean's response when he tried, diplomatically, to broach the subject.

'You shut yer mouth! If yer don't like it you can get off now and start lookin' for another job.' No doubt the trainee was wetting himself lest he become involved and jeopardize his chances of success.

As a captain, I too had to undergo checks with the Chief Pilot from time to time. I was surprised when he indicated he would occupy the left-hand seat for the return sector out of Hong Kong. When he told me to take his place on the jump seat I assumed he simply wanted to fly the leg himself. Colin, an experienced captain suffering in the right-hand seat with this company, continued with the co-pilot's duties.

There was no briefing. The departure, towards the hills, required a left turn at a specific height and needed to be accurately flown for terrain clearance and noise-abatement reasons. The Chief Pilot took off, called for the gear to be raised, then, a couple of hundred feet before the turn was due to be made, slumped in his seat to feign incapacitation. For a long moment, nothing at all happened. Colin did not move, but the aircraft was climbing on track towards the turning point – and towards the hills. I noticed the Chief Pilot open a nervous eye and look towards Colin. He knew something must be done soon. Then, very slowly, with a pained expression on his face, Colin began to fidget. He squirmed in his seat in an effort to reach the back pocket of his uniform trousers. As the turning point was reached, he stretched out a languid hand and rested it briefly on the control column. Even while he extracted a cigarette from the packet he had retrieved from his pocket and lit it with his trusty Zippo lighter, the aircraft rolled smoothly to the exact bank angle required, maintaining the correct speed impeccably. I had expected nothing less, but to the Chief Pilot who had hoped to catch Colin out, it must have seemed like magic. It was as if the aircraft would have flown the departure itself even if Colin hadn't touched it.

Nothing at all was said. Colin drew silently on his cigarette, squinting into the sun and blowing the smoke from his eyes. Much later, when he caught my eye, his raised eyebrow conveyed, eloquently, his opinion of the Chief Pilot's training methods.

Pilots do not always act in accordance with their public image. We rather like being thought of as modest and highly competent; the tall, greying figure in the half-moon specs and smart uniform, always cool and always in control. Whether we adopt the British way of speaking in clipped, self-effacing tones, or prefer the laid-back American drawl, we enjoy giving an impression of solid reliability when we speak to our passengers over the cabin address system. It is all an act. We are all quite capable of doing stupid things at times.

I remember a couple of such occasions that occurred while I was flying with my friend, Phil. Amazingly, he is still my friend. We were taxiing out for the first sector of the day in the Boeing 737. It was standard procedure for the co-pilot to check the flight controls for full and free movement. Phil duly operated the rudder, ailerons and elevator through their full range of movement but looked puzzled. He tried them again.

'Try these elevators,' he suggested. 'Do you think they feel stiff?'

I moved the control column fully forward and back.

'Nah,' I replied. It was early morning; we were on schedule and looking forward to a full day's flying. I was full of energy and confidence. I had recently bought a portable tape recorder in Singapore with the intention of recording every aspect of our lives in the Far East. Today it was strapped to the centre console of the flight deck and it had been running since we boarded. With luck, it had captured our pre-flight checks and the cabin report from Mariam, the number one cabin attendant; now it should record the take-off. I thought Phil was being oversensitive. No two aeroplanes are ever quite the same. This is a Boeing: nothing ever goes wrong with the flight controls and, anyway, you can't really evaluate the feel on the ground.

We lined up on the easterly runway and were cleared for take-off. The two Pratt and Whitney turbofans spooled up and we accelerated down the runway and into the air. At light weight, the 737 soared into the sky and I began an early turn left through 180 degrees to pick up our track to Singapore. With the gear up and flaps remaining at the take-off setting, she was nicely in trim. I hardly had to make any input on the control column. Then, as we started to increase speed and raise the flaps, I became conscious of a restriction in the elevator circuit. No doubt about it, they were stiffening up.

'You have control, Phil,' I said. 'Just try these elevators again.' He stretched out his long arms, applying only a suggestion of pressure to the control wheel, but his face told me his worst fears were confirmed.

'Ooohh, I don't like that,' he said lugubriously.

I took back control and realized the elevators were even stiffer now. While Phil got clearance for us to turn back to the airfield, I started to reduce speed and position for a straight-in approach to the runway from which we had so recently departed. The situation was unreal. We quickly completed the checks and then there was nothing else to do. The only help offered by an abnormal checklist was that we 'use such force as necessary' on the elevator. Neither of us spoke, but I knew Phil would be wondering, as I was myself, what we could do if the elevators seized completely. There was the trimmable tail plane, of course, but experimenting with that as the principal pitch control for landing was not something either of us would have relished. And anyway, which way did one move it? Such questions are easy to answer on the ground, but they can become devilishly difficult in the air.

Engrossed in these silent considerations, we watched the sparkling blue sea, the white line of surf and the golden beaches give way below us to the thick, deep green of the rainforest and, eventually, the airfield. Would we make it? It was such a lovely day to be faced with all this. We had set off with such enthusiasm. There was hardly a cloud in the sky, just some ethereal mist in the wooded valleys further inland.

How quickly these moments of profound introspection vanish upon landing. The problem is immediately forgotten and new ones demand attention. What is going to happen to the passengers? How to explain the symptoms to the engineers? Is there another aircraft? Can this one be fixed? How long will the delay be? Who needs to be told? What else must be done?

It was not a quick fix. We learnt later that it was a known problem with something called an elevator horn balance. Its beak is designed for a small clearance gap, but this had somehow reduced to nothing. Had it seized, applying a good heave on the control column would have separated the two halves of the elevator and left us with the more than adequate serviceable half, but it was all out of our hands now. We retired to my flat for a beer. I felt I owed one or more to Phil for ignoring his concerns before take-off. Halfway down the second bottle of Tsingtao, we remembered the tape recording and played it back. Our bright and busy pre-flight preparation, together with the cheeky repartee of the cabin crew, gave way abruptly to a terse discussion about the elevators, the deliberate recitation of the checks and the long, pregnant silence until the landing came. I was uncomfortably reminded of flight-deck voice recordings played back by accident investigators after a crash and I lost my enthusiasm for making recordings. I also vowed to pay much more attention to any concerns expressed by Phil in the future.

But, of course, I didn't. A month or two later we were taxiing out for departure from the old airfield at Singapore when it started to rain. Now, we were used to rain in those parts. It rained a lot and sometimes it was very heavy, but this was very heavy indeed. We were number two to a Pan American Boeing 747 and the captain of that machine, sensibly, refused the controller's invitation to take off. The long runway had become a river several inches deep with spray bouncing a foot above that. I had no hesitation in refusing myself when the controller suggested we line up in front of the Jumbo to take off; if it wasn't good enough for Pan Am, it wasn't good enough for us.

Eventually the rain eased and Pan Am took off. When we lined up in turn, the rain got heavier again and I thought I heard Phil say something. 'Er ...'.

I should have listened to him, encouraged him to voice his concerns, but instead I commenced the take-off run, eager not to lose any more time. As we accelerated, the rain got heavier and the visibility reduced. It was not until about 80 knots that I realized there might be a problem. Just before we reached 100 knots we lost all forward visibility. My focus had reduced steadily from the runway end, to the centre-line runway markings, then closer and closer to the nose of the aircraft until now all I could see was the inside of the windscreen. Phil was no doubt monitoring the instruments, but I knew he had looked up and seen the situation for himself. He didn't actually say anything – not even that he didn't like it – he just let out one soft, deep sigh.

'Ooohh.'

I had taken off on instruments before, but that was from wide grass fields in little aeroplanes that needed only a few yards' ground run and were airborne at 60 knots. The 737 weighed about 50 tons and travelled twice as fast on what, at these speeds, was a narrow runway. But to stop would be even more dangerous. Trying to keep straight on instruments while braking and using reverse thrust would be much more difficult. There was no guarantee either that, even if I did, we could stop before the runway end in these conditions. So I concentrated on maintaining an accurate compass heading and waited for what seemed a long time for Phil to call, his voice devoid of expression, 'V1' and 'Rotate!'

Once airborne, the problem of course disappeared. I flew a normal departure, deviating only to avoid the worst of the turbulence from the enormous cloud build-up that had produced the rain. Phil didn't say much. We both knew that, had we suffered an engine failure or even a tyre burst during those few seconds on the runway without visual reference, we would almost certainly have gone off the side of the runway with disastrous consequences. It was a sombre thought. But then we broke free of the cloud and the sun sparkled on the South China Sea and we were back in the familiar unreality of life in South-East Asia. It was all a dream.

Special occasions often seem to provoke calamities in aviation. It was a great honour to be chosen to fly the Head of State on an official trip to Singapore. We had been ready for hours. The official retinue was seated in the cabin. We pilots waited in our seats, in shirt sleeves and air-conditioned comfort while representatives from the airline management stood on the tarmac outside with the guard of honour, wearing suits in the 30°C heat and the 90 per cent humidity. The cabin crew were at their stations and, at the foot of the steps, the Fleet Captain stood to attention, ready to welcome the great man aboard.

A small crowd had collected on the balcony of the terminal building to cheer and wave the Sultan off. The scene was colourful and the atmosphere happy. The tiny state had had its troubles; an insurgency had been quickly suppressed and dissidents were still held in the notorious jail, Jerudong, a few miles from the airfield. Though the country remained officially in a State of Emergency, it seemed to me fully to justify its reputation as 'The Abode of Peace'.

The only unusual duty required of us that day involved the Royal Standard. It had been impressed upon me repeatedly that I must ensure that the flag was raised the moment the Sultan set foot on the aircraft steps, but there had been considerable debate about when it should be struck down. It had caused problems before. The flag was attached to a short pole and could be fitted into a socket by the captain's elbow so that it protruded from his open side window. The window had to be closed for take-off, but it would be preferable to do it much earlier. For one thing, the engine noise with the window open made it difficult for the captain to hear the radio. So it had been decided to get the flag stowed away and the window closed just before the aircraft moved off. It was agreed that Graham, the co-pilot, should start the engines and prepare to taxi while I looked after the flag. I had rehearsed the sequence mentally several times, but we had not actually tried it.

Exactly on time, I saw the military guard of honour lined up outside snap to attention and present arms as two long, black sedans swept onto the apron. The Sultan leapt from the first car and strode along the line in a brief inspection before moving quickly to the aircraft. He was impressive; though small and slight, his uniform was immaculate and he radiated energy and power. Here, clearly, was a man who demanded the best from everyone.

We had already completed the checks and had clearance to start from the tower. When the Sultan's foot hit the first step I opened my side window and Graham turned off the air-conditioning. The hot, humid air rushed in and perspiration began to soak our shirts as I pushed the flag out of the window and secured the pole in its socket. Then I nodded to Graham, who immediately began to start the starboard engine. The Sultan ran up the steps and entered the cabin, followed by the Fleet Captain and the moment the door closed, I nodded again for the co-pilot to start the second engine.

It was all going like clockwork until the flagpole stuck in its socket. I don't suppose I struggled with it for more than a few seconds, but the slight delay threw our carefully arranged procedure off track. Graham, quite reasonably, continued with the engine start process. By the time I had freed the pole and stowed the flag, he had completed the after-start checklist, which included turning the air-conditioning, now powered from the main engines, back on.

Even as I was sliding my heavy side window shut, my relief at retrieving the flag was tinged with an uneasy feeling that I was doing something wrong. Within a second of the window locking closed, the truth dawned. The conditioned air that the two Pratt and Whitney engines were pumping into the airframe with such vigour, normally a welcome relief, had been escaping through my open window in preference to the normal pressure-relief valve in the tail. This valve, well damped and slow moving to avoid surges, had consequently stayed shut. Now there was no escape route for the air and the fuselage was suddenly being pressurized. Deciding what to do about this situation was made difficult by the searing pain I was experiencing in my ears. It was like suddenly being plunged several fathoms to the bottom of the sea. Dimly, through my pain, I realized that everyone on the aircraft, including the Sultan, was suffering the same torture. Before I could react, the pressure, and the pain, eased. There was just time enough to think that the problem had resolved itself, to share an embarrassed smile with Graham, before it returned, stronger than before. We must have endured three or four cycles until we, or more probably the automatic controller, had the system stabilized.

There was nothing to be done except to get on with the flight. There were no more dramas and the trip to Singapore was smooth and uneventful. We arrived on schedule and the Sultan was whisked away in another black sedan. But I felt depressed; surely both my stupidity and my assault on the Royal ears would not be forgotten.

Still, nothing was said and as the days passed I began to think I would not hear any more about it. A few weeks later, however, I chanced to meet a senior member of the Sultan's staff who had been on board the aircraft that day. He smiled when we were introduced and shook my hand.

'About that flight,' he said. 'The Sultan has asked me to tell you it won't be Jerudong for you – this time. But if you ever do it again …'.

Moments of humility such as this are part of a pilot's life, so I learnt to take quick advantage of good fortune. We used to encounter high-level turbulent cloud over the South China Sea. It was never severe, just a most unpleasant, continuous and unpredictable shaking. There would be ice too, even at 30,000ft. Sometimes these conditions would persist for days, making the crews and the passengers fed up and cross on every flight. On one occasion, we left Singapore heading east and ran straight into it. I spent the whole trip fiddling with the weather radar. I know no one will believe me, but I reckon those older monochrome analogue sets actually provided more information than the later, colour digital type, so long as you constantly adjusted the gain and tilt of the scanner.

The thicker cloud seemed to lie in a vast wedge off the Borneo coast and we were forced off track, further and further north, but we could not free ourselves from the solid, grey, wet and uncomfortable blanket. My co-pilot on that trip was new and must have wondered whether he was really going to enjoy flying these routes. The coffee got spilt, the passengers complained and the cabin crew were grumpy, but there was nothing else we could do.

Eventually, tired of the discomfort myself, I decided to go direct and put up with the bumps. After all, we had to land at our destination eventually and if we carried on like this we would end up in the Philippines. I spun the heading bug and the autopilot turned us right through 90 degrees. Immediately we broke out into clear, smooth air. We burst into a vast sunlit valley with dazzling white cloud on either side, clear blue above and the blue sea sparkling below. I called for the descent checks, but my companion was open mouthed.

'How on earth did you know that was there?' he asked.

'Ah,' I replied, assuming an air of mystery. 'It takes years of experience.' And kept my silence as we descended towards the golden beaches and dark forests of Borneo.

Weather provides the physical indications of the pilot's element. Air is transparent, colourless, odourless and pretty insubstantial on its own. Yet a few drops of moisture and some variations in temperature can produce dramatic changes in the stuff. Flying over a typhoon or tropical revolving storm above the seas to the south of China is fascinating. A great circular swirl of cloud, flat on top like a white gramophone record with a hole in the middle, it radiates enormous power. Above 30,000ft the whole thing can be seen, even though it might be 200 miles across. We know that winds near the centre may reach well over 100mph and that, on the surface, the seas will be whipped up into mountainous waves, making survival problematic for any vessel unfortunate enough to be caught there. Yet often the air above is smooth.

If your route takes you right across the storm you will notice the drift increase as the wind gets stronger towards the centre, the nose pointing more and more to the left to stay on track. Then, as you reach the eye, the wind suddenly drops and the heading bug must be zeroed. You may, for a minute or so, be able to see clear down to the surface of the sea below. Even from this height you can see chaotic waves with fierce white crests. Then you are past and into the same strong winds, but from the right this time. The heading bug must be turned decisively to swing the nose to the right to regain track. As you fly towards the edge of the immense white disc of cloud, the winds grow lighter, the drift reduces and things return to normal, except that you are left with a deep sense of awe, and of privilege, at having witnessed the power and grandeur of it all.

One particular trap that the weather held in store for us was deceptive in its simplicity, but deadly enough to catch out better pilots than me. Showers, often quite heavy, are a characteristic of the tropics and anyone flying in the countries around the South China Sea for any length of time becomes accustomed to coping with them. They are usually isolated, easily seen and moving quite slowly. At low level it is easy to avoid them, except when actually lined up with a runway to land. There is always the option to hold off and wait for the shower to pass, of course, but this has to be balanced against the need to conserve fuel and to operate on schedule.

The pilot can have the aircraft stabilized on final approach, with the runway in clear sight, and watch the wall of rain approaching. It is only rain, but when it actually reaches the aircraft several things happen at once. First, dramatically, visibility is reduced and the pilot's focus switches involuntarily from the runway touchdown point to his windscreen, which is now streaming with water. The light level reduces and the noise of the rain hitting the fuselage may be unexpectedly loud.

It takes only a fraction of a second for the pilot to refocus on the runway, but now he is looking through half an inch of water in addition to the thickness of the glass in his windscreen. The alteration in refraction caused by this layer of water on the screen changes the appearance of the runway on which he has been judging his approach. The arrival of the rain may also be accompanied by a change in the wind strength and/ or direction, so that the aircraft is destabilized. None of these events have major effects by themselves, but at smaller airports with no form of electronic glide slope indication, the combination of different visual aspect and change in airspeed will lead to a change in flight path.

What usually happens, even to experienced pilots, is that the rate of descent reduces and within seconds the aircraft is above the ideal glide slope. Power needs to be reduced and the nose pitched down decisively to regain the glide slope and then, just as quickly, power must be restored and the aircraft retrimmed so that it maintains the correct speed to the touchdown point. In order to do it quickly enough, the pilot really needs to have anticipated the need. The slower he reacts, the further the aircraft is displaced and the greater the correction required. But he is now faced with a landing on a short runway streaming with water and he needs to touch down in the correct place at the correct speed; large corrections to the flight path at just a few hundred feet above the runway make it very difficult to achieve the required accuracy.

There may be all sorts of other pressures on the pilot and he will be trying to concentrate on completing the landing. If the aircraft has been too destabilized he now needs an alert, competent co-pilot, whose flying judgement he respects, to shout, 'Go-around!' When he doesn't get it, or doesn't heed it, the chances of touching down fast and long are high and we see the results too often. There is something very depressing about an aircraft that has slid off the end or the side of the runway, stuck in the mud at an unnatural angle in the pouring rain. At best, it is humiliating for the pilot, at worst it is a tragedy.

My years in Brunei did not involve any great changes in technology. Jets were now in use everywhere for all except the shortest routes. It seemed to us, if we thought about it, that the development of the jet airliner had reached a plateau. It was difficult to imagine what might come next. In Seattle and Toulouse, the engineers were exploring new frontiers of which we knew nothing. Before I returned to work in Europe there were new experiences waiting for me in mysterious and exotic parts of the Far East and other parts of the world. The march of technology would even go into reverse for a while, but, after seven years as a captain, I would move back to the right-hand seat as a co-pilot and that too would be a challenge.

CHAPTER 8

The Mighty 707

Before we can go forward, it is sometimes necessary to go back. I suddenly found myself sitting in the right-hand seat, flying as a co-pilot again. Some of my colleagues suggested that it might be difficult to adjust to that situation, but in fact I experienced very few problems. The adjustment was made easier by the amount I had to learn: four engines, three crew and new, long-haul routes would have kept me quiet anyway, but mastering the mighty Boeing 707-320C was an additional challenge. Some aeroplanes earn a special place in airline pilots' hearts and the 707 is one of them. It was already a legend by the time I came to grips with it. It seemed enormous after the 737 and even though the -320C was the final developed version of this great aircraft, it had an air of antiquity about it. Ailerons and elevators were manual, only the rudder being fully hydraulically powered. This, given the weight and inertia of the beast, its large speed range and powerful flaps, meant that it was essential to keep the aircraft in trim. I soon found it was possible to set up a situation that demanded so much strength through both hands on the control wheel that I could not move my thumb onto the electric trim switches to adjust the tail plane. I was in awe of the Training Captains who could throw the machine around in a truly spirited fashion in the restricted confines of the old Kai Tak airfield at Hong Kong.

When you got to know this aeroplane, you could do almost anything with it. But it took time. It operated effectively on short sectors, but really it was a long-haul machine. When heavily loaded for a full 6,000-mile leg with the great centre tank full of fuel, it had great stability. During take-off at a high temperature in one of the Persian Gulf airfields or in Australia, everything seemed to happen in slow motion. It was like watching a film on aerodynamics: rotate at exactly the correct speed and note the speed achieved when the initial climb attitude is reached; call for the gear up and watch the speed drop by 4 knots due to the extra drag when the gear doors opened; then watch the speed return, plus a few more knots when the gear was fully retracted.

The air at desert airfields would cool dramatically overnight, so during an early morning take-off the performance, though never spectacular in a loaded 707, would be solid, with a workmanlike rate of climb, until we reached the inversion. The great air mass covering the region maintained its heat; only the relatively shallow layer close to the earth cooled overnight. At 1,000ft or so, we would encounter warmer air and the rate of climb would drop away. Sometimes it was necessary to fly level for a while, allowing the speed to increase before we could climb at all. But all this was so predictable and became so familiar over time that it was almost reassuring. The old girl would do the job, but she would do it in her way in her own time and there was to be no rushing of her. She was full of character.

The flight deck had been designed to accommodate a navigator in addition to the two pilots and the flight engineer, but we rarely carried one. The navigation equipment included the usual VOR, ILS, ADF and DME, but was supplemented by a clever Doppler system for use when the route lay outside the range of these devices. Four radar beams were directed at the ground or sea beneath the aircraft and by measuring the Doppler shift through the change in frequency of the returning signal the computers could derive track and ground speed. The non-handling pilot set up the two computer controllers with required track and distance to run for the current leg and the next one. At each waypoint the system switched automatically to the second controller and the first one, now the inactive, could be set up for the following leg. The controllers displayed track error in miles left or right. These displays were zeroed before each leg and the pilot setting them confirmed this had been done by calling out the two 'R' and '00' readings as 'Roo, Roo!' in as good an imitation as he could manage of an Australian accent. It was an excellent system, simple and reliable. The radar returns from the glassy surface of the South China Sea were sometimes weak, but even so we were rarely more than a couple of miles off track.

Perhaps the biggest operational difference for me to get used to on this aircraft involved the presence of a flight engineer. The company had an enlightened policy about how these specialists should be incorporated into the crew and it worked perfectly. There had been a lot of discussion about the value or otherwise of flight engineers on civil aircraft – even a US Presidential Committee of Investigation – and I was keen to see for myself how it worked. With virtually all airliners nowadays designed for a two-pilot crew, the argument might appear to be over, but anyone who has flown three-crew, in a well-designed and disciplined operation, knows how much safer it is.

All sorts of philosophies have evolved to eliminate the problem of flying with just two pilots, but I have yet to see one that works naturally. While everything in the aircraft is functioning as it should there is no problem. But when a failure occurs there are three jobs to be done. On a three-crew flight deck, each crew member simply continues with his primary job: the handling pilot concentrates on flying the aircraft; the engineer troubleshoots the problem; and the non-handling pilot deals with communications while monitoring everything that is done by the other two.

However well-disciplined they are, both pilots on a two-crew flight deck will be naturally inclined to respond to the failure. Indeed, the warning systems are designed to get their attention. Both pilots respond to the master warning, both look at the specific system panel or caption to get details of the failure and at that moment we have two people doing the flight engineer's job. No one is concentrating exclusively on flying the aeroplane and no one is monitoring the flying.

It takes only a moment for the captain or handling pilot to create order out of this situation. He returns to the primary task of flying the aircraft, calls for the relevant checklist and usually assumes responsibility for communications. The non-handling pilot carries out the checklist drill. 'Aviate, navigate and communicate!' is the mantra that reminds them of their priorities. If the failure is a simple one, which they have rehearsed in the simulator, the procedure seems to proceed smoothly under full control. But still they are both doing at least two jobs because they are supposed to monitor each other at all times. The handling pilot is flying the aircraft and monitoring the actions of the non-handling pilot, while the non-handling pilot is monitoring the flying and carrying out the checklist drill. This is not difficult, providing the autopilot remains engaged and continues to do the job it was programmed to do. But if the fault is more complex, a major hydraulic or electrical malfunction, say, which causes the autopilot to disconnect, the workload for both pilots increases significantly.

One of the secrets of a well-run two-pilot crew is the recognition that there is no merit in troubleshooting by pilots. Even if they have enough technical knowledge to work out what has caused the failure, they almost certainly will not be able to do anything about it. It is far better to forget whatever has failed, switch it off and concentrate on managing the flight without it. Even when the drills have been completed and the new plan of action has been put into effect, any spare mental capacity is better spent trying to anticipate the consequences of any subsequent failures than investigating the first one.

The presence of a flight engineer on the flight deck, a proper engineer, that is, not another pilot operating the systems panel, makes for a more professional operation. Even though a high proportion of the engineers I flew with had gained their Commercial Pilots' Licences, their background was different to ours. They reported to a different manager, their career structure was quite different and this made for more formal relationships among the crew.

The arguments against the employment of flight engineers are entirely economic. It is assumed that the extra salary and training costs, along with the costs of providing an extra seat and panels on the flight deck, can be avoided. But time and again flight engineers proved their worth by avoiding delays on the ground. While the pilots continued to do their checks and set up the navigation systems, the engineer could investigate and sometimes fix faults that threatened to cause a delay. They were also useful when there was trouble with unruly passengers. What they really brought to the operation, though, was a different viewpoint. They saw things with an engineer's eye. While a co-pilot, with similar training and expectations to those of his captain, might misread an approach chart in the same way, or misinterpret a controller's instruction in the same sense, an engineer might spot the ambiguity. More importantly, he would have no inhibitions about voicing his concerns.

There remains the question of what a flight engineer would do during a routine flight on a modern aircraft when all the systems are automated. It provokes the question: should all the systems have been automated? When we lost a hydraulic system on the 707 at lift-off from Bangkok one morning, I was amazed at how easily we were able to deal with the situation. Everything seemed natural and logical. There was no rush, no hesitation and no confusion at all. The captain had plenty of time to consider his options and to discuss them with both the engineer and me before making his decisions. It was a non-event. The same event would have been dealt with effectively on a two-crew aircraft, but the workload for both pilots would have been significantly higher and there would have been a need for more conscious and disciplined role changes.

In addition to mastering the aircraft, in my new role there were new routes to learn. This was made easier because I already knew Hong Kong and enjoyed the challenges of operating from the old Kai Tak airfield, which was squeezed onto the edge of downtown Kowloon. As a Line Trainer with my previous company, I had been responsible for checking out new pilots to the airfield. The landing to the south-east was famously spectacular. The proximity of Lion Rock Hill prevented the usual ILS from being aligned with the runway. Instead, it was aligned parallel to the hills, pointing towards a large chequerboard that had been erected on the edge of the built-up area. On reaching minimums, a wide turn had to be made to line up with the runway and, since the high-rise buildings extended to the airfield, images of large aircraft apparently turning down amongst the buildings were popular with photographers.

This, I was often told, was an optical illusion, of course. We weren't really that close to the buildings, were we? All I can say is that kite flying is a popular pastime with Chinese children, who often flew their home-made creations from the tops of the high-rise buildings and it was not unusual, on checking the aircraft after landing, to find yards of string wrapped round the undercarriage.

Landing the other way, to the north-west, involved an approach between hills on the mainland and those on Victoria Island, through what is known as the Lei Yue Mun gap. I heard one British pilot, asked for his impressions after his first visit to Kai Tak, sum up the situation.

'Well,' he said. 'You don't want to be off to the left on either runway, do you? On the other hand, you don't want to be off to the right, either!'

Other airfields on the company's routes posed their own problems. Jakarta was short, narrow, incredibly bumpy and usually wet. If the mighty 707 was going to be stopped safely within its confines it was essential to touch down at exactly the correct point and exactly the correct speed.

There was nothing special about the airfield at Kaohsiung situated on the south-western tip of Taiwan, but its proximity to Hong Kong and the division of the airspace between the two called for decisive and spirited handling of the aircraft. Air Traffic Control always seemed to delay the start of our descent and I was to see a number of pilots get themselves into a tangle there. My first attempt came at the completion of initial base training (six landings) with a pair of Australians. The first, a crusty Senior Trainer, was in command in the left-hand seat. The second was a much younger and more reasonable individual who was scheduled to take over my line training. He was observing my performance from the jump seat.

I had done my homework and was determined to get the aircraft descending promptly and steeply to give myself the best chance of making a stable final approach. Even while we were waiting for the delayed descent clearance, however, the ancient trainer suddenly decided he should explain to me, there and then, the company-approved method for calculating the optimum descent point. This was a complicated formula that involved dividing the flight level by ten, multiplying by three point three, applying factors to allow for landing weight and average antici-pated head or tailwind and measuring the answer back from the final approach fix in nautical miles. Never having heard of this procedure before, I found it hard to assimilate, while desperately trying to coax the unfamiliar aircraft through the manoeuvres required and calling for the checklists at the appropriate times. At some point it all became too much and I simply switched off to everything except the handling problems. Somehow, at the end of a hectic descent, I managed to get the aircraft onto the runway in a passable landing. The old Aussie was still talking, but I hadn't heard any of it.

Fortunately, when we reached the hotel at the end of the trip, Hal, the younger trainer, took me to one side. 'You didn't understand that descent calculation, did you?' he asked. 'Not a word,' I replied. 'No, thought not,' he nodded. Then he took me for a beer so that he could explain it all in a calm, rational manner.

Whatever their personalities, most of those Aussies could fly. There was a highly disciplined, straightforward approach to airline flying that reduced every procedure, wherever possible, to numbers. The airline had a rule of no drinking for ten hours before reporting for duty and it was common for whoever had noticed the time while engaged in convivial argument in the bar to shout 'Ten hours, fellers!' and the whole crew would put down their glasses unfinished and go off to their rooms.

Even the complex art of taking off in the 707 in a strong crosswind was reduced to numbers. Estimate the crosswind component of the wind in knots and turn the control wheel towards the into-wind wing by that number of degrees. So if the crosswind is 20 knots from the left, turn the wheel 20 degrees to the left and hold it there during the take-off run. Then, as you pull back the wheel to rotate, double the angle to 40 degrees. In fact, because of the geometry of the bones in the human arms, there is a natural tendency to allow the control wheel to return almost level while pulling back on it. Making a positive mental resolve to double the angle usually results in just maintaining the original 20 degrees, which is exactly what is required to hold the into-wind wing down and prevent an unwanted roll at lift off.

The competition between the British and Australian crews was funny and the banter unrelenting. The company had an 'open door' policy on the 707 fleet; passengers could saunter up to the galley area at the front of the first-class cabin and peer in to watch us at work on the flight deck. Sometimes the engineer would invite one or two in and treat them to an explanation of what was going on. It whiled away the longer, empty stretches and was supposed to be good for passenger relations.

On one trip with a British flight engineer and an Australian captain, I heard a little old lady chatting to the engineer ask '... and are you boys British or Australian?'

'Well, the company employs both,' said the engineer, 'but as it happens, we're all Brits today.'

The captain spun round in his seat. ''Ere,' he said indignantly. 'I'm Australian!'

'Sorry, skipper,' replied the engineer smoothly. 'I thought you were English. I'm sure I saw you eating your lunch with a knife and fork.'

My first trip to Australia was an event I had been looking forward to. An eleven-hour overnight flight from Hong Kong to Sydney, it was my first maximum-range trip and my first as a full member of a crew after completing my training. The captain and engineer were both Australians and typically businesslike and professional. As soon as we had reached cruising altitude and completed the routine checks and paperwork they explained a little wager they usually made. Each of us was to put one Australian dollar on the centre console together with a written estimate of exactly what time we would cross the equator. I was happy to join in and put my dollar alongside theirs, but I was surprised they were being so generous. I was, after all, responsible for the navigation and ought to have an advantage in predicting the time. Even if my guess was not the best, it would be up to me to announce when we actually crossed the line. Yet they seemed surprised and disappointed when I won.

When they discovered it was my first visit to their country they fell to extolling the virtues of Australian beer. 'Oh, its wonderful beer,' they claimed. 'Served cold too, not warm like that English muck.'

'How strong is it?' I asked.

'Strong? You better watch out. You pommies are not used to drinking lots of strong beer like we Australians are!'

It was about nine o'clock in the morning when we checked into the Hilton in Sydney and I was tired and dehydrated.

'Are you blokes going to show me how good this beer is then?' I suggested.

'What, now?' they chorused.

'Why not?'

'Aw, look …'. But we got changed and adjourned to a nearby bar where we started to drink schooners of some tasteless weak lager that was so cold my fingers stuck to the glass and my throat was anaesthetized after a couple of them. We started at a brisk pace and then I tried to up the rate, but they couldn't keep up. First the skipper and then the engineer gave in and returned to the hotel. I enjoyed a couple more and then had some lunch before turning in for a nap myself.

We had two or three days in Sydney and while I tried to acclimatize myself for a morning departure back to Hong Kong, I discovered the sport channel on the hotel TV. I rejoiced to see England winning a test match against the Australian team. Naturally my crewmates were not too pleased to hear my joyful account of the match when we reported for the return flight. They were even less pleased when I won the equator crossing competition on the way north as well and they were muttering darkly about lucky poms when we finally parted.

Life as a 707 pilot operating out of Hong Kong was good. The company was well organized, but demanded its full pound of flesh from the crews. We flew a full eighty hours a month, long and short haul, passenger and freight, and slipped overnight away from base for more than half the time. But the scheduling was generally sensible and I found myself falling into a pleasant routine. The days back in Hong Kong were like little holidays, while the time down route was a different world of flying and resting and adjusting to irregular sleep patterns.

Each take-off returned me to the never-sleeping world of Radio Telephony. The harsh crackle in my earphones was going on before I got airborne and continued after I landed. It might be a frantic gabble of distorted voices, or cheerful controllers greeting us all with crisp pleasantries. They might be overly polite, speaking with curiously old-fashioned courtesy, or the phrases they used might be curt, stressful and charged with impatience. But it was a never-ending world of chatter, clearances and exchanges.

Whatever the character of the day, I was immediately a part of it. It was my world and I returned to it as to a familiar office. Only in the far reaches of the world, the backwaters of the world's air routes, did the radio fall silent and then it was threatening.

Without contact, pilots are for once aware of the immense distances they travel. Then it is possible to feel remote and alone. We made position reports anyway, in case another aircraft was within range to hear, however unlikely that may have been. I always felt embarrassed doing that, calling into the void. It was as if I was trying to remind myself I was alive and human, as if I was betraying a childish need for someone to hear and respond.

Autopilot problems are rare, but they fall into a category where one failure can be disturbing. On a night return from Port Moresby to Hong Kong I had little to do as handling pilot. There was no moon and the old 707 sat motionless at her cruising altitude, the miles ticking away on the Doppler navigation computer the only sign of progress. Every few minutes I adjusted the weather radar to scan the air ahead for cloud build-ups, but all I saw on the screen was a random pattern of small islands. We were in the no-man's-land between New Guinea and the Philippines with a profusion of scattered islands to our left and the vast expanse of the Pacific stretching away on our right. From time to time the captain gave a position report, broadcast into the empty ether because we were well out of range of any receiving station. The engineer was silently engrossed in the tiny pool of yellow light on his table behind my seat. We had not heard another aircraft for a long time.

The first phugoid the autopilot made in pitch was so shallow, so gentle, that I wasn't sure whether I had imagined it. The nose dropped almost imperceptibly, the speed increased by a knot or two, then the nose rose again through the level attitude and the speed fell back until it was a couple of knots below the cruising speed.

I adjusted the tilt of the radar scanner again, checking that we were not overflying a cloud I had missed, but there was nothing there. Perhaps just the cabin crew or some passengers moving about in the cabin, I thought. Then I realized the cycle was continuing, the nose pitching down again, more definitely this time, with a corresponding change in airspeed. Still it was smooth and gentle and I watched in fascination as the nose rose again, higher this time and the cycle continued. It wasn't until the peak of the third cycle that I realized the amplitude was increasing at an alarming rate. By the time I decided I must do something the aircraft had crested the top of another wave and suddenly plunged downwards into what threatened to be a violent dive.

I pressed the button on the control wheel to disconnect the autopilot and was surprised how much strength I had to use to counteract the out of trim forces. It took a little while to restore the heavy aircraft to its stable equilibrium, but I managed it without any more excursions. The passengers would have felt only the initial jerk when the autopilot came out. I continued to hand-fly for a few minutes, stroking the trim wheel to correct even the slightest, imagined movement. Nothing. The old aeroplane sailed on like the liner she was. There wasn't a ripple in the black sky and I could detect no movement in the cabin.

Gingerly, I re-engaged the autopilot and watched, alert and fully awake now, for any signs of instability. But the old aircraft roared on serenely and there were no more excursions of any sort.

No one had spoken on the flight deck. Not a word was said by any of us, though I knew that both my colleagues had been aware of what was happening and were watching with keen interest. But we cruised on. And the autopilot behaved impeccably. Still we didn't speak. And when the sun came up and we drew close to Hong Kong and prepared to make our approach and landing, we forgot about the autopilot's aberration. As far as I am aware it never gave any problem again. But sometimes I think back to that black, silent night long ago in one of the more remote corners of the world and wonder what caused that divergent phugoid and what might have happened had I not intervened when I did. Perhaps we would have starred in one of history's great, unsolved mysteries of the air. Today there would be formal reports, an investigation and the incident would be taken seriously. Then, while the autopilot was capable of flying the aircraft from shortly after take-off to decision height on the approach, it was not relied upon and most climbs and approaches were hand-flown. The pilots enjoyed it; it gave them practice and currency and they felt they were better in touch with the aircraft and the weather. The autopilot was a device primarily for the cruise. Anyone who made full use of the autopilot was looked upon with a degree of suspicion. Wasn't he entirely happy about his own handling ability? Certainly, if something went wrong, any sort of failure or doubt about exactly what was happening, the instinctive and recommended first reaction was to disconnect the autopilot.

The 707 has been described as a 'flexible' aeroplane in more ways than one. The term is often used of aeroplanes that are suitable for many different roles: short haul; long haul; passenger; freight; and diverse specialist roles. The 707 certainly qualified by that yardstick, but the term was apt in strictly physical terms too. I turned round to peer out of my side window at the starboard wing when we were experiencing some heavy clear-air turbulence one day and gaped in amazement. The extent to which the wing flexed and how much the engines yawed and danced on their pylons was astonishing. The flight engineer must have noticed my open mouth, realized the cause of my concern and was able to offer me some sound advice: 'Don't look,' he said.

It was a tribute to the Boeing designers and engineers, and the secret of the 707's success, that they had been able to fabricate a structure that was so light and yet strong enough to withstand enormous aerodynamic loads.

On one occasion, in the freighter on an almost empty leg, I calculated that our optimum would be the aircraft's maximum, 41,000ft. I had never flown that high before, so I wasted no time in requesting the level. The skipper checked and then agreed. The engineer, however, was not so enthusiastic. He didn't voice his objections except to remark, as we set off for the high, thin air, 'This is a very old aeroplane, you know.'

The 707 had no trouble reaching the altitude and, apart from a minor lessening of stability, the slightly less well-damped movements that are characteristic of an aircraft at its operational ceiling, cruised there serenely. In later years, in a different aircraft, I was to fly routinely at 41,000ft, but in the old 707 it was an event. I could not forget the engineer's reservation, though; it made me think and rather took the edge off my enjoyment of the experience.

I missed those bright, blustery days of Europe's more temperate climate. I had always enjoyed flying when the wind had scoured the sky clean and every detail of the earth could be seen in sharp detail to the furthest horizon. Thunderstorms, though not as big or as frequent as in the tropics, seemed more dramatic, somehow; they billowed and stretched into the blue, dashed their rain and hail to the ground from purple-black bases, splitting the wind into chasms and edges through which the aircraft bumped and swung. It requires deft handling to land the aircraft safely in that weather. Even today's fly-by-wire creations, designed for autoland, need a human input. Despite all the marvels of modern technology, the pilots, and therefore the passengers, are forced to rely on that old-fashioned concept, skill. It needs a complex fusion of muscle, brain and eye. The machine must be coaxed down the turbulent approach path at a crab angle. Nothing is constant, everything is in flux – attitude, heading, power, trim, speed and rate of descent must all be smoothed into compliance. The aircraft is coaxed into a precise point in space and time just above the runway so that the wheels can be placed on the tarmac under firm control. It's not all over then, however. Slowing several tons of fast-moving machinery on a soaked, wind-swept surface until it ceases to behave like an aeroplane and begins to resemble a land vehicle over which something like normal rules of control exist takes skill too.

Then you feel the tension flowing out of your body like the rain that is streaming off the fuselage and wings and you can relax. You might steal a glance at the other pilot, perhaps exchange a sheepish grin, and remember why you do this job.

Nevertheless, we did occasionally encounter crosswind landings in the 707 and its reputation was enough to infuse them with a special excitement. When an aircraft with an approach speed of 120 knots experiences a crosswind of 25 knots, the drift angle required to track in line with the runway is about 12 degrees. It does not sound much, but, in order to ensure that the wheels are aligned with the runway during the actual touchdown, the aircraft must be yawed, that is flown sideways, by 12 degrees. There are various techniques the pilot can use to achieve this feat. He can wait until the last minute, holding the drift angle until he begins the flare to land, then squeeze on enough rudder to bring the aircraft in line with the runway for just long enough to complete the landing. The aircraft's inertia will keep it tracking down the centre line for a second or two before it starts to drift downwind and there will be just time enough to place the wheels on the tarmac, where the undercarriage geometry will help to keep it straight.

The timing has to be right, but just applying rudder is not enough. On its own, this would induce a roll lifting the into-wind wing and turning the aircraft towards the downwind edge of the runway. So, if the wind is from the right, the pilot must apply rudder with his left foot and hold the wings level by applying aileron to the right. He will usually try to ensure that he overcompensates slightly in roll so that the aircraft is banked a degree or two into the wind and that the into-wind main wheel touches down first, because if that wing rises the plane will start to drift downwind and all sorts of chaos can result.

It's a clever trick and a joy to watch when it is done well. Of course, it is only really necessary when the wind is strong, which usually means it is gusting and turbulent and a multitude of small corrections are needed at the same time. Nor is it possible to use a much higher approach speed. The fact that the wind is across the runway means that there is no head wind component to reduce the ground speed. In fact, it is entirely possible that a tailwind component may be present at touchdown and for the rollout, so the available landing distance may be critical.

The 707 was no different to any other aircraft in that it obeyed the same rules of physics and aerodynamics, but several features combined to give it a fearful reputation. It was, of course, large and heavy, and runways were more often limiting. It also had a highly swept wing, probably the highest sweep on any western-built airliner, which magnified the 'further effects of rudder', so that roll, when rudder was applied, was pronounced. It also had a wide wingspan and the low-slung podded engines offered little clearance above the runway. If landing occurred with more than a few degrees of roll angle, the outer pod would scrape the runway. The few incidents where pilots had scraped pods were enough to warn us of the career-damaging consequences.

Another technique, which has the advantage that it doesn't call for such precise timing, is to set up a sideslip while still a few miles out on the final approach. Rudder is used to align the aircraft as before and opposite aileron is applied to keep the wings level, so that the aircraft is in effect flown sideways down the approach in order to stay aligned with the centre line. It takes some practice and feels unnatural at first, but it allows good control and makes less of a demand on the pilot's judgement. It reduces the need for precise timing during the flare, so this method, or a combination of the two, was normally used on the 707.

In fact, the amount of roll needed to scrape a pod is quite considerable. I witnessed a remarkable arrival on the bumpy surface of the runway at Kaohsiung in Taiwan once when the old Boeing demonstrated the flexibility of its airframe in a violent series of bounces, pitching and rolling alarmingly while the captain stirred the controls in a frenzy and the engineer hastened to get the engines into reverse and get the machine slowed down. We looked carefully during the turnaround, but were surprised and delighted to find not a scratch on the pods.

Why not just fly the aircraft onto the ground and allow the undercarriage to straighten it up? Well, you can do that too. It was actually the recommended method on the Boeing 737-300 series, but I suspect that owed something to the fact that the manufacturer wanted to clear the aircraft for autoland and the autopilot did not have a rudder channel. There is little likelihood that, in the very low visibility when autoland is needed, strong winds will be present. Most of the systems in use today, which do have a rudder channel to align the aircraft for touchdown, are limited operationally to 10 knots of crosswind. Boeing had demonstrated that it was acceptable to land the 737 with the drift on in crosswinds of up to 30 knots, but I never met anyone who had tried it. Real pilots are far too sensitive. The thought of flying onto the runway sideways sets our teeth on edge.

However you do it, there is immense satisfaction in getting a crosswind landing right. It requires skill, understanding, a high degree of coordination and judgement. If it all comes together so that, out of the turbulence and confusion of the last few feet, a smooth alignment and gentle touchdown emerges, it feels wonderful.

The long-haul routes we flew reintroduced me to that old enemy, fatigue. Attitudes to fatigue on the flight deck have changed over the years. There is much more awareness now; it is acknowledged and discussed. I flew with captains on the Boeing 707 who expected the co-pilot, when he wasn't actually doing anything else, to maintain a continuous watch for other aircraft; sit up straight, be alert and sweep the sky ahead with his eyes throughout the long hours of the night even over the vast spaces north of Australia where the chance of encountering another aircraft was very low.

Others, more realistic, would say, 'If you feel tired, don't bother to tell me, that will wake you up again and make you feel worse. Just let yourself fall asleep.' Their thinking was that it was far better to have ten minutes' real sleep and be refreshed for the next few hours than to struggle through the night feeling awful. Only twice in over thirty years have

A fine study by my colleague Kurt Lang of a Handley-Page Herald of Autair, in good weather for once, near our Luton base. For pilots, its best feature was its two Rolls-Royce Dart turboprops; for passengers, the comfortable cabin with large windows.
KURT LANG

Court Line revolutionized holiday travel, not only with the introduction of the jet BAC 1-11, but also with its corporate image. The vibrant colours of the aeroplanes and fresh designs for the crews' uniforms helped to popularize foreign travel. KURT LANG

Royal Brunei Airlines started operations from Brunei in 1975 with two Boeing 737-200 aircraft. Thus began my fascination with South-East Asia, my friendship with and respect for the people of the region, and my love affair with Boeing's products. JON CHARLEY

The Boeing 707 was already a classic when I got to fly it with Cathay Pacific Airlines. It could carry up to 200 passengers over 6,000 miles and is seen here crossing Boundary Road on the way into the old Kai Tak airfield. AUTHOR

Orion Airways' European Airbus A300-B4 was my introduction to a line of very capable airliners from Airbus that has transformed the world's hierarchy of aircraft manufacturers. Its size was impressive but flying it was very straightforward.

An Airtours McDonnell Douglas MD 83, a classic aeroplane developed from the Douglas DC-9. Built to last, it was a delight to fly but the European inclusive tour business pushed its performance and range to the limit.

The Boeing 757-200 was designed to be almost indistinguishable from the Boeing 767 from the perspective of the pilots. This gave the airlines great flexibility and provided the pilots with two exceptionally fine types to fly. DEAN MORLEY VIA FOTER.COM

The Airbus A320 – airline flying enters the digital age. A superb example of the aircraft designer's art, the engineer's ingenuity and a model of operational efficiency. But the interface with the imperfect human pilot leaves much to be desired. WILTSHIRE SPOTTER VIA FOTER.COM

I woken with a start on the flight deck and looked round to find that the other two were fast asleep, too. The first time I was shocked and filled with guilt. The second time it didn't bother me. By then I knew that, had anything happened, had the autopilot dropped out or a system failed, we would have been awake instantly.

In the days when autopilots were less reliable and navigation required frequent human input, we were attuned to the needs of the aeroplane and the rhythm of the tasks to be performed. If we slept, it was like a laptop computer going into power-saving mode, restored to full functionality as soon as it is touched. We didn't close down completely.

My spell back in the co-pilot's seat gave me another opportunity to observe different captains at work and reinforced my existing beliefs about command. The best captains, the ones who make the safest decisions, who operate economically and best look after their passengers' interests, are the ones who can handle the aircraft best. Those pilots who were very well trained in basic instrument flying and who can achieve remarkable accuracy with relatively primitive equipment seem to have a better awareness of the situation and to have more time for rational decision-making.

Unfortunately, present-day pilots do not get that sort of training. They don't get enough practice at raw instrument flying and they are going to get less under future licensing arrangements. It is argued, of course, that they do not need that level of skill, but their knowledge and understanding of their aircraft and its environment does not develop. Their awareness of what is happening to the aircraft has to rely on the interpretation of information at a conscious mental level, rather than becoming instinctive. Thus they have less spare mental capacity for strategic thinking and their captaincy skills suffer.

While I was flying the 707 in a disciplined, even rigid operational environment, I was unaware of worldwide social changes impinging on how airline pilots did their job. But now, looking back, a drift from personal responsibility and autonomy to central control and the limitation of authority is clearly apparent. In the olden days of airline flying, once the designers and engineers had created the hardware, safety was largely left to the crew. It was the skills and attitudes they developed, coordinated and enforced by the Chief Pilot and Training Captains, that prevented accidents. Clearly it was a far from perfect system, but in the story of the progression from autonomy to central control, Cathay Pacific had got it pretty well right.

The 707 crews' actions were prescribed in detail from the moment they 'signed-in' for the flight in the crew room through pre-flight preparation, aircraft operation, navigation and communication activities to the final filing of the paperwork at the end of the trip. There were very few decisions to make: the SOPs described how a thing was done, so that's the way you did it. But the rules were simple and they were kept to a minimum. They were designed to encourage best practice in a multitude of common circumstances so that good habits developed across the fleet. Everyone did things in the same way, the way that had been proved to be the best, so that it did not make any difference whether the crews had flown together before or not. The handling of irregular events and unexpected situations was left entirely to the discretion of the captain. It was assumed that he was the most qualified person to assess the situation because he was the man 'on the spot' and he carried full responsibility. If the outcome was reasonably satisfactory, nothing was said. In fact, the company management would go to some lengths to support a captain's decision and to defend him against critics. If the captain really got it wrong, then he was assumed to be 'not up to the job' and was demoted or fired.

The tendency in recent years has been away from individual responsibility. SOPs are less prescriptive of simple basic chores and have infiltrated the realm of decision-making and responsibility. This does not just mean fewer and less colourful 'characters'; it also inhibits the development of decision-making skills and of initiative. There is no longer much scope for individual interpretation. Furthermore, the captain is encouraged to ask for help. In addition to the emphasis on Crew Resource Management is added a requirement for frequent and detailed referral to his company's operations centre. Proponents of these developments will point to improving safety statistics and perhaps they have some justification. There is no doubt in my mind, however, that it is possible to carry this process too far, blurring the lines of responsibility and weakening the benefits of leadership and initiative.

Such matters, while of interest to the airline pilot, do not play a large part in his day to day concerns. Humour is more important and it does not really matter if it is not absolutely Politically Correct. Trudging through the airport terminal building in Bangkok before dawn, crew morale was not at its best. No one had slept well and we had a long day ahead of us. We had fallen into single file to negotiate the corridors, with our twelve female cabin attendants in front, dragging their wheeled overnight cases, followed by the engineer, myself and our captain. The airline was famed for its very attractive Asian cabin crew and I must say they were impressively turned out, looking very smart and pretty in their immaculate uniforms, in spite of the early hour.

Coming the other way, having presumably just completed a long overnight flight, uniforms crumpled, was the crew of an American airline in a similar formation. Cabin crew members in the US had, a few years previously, successfully challenged the law forcing them to retire early. They could now continue working to, I think, fifty-five years of age.

The two lines passed in silence, without acknowledgement until the two captains at the end of the lines were level. Out of the corner of my eye I saw the slim, grey-haired American lean slightly towards us, peering over his half-moon specs, and heard him say in a low voice, 'I'll swap you all of mine for one of yours.'

Both lines of cabin crew turned with rather sullen, puzzled expressions to discover what had caused the three of us to double up in laughter. We never told them.

Airports get more uniform as aviation develops. It is sometimes difficult to distinguish one from another, with the same architecture, shops and cafés. But you may notice one feature that they all have in common: there is always a change when you pass through check-in and security to reach the departure lounge. You are relieved that the stress of getting to the airport and checking in on time is over, you begin to relax and perhaps you rediscover the excitement of going on holiday. But there is something else – the atmosphere on this side of the formalities is different. You have left the ordinary world behind. You are now 'Airside'; you have entered that part of the airport reserved for those directly engaged in the business of flying. Ordinary mortals, those who do not have a ticket or an airport worker's pass, are forbidden to come here. Airline pilots, who spend their working lives on this side of the fence, sometimes refer to passing back through the controls to the public areas as 'going ashore'. It is a reminder of the magic of flying.

The great British air pioneer Sir Alan Cobham writes of 'the poetry, the romanticism of flying'.[5] He linked his love of flying to his passion for gardening and his love of nature and the countryside. He wrote: 'There was something in me that loved aeroplanes in just the same way as it loved horses.' I, too, see flying as part of the natural world and always have. The connection was clear in the early days of my career, but it became elusive later. That poetry and romanticism is easier to find now in sailing or motorcycling, or just walking on the West Coast of Scotland. For me, flying was an adventure in the wide, wild world, learning, if not to master it, to stay alive in it.

There is another moment during the preparation for flight when everything changes. The refuellers have topped up the tanks, the engineers have done their checks, the cleaners have reinstated orderliness in the cabin and the caterers have replenished the bars. The passengers are on board and are settled in their seats, the pushback is complete. The engines are started, the generators come on line and the air-conditioning is boosted, powered now by the main engines. All the ancillary equipment is withdrawn from the aircraft and the last connection is broken when the crew chief overseeing the departure unplugs his headset from its socket under the nose and stands aside, ready to indicate that all is clear for the aircraft to taxi. Clearance is obtained and when the captain releases the brakes the aircraft begins to move forward under its own power, an entire and independent, living entity at last. The crew chief and the captain may exchange a salute, even in this age of informality, because they sense that this is a special moment. At some airfields where uniformed security police guard the process, they form a line and present a formal salute. What was part of a transport system, indistinguishable from the other infrastructure and paraphernalia of airline travel, is now an autonomous flying machine in the charge of a unique crew. That moment, that comradeship, that bonding of highly trained individuals united by a desire to do a thoroughly professional job, is what I miss now.

Night flying provides more memorable sights than you might expect. Perhaps things seem more significant because we are awake while so many are asleep. The feeling will be familiar to anyone whose job involves working during what are called, 'unsociable hours'. Golding's character, Edmund, in his novel, *Fire Down Below*,[6] expresses it well when he is called to stand the dog watch as a midshipman on a beleaguered sailing ship: '... the idea of staying up all night has a mysterious attraction ... something – adult about it ... an invitation to the world of men who are doing this strange thing not as a dare or discovery but because it is their duty.' It is an unnatural time to be working and our normal daytime defences are lowered, our imaginations are freed and our emotions are nearer the surface. Perhaps it is because on a long overnight flight nothing much happens and anything that does happen acquires unusual salience.

The Boeing 707 overnight from Hong Kong to Sydney usually took over eleven hours. Traffic on the route was sparse and radio contact minimal. After dinner had been served to the passengers, the lights in the cabin were dimmed and most people slept. On the darkened flight deck we worked through our routine duties with slow deliberation: monitoring the systems; keeping the log; and resetting the Doppler navigation computer as each waypoint was crossed. I came to look forward to, and relish, the wonderful moment when the engineer threw a series of switches on his panel behind me and announced in a nasal, Australian drawl, 'Centre Tank's empty. We must be halfway. Can you see Darwin?'

I would lean forward in my seat, shielding my eyes with my arms from what little light there was inside, and peer down on a loose cluster of orange-yellow lights in the blackness far below, on the edge of a mighty continent.

Airline companies have tried, with varying degrees of success over the years, to influence the way in which their crews relax in their own time, but crews have a different attitude to their jobs now. They tend to expect a life outside, distinct from the airline world. At their main base they generally split up and go to their own respective homes or social centres. They expect some sort of normality in their lives without the all-consuming commitment to flying that used to be normal. It used to be every pilot's burning desire to be promoted to captain. Now the benefits of command are weighed carefully against the other things in life. It was not unusual in the later years of my career for a co-pilot to refuse a command – at Glasgow, say – because his partner did not want to move home. His salary would have been half as much again and he would get to be, at least while the wheels were off the ground, his own boss, but he would remain unmoved. Perhaps it indicated a healthier attitude to work and life; it certainly showed that the pilots recruited today have different values to those held by previous generations. I, and my contemporaries, simply shook our heads and could not understand.

But whatever the priorities, there are still popular, unofficial meeting places round the world where crews in transit go to relax and, occasionally, meet up with old friends. These bars, clubs and restaurants are known or discovered by long-haul crews as if by instinct. Singapore, Bangkok, Hong Kong, Seattle, Montreal, Manchester, Toulouse, Bahrain; wherever they find themselves, pilots will find each other. A hotel in Narita, Tokyo, provided a twenty-four-hour bar for aircrew guests. Furnished in stainless steel, so that cleaning was easy, it had machines to dispense beers and spirits so that a barman was not always necessary. It sounds a soulless place, and it probably would have been if ever it had been empty, but there was a constant flow of pilots and cabin crews from around the world passing through and it was an excellent place to meet up with lost friends or to make new ones.

People I meet are often surprised to learn that pilots, too, spend a lot of time travelling in the passenger cabin. The situation is common enough to have spawned its own terminology. Whether positioning as crew or simply going on holiday, crews who are not on duty are said to be 'dead-heading'. So we know that it is not absolutely essential to sit at the front to get a good view from an aeroplane. Returning to the UK as a passenger from one of my stints in the Far East, I was not at all unhappy when our Boeing 747 had to hold at low level, circling central London on a fine morning. It was good to be home and to see all the familiar landmarks again. I became aware that the pretty Singaporean teenager sitting next to me was straining to see what she could and I was able to swap seats so that she was next to the window. For fifteen minutes we were given an unprecedented tour of the city. I pointed out the Houses of Parliament, Tower Bridge, Buckingham Palace and everything else I recognized, delighting in her excitement at seeing all these famous places for the first time in such a novel way.

Back at work in Hong Kong, I found that my new company was no different to any other in having its share of organizational politics. The knowledge and patience I had learnt while bidding for my first command was to come in useful in other circumstances, although tact was never my strong suit. On an early simulator session on the Boeing 707, I was paired with a very experienced Line Captain. The captain assessing both of us was himself being checked by a second Training Captain. During a short break, a senior Management Captain joined us. I saw an excellent opportunity to get a definitive answer to a problem that was bothering me and, I knew, lots of other pilots on the fleet. I opened the company manual and asked, 'Can you gentlemen explain this? One paragraph seems to contradict another; what is the correct procedure?'

The Management Captain spun on his heel and left the office. The two Training Captains glared at each other, their faces turning red and then purple, before they too left the room.

'Oh dear, I wish you had asked me about that first,' said the Line Captain. 'It's very contentious. No one talks about it. We'd better get back in the simulator and see if anyone turns up to finish the exercise.'

I never did get an answer and learnt to avoid the question like everyone else, or to accept an admonition in silence if I offended any captain by adopting the opposite procedure from the one he championed. Feelings ran high. It was a fundamental issue, but the fact that I can't now remember the details suggests it was not important in the overall run of things. Personalities had been allowed to obscure common sense.

For a pilot, real life occurs only on the aircraft, in the air. There we work, laugh and experience the joys and triumphs that make life worthwhile. But we also need to eat and airline food is not always of the very finest quality. There are exceptions, though, and sometimes we were spoilt.

The best food is invariably enjoyed on freight flights. Where we carried an engineer, as on the 707, he would usually take responsibility for the cooking and we could make up our own minds when we were going to eat. Apart from an occasional oily fingerprint or two on the edge of the plate, the service was excellent.

It never did to expect such things, however. If you looked forward with too much anticipation you might be disappointed. A schedule out of Hong Kong on the Boeing 707 took us to Kuala Lumpur and then to Jakarta, where we slipped for two days before continuing on to Perth in Western Australia. It was a leisurely trip, popular with crews because of the slips, but the return was done all in one day, which meant about fourteen hours on duty. One bad-tempered skipper with whom I flew the schedule brightened up after KL outbound and proudly informed me that he had ordered a dish of king prawns to be delivered to the aircraft for him on the return flight.

'Best prawns in the world,' he boasted. 'Makes that long three-sector day worthwhile.' I was glad he was in a better mood, but noted that he had not told me, or the engineer, about the prawns in time for us to order any ourselves.

I relaxed in Jakarta and Perth and would have looked forward to the long flight back to Hong Kong with any other captain. Some people are hard work to fly with. We were delayed a bit out of Jakarta and we rushed to make up time on the turn-round at Kuala Lumpur, sweating in the high humidity and early afternoon sun. The captain fumed while we waited for the load sheet, boorishly berating the hapless handling agent who waited with us on the flight deck. At last a slight figure appeared sauntering across the tarmac towards us in the brassy sunshine. He carried the piece of paper we needed and he moved slowly, indolently, as if he was immersed in warm oil.

'What the Hell's he doing!' roared the captain.

'That,' replied the patient handling agent, 'is a Malaysian sprint.'

On our way again at last, the skipper climbed the aircraft at high speed and insisted on setting the throttles for maximum speed in the cruise, overruling the fussy concerns of the engineer. He was convinced he could reach Hong Kong on schedule and did the calculations on a piece of paper to prove it. He was mightily pleased with himself when he slid back his seat and pressed the cabin call bell. The beautiful Asian stewardess had been laughing happily with her colleagues when she came onto the flight deck and, I thought, eating something.

'I'll have my prawns, now!' boomed our wretched skipper and out of the corner of my eye I saw the stewardess's face change. She put a hand to her mouth, her eyes went big and round, and she seemed to swallow with some difficulty. But she composed herself quickly.

'... er, prawns, captain?' she said, the picture of innocence.

'My bloody prawns from KL,' the skipper shouted. 'The agent promised they were on board. I paid for them on the way out.'

'Don't know about any prawns,' she said. 'I'll ask the others but I don't think we uplifted any prawns,' and she disappeared with some haste.

Staring stiffly out of my side window, I tried desperately to keep a straight face. I could picture her rushing to warn the rest of the crew not to let slip that they had eaten the captain's prawns. I dared not look at the engineer or at the captain who was now in a purple-faced rage. He fumed and swore until we reached the Hong Kong control boundary, where he descended the aircraft with the high-speed warning bell ringing continuously in an effort to overtake a Malaysian aircraft ahead of us. Just when it looked as though he might have succeeded, the radar controller came up with vectors for both aircraft and positioned us firmly as number two. We would be late.

That captain's rages never bothered me again. Whenever he started to get on my nerves I would remember his prawns and the secret smile I had shared with the beautiful stewardess as we parted.

CHAPTER 9

Trainer

Back in Europe, and back on the Boeing 737, the navigation equipment provided was beginning to seem out of date. Other aircraft were entering service with INS that allowed very accurate navigation over long distances out of range of ground beacons. Air traffic controllers in France and elsewhere found that they could clear aircraft direct to reporting points hundreds of miles away and aircraft could be relied upon to navigate accurately over these routes. It saved time and fuel for the aircraft and relieved the pressure of traffic over the established airways system. We found we were being offered such routings routinely, even though we had not got the necessary equipment and, always ready to meet a challenge, we accepted them anyway. We often received clearances, particularly at night, from south of the Alps direct to Cherbourg, or from over the north-west of Spain direct to Southampton.

So began a short period of old-fashioned navigation for jet pilots where we found ourselves drawing lines on charts, measuring or calculating new tracks and attempting to follow them by means of dead reckoning, position lines from off-track beacons and coastal returns from the weather radar. For a year or two we became quite proficient at this 'off the cuff' sort of navigation. The techniques we used would have been familiar to any enthusiastic weekend sailor. We became adept at calculating the wind we experienced at altitude, at developing our own store of modified charts and at such ancient, arcane arts as the transferred position line.

Of course, the authorities, when they realized what was happening, could not let this situation continue. It worked quite well for a while, with very few aircraft getting seriously off track, and Air Traffic Control usually had radar to monitor our position, but it was clear that some proper sort of longer-range navigation system must be provided for us. As usual, most of the equipment on offer was expensive and could not be justified until a new version of the Boeing 737 with up to date equipment came into service, so we got the Marconi Omega system installed instead. This equipment certainly had a long-range capability; it depended on very low frequency radio signals and had been originally developed for submarines, but we did not get on with it very well in the 737. Most of us soon reverted to our own, imprecise but entertaining and satisfying methods.

Being in at the start of a new company is always exciting; optimism is high and a great spirit of cooperation is apparent in all departments. Even the old stagers are hoping that, this time, things can be organized on a professional basis before disillusionment and cynicism take over. Things had changed in Europe while I had been away. Airline management had moved away from a perceived amateurism and had come at last to conceive of airliners as expensive 'plant' that must be worked hard to achieve a good financial return. Unfortunately, some had not understood that employees need to be treated in a more sympathetic manner. The idea grew in the industry that pilots too were expensive and that their utilization should also be as high as possible. Chief executives saw it as their job to achieve as high a return as possible. They saw their responsibility for safety in terms of ensuring that the company complied with current legislation. It was not, they reasoned, their job to set safety standards themselves, as this would put them at a financial disadvantage to the competition.

Formulating legislation to govern pilots' working hours is not easy. Any framework needs to be very flexible to allow for different operations, different working practices and unpredictable events. It would be unreasonable to force a crew that had started a four-sector duty at eight o'clock in the morning to stop work at eight o'clock in the evening, when they might be only a one-hour flight from home due to a technical delay. The crew might feel they had enjoyed plenty of rest; they may be happy to continue and the weather might be benign. The cost of night-stopping would be considerable. There would be the cost of hotel accommodation for the crew and the passengers of course, but the disruption of the crewing and aircraft utilization schedules would be a bigger penalty. And the passengers would not be where they had paid to be. So captains must be allowed some discretion. Problems arise when the airlines come to rely on the captains using that discretion in order to make the programme work.

The legislation drawn up by the Civil Aviation Authority was a creditable attempt to deal with these different situations. It consisted of two parts: first, a general, overall policy stressing the need for a regular, stable schedule to give pilots a sensible lifestyle; and second, a list of specific limits on flight times, duty times, night flying, and so on. However, most employers completely disregarded the first part and used the absolute limits in the second part as targets or a measure of efficiency. Pilot unions should have resisted these interpretations, but they were swayed by short-term considerations. In many cases, they simply did not appreciate the effects of the regulations. Often the promised safeguards never materialized.

Commercial pressures are of course inseparable from airline flying. It is always interesting to watch an airline executive speaking to the press after his airline has suffered some embarrassing incident or an accident. The phrase that trips most readily off his tongue is, 'Safety is our first priority!' But of course it isn't. How can it be? If the most important thing to us is that no one should be killed or injured in an aeroplane crash, we could ban aeroplanes and guarantee 100 per cent success. No, there are three priorities: getting the passengers where they have paid to go quickly and comfortably; doing it economically so that the airline survives and prospers, people keep their jobs and the shareholders get a good return on their money; and doing it safely. These three requirements can all be achieved and they often complement each other. Accidents are very bad for business. They are very expensive, they disrupt the programme and they put the passengers off travelling. But to achieve an acceptable level of safety requires everyone in the company to work tirelessly towards that end. Leadership in this, as in everything else, must come from the top. Unfortunately, awareness of safety culture does not seem to figure highly in any MBA curricula.

There is a widely held view in all industries, not just aviation, that safety is an absolute – the operation is either a safe one, or it isn't. It is a convenient view, because once you are satisfied that your personal operation is 'safe', you can forget about it and concentrate on some other feature of the business. But the level of safety achieved in any undertaking can only exist in a continuum; it will always be somewhere between 'as safe as human beings can make it' and 'downright bloody dangerous'. And it will vary from day to day, minute to minute, as conditions change and people concentrate or drift off into inattentiveness. It takes time to educate people into recognizing this fact and into adopting the mindset that keeps safety at the higher levels. A culture has to be created where everyone involved is aware of how fragile the state of safety is, so that they are constantly watching themselves and their colleagues for signs of its deterioration and ready to shout for help if it is needed.

Of course, people won't call for help unless they expect a sympathetic response. Often the perception is – justified or not – that it will be seen as a sign of weakness, a nuisance and another negative to be considered when promotion or redundancy is in prospect. Then there is the guilt of calling out one of your colleagues – you may be asking him to fly more because you can't cope. The fatigued pilot has to weigh these factors and make a decision when he is at his lowest ebb.

The difficulties of maintaining a high level of care are increased when the level of safety is already high. If the safety system is fundamentally a good one, so that accidents or incidents are rare, it is difficult to motivate people to be vigilant. It also means that standards can fall a long way before an incident occurs to focus minds back onto the important priorities.

Enormously successful safety cultures have been built up and maintained for long periods, only to be thrown away in a thoughtless act. We saw it happen in NASA, when the triumphant development of the Space Shuttle was passed to a new management team who had not developed that safety culture. They lost one Shuttle spacecraft and even after long, expensive, exhaustive investigations and reorganization, lost another, because they did not have the culture anymore. We have seen it in the rail transport industry in Britain, where privatization led to outsourced contractors being made responsible for track maintenance. Even though statistics show an overall improvement in rail accident rates, the employment of itinerant workers with no sense of ownership of the task and no safety culture appears to have contributed to the accidents at Potters Bar in 2002 and Cumbria in 2007.

Changes that threaten the safety culture are not at all obvious. In the airline industry, independent, professional pilots should constitute the greatest safeguard to the erosion of safe standards, but independence is a threatened concept. For a multitude of reasons there will always be a few pilots prepared to nail their colours to a particular management mast. Some, often with military backgrounds, have a misguided notion about total loyalty to management. Others are swayed by ambition or money. And aviation has always attracted more than its share of oddballs.

At least training within the airlines had improved. Classroom or computer-based ground school was followed by extended simulator training. Suitable courses and formalized standards for instructor training approved by the Civil Aviation Authority (CAA) had removed some of the variability.

Even so, it was already becoming evident that the overall standard of flying, that is pure aircraft handling, was certainly not improving during the rapid expansion of the jet age. On their biannual competency checks, pilots were having difficulty in two main areas: the ADF approach; and, on the Boeing 737, the two-engined go-around. Simulators had improved enormously, but the time pilots spent in them was seen as expensive, non-productive downtime. We were now expected to avoid unnecessary periods in the simulator and to make best use of what time was allowed. The result was a concentration on the abnormal and emergency procedures required by legislation; after all, the pilots spent their normal working day operating the aircraft in routine procedures, why did they need to do the same in the simulator? However, there are procedures, considered ordinary and routine, that do not get done very often and one of these was the two-engined go-around.

The problem arose because of the superb performance given to the 737 by its Pratt and Whitney JT8D engines and the fact that pilots rarely used all of the power available to them, even when the aircraft was heavy. De-rated power was usually used for take-off in order to extend the life of the engines. Pilots entered data tables with details of the aircraft weight, the outside temperature and altitude of the runway in use to give an engine-pressure ratio indicating maximum thrust. But instead of using the actual ambient temperature, the maximum temperature at which the aircraft was allowed to take off at that weight was used, resulting in a reduced, but still safe, thrust.

Go-around is the term used to describe a discontinued approach. It can be a fairly leisurely affair when done at a safe altitude or in visual conditions, but it needs to be done smartly, with full power, at the decision height of an instrument approach if visual reference has not been obtained. Pilots may fly for months or years even, without having to do a go-around from minimums in anger. When they do, it is at the end of the flight when they may be tired, most of the fuel has been consumed and the aircraft is much lighter. The low-slung engine configuration of the 737, combined with full landing flap, also produced a strong nose-up pitch change. Applying full power at minimums, pilots suddenly found themselves wide-eyed, pushing on the control column with all their strength, while the aircraft took off skywards at a startling rate. There were a number of incidents where they failed to get the aircraft properly under control before climbing above their cleared altitude, causing potential conflict with other traffic.

The answer was simply to practise the procedure, several times if necessary, in the simulator every six months. If the effects of full power were anticipated, a slightly less aggressive technique used when applying the power and prompt action taken to reconfigure the aircraft once it was established in the climb, order would be restored. This was not the solution favoured by the engineers or the accountants, however. Later on, with the introduction of the 737-300 series, the manufacturer resorted to technology to tackle the problem. First, the power delivered by the engines when go-around power was selected was automatically reduced to a level that restricted the resulting rate of climb to a maximum of 2,000ft per minute. Second, the upgraded autopilot could remain engaged to fly the go-around itself. It looked as though the problem had been solved, but subsequent incidents and accidents in recent years show that the all engines operating go-around is still a higher-risk procedure. The hypothesis is, if you get the autopilot to do the mechanical flying, the pilot then can concentrate on the thinking. Unfortunately, unless he is fully competent and current in manual instrument flying, he will not be completely aware of the environment or the situation through which the aircraft is moving. It is then easy to become disorientated. Analysis of recent events points either to the pilots' lack of understanding of the automatics, or to their lack of skill.

The difficulties pilots had flying ADF approaches were partly a result of infrequent practice and partly historical. One of the earliest radio navigation aids dating back to the 1930s, the ADF, or radio compass is, at the same time both a remarkably simple, reliable and versatile instrument and an anachronistic nightmare. It consisted originally of a needle on a dial showing the direction of the tuned radio station, or NDB, relative to the aircraft. Later developments incorporated a compass card so that the pilot could read directly the magnetic bearing to the station. Apart from the fluctuations of the needle caused by atmospheric interference and other errors, the system can provide good bearings at a glance. In order to follow an accurate track towards or away from the station, however, allowance must be made for the wind. This requires some mental agility from the pilot to calculate his drift and to add or subtract it from the reading shown by the needle to determine the heading he should fly. It is the old problem of being able to fly and think at the same time.

Flying an instrument approach based on the NDB and ADF has always been a demanding exercise. It was demanding in the slow, piston-engined aircraft in service when it was originally introduced and it was still demanding in the slow, piston-engined training aircraft on which most of us learnt our trade. By the time the jet came along, ILS and radar approaches were the norm, so opportunities for practice on the line were limited. Major airfields around the world were usually equipped with more than one ILS, VOR/DME and radar and jet pilots rarely had to resort to ADF approaches with their higher minima and the low rate of landings they allowed. Operating into secondary airfields, however, meant the pilots would often find that an ADF approach was the only instrument procedure available.

While conducting pilots' biannual checks in the simulator with different airlines between 1981 and 1998, I found it instructive to observe the varying accuracy achieved. The sort of task I set involved a normal take-off, radar vectors towards the beacon to hold, an ADF approach to minima of, say, 400ft, followed by a landing or a go-around. The airfield selected would be one known to the candidate. No aircraft failures would be introduced and the weather would be benign except for a brisk crosswind relative to the final approach track and the cloud base set at about 50ft above the minima.

Few pilots achieved a satisfactory approach at their first attempt. I did not keep continuous records, but it was certainly less than 50 per cent. Allowance must be made for the fact that the pilots were on check. No matter how experienced they are, how many times they have done it before, professional pilots are still nervous for the first few exercises in the simulator. It is also necessary to remember that the simulator, however faithful it is to the real aircraft, is not the real aircraft; it is not as stable and the motion clues are not exactly the same, so it takes a bit of getting used to. Even so, the chances of landing off an unexpected ADF approach to minima on the line must have been slim.

The failures I observed would very rarely have resulted in an accident.

After a brief rest and discussion, the second attempt was usually fine. And that was why we were doing the exercise after all, to correct errors and to restore performance back to an acceptable level.

The difficulties encountered in intercepting and maintaining an accurate track to or from the beacon seemed to stem from the pilots' original training on slower aircraft. If there is enough time, it is possible to make a series of small corrections of heading to establish accurately on track and to stay on track. In a jet, even in the approach configuration at between 140 and 180 knots, there simply is not time for this sort of refinement. It is essential to anticipate the drift that will be experienced on any particular track, to take up the estimated heading and to stick to it. The brain is then free to concentrate on the vertical profile in order to set up a suitable rate of descent quickly and accurately. By knowing the power settings and attitudes of his aircraft in a range of situations and making reasonable estimates of the drift to be experienced, the pilot can reduce his workload to the point where he has plenty of spare mental capacity for self-monitoring and decision-making. If he is given enough practice, an average pilot should be able to make a good ADF approach, every time, even when flying with one engine shut down. Unfortunately, I never encountered an airline that adopted such a requirement; it is a useful and highly satisfying exercise, but, I'm told, it would take up too much time and cost too much.

Another problem was encountered at the point where the aircraft emerged from the cloud base and the pilots got visual contact with the runway. For a straight-in landing, the aircraft must be close to the runway centre line and at a suitable height and speed. Any attempt to land from a less than ideal position would be dangerous. Even when perfectly positioned, it was essential that the first reaction was to do absolutely nothing. In a strong crosswind the runway would appear off to one side of the windscreen; turn towards it and it would swing smartly off to the other side and the chance for a landing was lost. A safe go-around from such a position, however, was not considered a failure.

On later aircraft such as the 737 NG, the introduction of sophisticated autopilots, Flight Management Computers, highly accurate navigation systems and large, clear map displays, made it possible to set the aircraft up to fly the ADF, or any other sort of approach, automatically. The ADF needle could be displayed, superimposed on the map screen, simply to confirm that the aircraft was indeed following the correct track. Life for the airline pilot would become easier, but he would lose far more than he had gained.

The simulator was a useful tool, but the transition to the actual aircraft was still a challenge for some. The company recruited pilots from many different backgrounds. Those from the RAF sometimes had difficulty adapting to the civilian world. They may have achieved a high rank and enjoyed considerable authority in the military, but now they were the most junior co-pilots in the fleet. Some coped by finding fault with everything. Others were very professional; they realized there was a lot to learn and quietly got on with it.

Some came from other airlines, from air taxi firms, or even directly from the initial training schools. They might be overconfident, nervous, or overawed, but every one of them was interesting and I made good friends with many of them.

One young man, I will call him Ian, had been an instructor at a civilian flying club, just as I had been many years before, and he impressed me immediately with his quick intelligence and sound knowledge. He had a reputation as a bit of an aerobatic ace too, but almost all of his flying had been on tiny, single-engined machines. He had accumulated only five hours on a light twin-engined aircraft to gain his Instrument Rating.

Now, the principles of flying a jet transport aircraft are exactly the same as those for a small training machine. Some say the larger aircraft is actually easier to fly because a jet does not suffer the gyroscopic and slipstream complications introduced by a propeller. It is also more stable, but that can cause problems too. A jet is heavier: around 50 tons, as opposed to less than 1 ton. And of course it is faster, so it has a lot more inertia. Nevertheless, the flight controls are arranged in a similar fashion to a trainer and they are more powerful, helped by hydraulic power, so many pilots convert from one to the other with little difficulty.

Training on the actual aircraft is expensive and potentially dangerous, so we trainers were always under pressure to keep the flight time to a minimum. As soon as each trainee was able to perform the required exercises to a satisfactory standard he was replaced by the next in line. And if he could not reach that standard in a reasonable time, it would be cheaper for the airline to let him go.

I took Ian's group to Ibiza where the blue skies and sparkling sea made an invigorating contrast to the East Midlands airport in the winter. They made generally good progress. We flew round and round, flying instrument approaches, carrying out landings and rolling immediately into take-off for visual circuits. Occasionally I throttled an engine back to simulate a single-engined condition.

When Ian strapped in for his turn I suppose I was expecting something special. He had all the attributes of an above average pilot and the confidence to go with it. But things went wrong from the start. He just could not come to terms with the inertia. No doubt his touch had been quick and light on the small aeroplanes he was familiar with, but a more patient and smoother technique is needed on the jet. He just could not get it. He pulled and struggled with the controls. He tried harder and things got worse. He got frustrated and tense, so I took control and told him to relax while I flew a circuit and tried to explain the different technique required. When I handed control back to him he was a little better, but the aircraft movements were still rough and unnatural.

I sent him back into the cabin for a breather while I pressed on with another trainee. I hoped he would relax, but I think he brooded about his lack of success. As a result, his next session fluctuated between rough, barely acceptable competence and wild overcontrolling. The guys in the back could tell things were not going well and he knew what they would be thinking. I tried all I could to reassure him, to relax him and to take the pressure off him, but he knew there was a limit to how much time he would be given.

By the end of his third session he had used up more time than I could reasonably allow and, with sweat on his brow, he had achieved a standard that, if I was generous, I might accept. I could sign his training file and pass him out for line flying, but both he and I knew it was a marginal performance. He was tough and determined and he would not give up, but he was bemused. He was so used to being the best that he simply could not understand what was wrong.

I finished off the last of the other trainees and landed to hand over the aircraft to the next trainer and his charges. We had been on duty long enough and we were all tired, but Ian's poor performance cast a shadow over the day for me. I slid my side window open as I taxied towards the terminal and savoured the fresh air. I reckon I can tell where I am in the world by the smell; Spain is a mixture of sun cream and cigars.

'Come on, Ian,' I called. 'Two more circuits.' And the others groaned as he came willingly enough, with a sheepish grin, and strapped himself again into the right-hand seat.

We did at least four circuits. I no longer cared about cost because halfway round the first one Ian suddenly discovered what jet flying was all about. His control movements smoothed out, the aircraft settled into a steady groove and I found myself watching an expert at work. The expression of relief and pure joy on Ian's face was a delight to behold. I will never know exactly how it happened and I can claim no credit for it other than having made the decision to give him one more try. That decision was vindicated now. To Hell with the cost! I'll pay for it myself if necessary; it's worth it.

Later, back on the ground watching the next crew go through their stint as the light began to fade, I was reflecting on that moment and thinking I would never forget it. Such rewards are rare, but they are what make being a trainer worthwhile. Another of my trainees detached himself from the group. He too was a low-time pilot, but his sessions had been unexceptional. I was sure that in time he would develop into an excellent pilot, although, for the moment, he could only be classified as average.

I was surprised when he put his hand out to me, but I took it automatically. 'I just wanted to thank you,' he said. 'That was the most wonderful experience of my life.' And I was reminded that it wasn't just the exceptions; every day was special in this job.

My return to European flying after only a few years' absence made me aware of the rapid growth of the major cities. The urban sprawl was most particularly noticeable at night. Genoa used to be like a handful of gems cast onto a cloth of black velvet, an image in sharp contrast to the noise and pollution apparent when the industrial port is seen at close quarters in daylight. Now the lights spread out and merge with others, spoiling the effect.

Paris used to be tiny. Only thirty years ago visitors to the flight deck at night were disbelieving when we pointed it out. 'It looks like a village,' they would say. Now it is a sprawling metropolis. It doesn't match the ocean of light that is the Low Countries where Belgium, Germany and the Netherlands meet, or the ever-extending expanse of London, but you have to look carefully now to spot the more brightly lit centre of the old city.

The combination of enlarged cities and the growth in jet traffic brought the problem of noise to more people. Complaints about noise seemed to peak in the 1970s and there are plenty of people for whom the roar of an aircraft overhead, even today, is intolerable. But improved engines, more precise noise-abatement routings and operational techniques have lessened the problem. The people who are opposed to aviation are now more likely to apply themselves to its supposed effect on atmospheric pollution, pillorying passengers for selfishly destroying the planet on their way to a foreign holiday. Frustrated to learn that aircraft contribute little to carbon emissions compared with other forms of transport, they identify it as the fastest growing contributor, ignoring the fact that aero-engine manufacturers are spending vast sums on ways of reducing those emissions.

It was always the same. In his book of 1934,[7] Captain Olley celebrated the reliability, convenience and comfort of 'modern' aviation. He delivered a tirade against people who complained about aircraft overflying their land or about the noise. To his mind, they were just a few killjoys holding back from the many the great benefits to come from the development of air services.

Pilots did, and do, take the problem of noise seriously. Every effort is made to keep things as quiet as possible. But a lot of the people who complain are guilty of exaggeration. Aircraft noise becomes a focus for them out of the many other, unconnected, random discomforts they suffer. On two occasions, groups protesting about the noise from airports I flew from arranged for monitoring equipment to be positioned under the flight path to provide scientific evidence to back up their complaints. Both trials were unsuccessful because the noise of the aircraft was drowned out by the noise of lorries grinding up the hill on which the equipment was sited.

I was called to my local pub one evening (such a chore) to settle a dispute. A local councillor had said he intended to object at an airport expansion enquiry, not only about the noise, but also about aircraft dumping fuel over the village on their approach to land. Half of the front bar agreed with him, claiming that they had seen the vapour pouring from the fuel tanks of 737s; the other half didn't think it could happen.

I spent a quiet, liquid hour explaining to the councillor that any aircraft that did dump fuel (in emergency only, it's expensive!) did so under strict control, preferably over the sea and at such an altitude that the fuel would evaporate before it could reach the surface. The Boeing 737, designed as a short- to medium-range airliner and capable of landing at or near its maximum take-off weight, was not equipped with the mechanisms necessary to dump fuel. The vapour people saw was in fact water in the atmosphere, condensing out in the vortices shed from the aircraft's flaps. The development of airfoils and high-lift devices has meant an increase in lift coefficient, which in practical terms means the pressure differential between the top surface of the wing and the lower. Nature will try to equalize any such difference; the air bleeding round the outboard end of the flaps from the high-pressure side to the low creates these vortices.

The councillor and I parted eventually in a spirit of great bonhomie and I was satisfied he now understood the facts. But I was saddened later, and had my prejudices against politicians reinforced, when I heard he had stuck to his original speech and publicly condemned the airlines for dumping fuel over the village.

On subsequent occasions, I confess, when tipped off by a controller that noise-measuring equipment had been positioned at the threshold of the runway to record our arrival, I have flown round the circuit and landed on the other end.

This was a busy time on the 737 for me. My duties involved the simulator, aircraft conversion training and line training. There was always something happening. I witnessed another autopilot malfunction on a Boeing 737 after take-off from Munich. The co-pilot was new, just out of the RAF and struggling with the transition to civilian flying. Not that he had any technical problems; his flying and knowledge were fine. But after a long career as a hotshot fighter pilot, he hadn't yet come to terms with his position as a new boy. He hadn't yet understood that he had a lot to learn. Surely this 'transport' flying must be simple after air-to-air combat and low-level attack? Then there was the rank thing. In the RAF, everyone knows his position and status. Things are less well defined in the civil world. He had already upset the cabin crew by trying to order them about. Perhaps that was a symptom of his new insecurity. The fury with which they responded had clearly confused him. I was trying to help him adjust and to offer some gentle advice from time to time, but it wasn't easy. And perhaps I wasn't the best person for the job. He had a lot of natural aggression – ideal I would have thought for a fighter pilot – but not the best trait in an airline pilot. He tended to attack the problems he encountered aggressively and was struggling to understand why this was often counterproductive.

The Standard Instrument Departure from Munich was combined with a noise-abatement procedure and routing that made the first few minutes after take-off busy and demanding. The new boy was tense, desperate to perform well, as no doubt he always had in his RAF career. A previous trainer had told him to make full use of the autopilot, so, against his natural instincts, he engaged it as soon as practical after take-off. But when it ran away into a hard left roll the workload was close to overwhelming him. He reacted like any good pilot by assuming the aberration was due to some mistake he had made. The air was blue and his hands flashed round the cockpit as he desperately fought to keep the aircraft within the confines of the procedure, get everything under control and finally re-engage the autopilot.

It is always much easier for the one who is watching than the one who is flying. I realized immediately what had happened and watched his struggle with mounting amusement. When the autopilot ran away in a left roll for a second time, his mighty oath was matched by my guffaw. This gave him a new and perhaps more legitimate target for his wrath and he cursed me without restraint for the rest of the trip.

A couple of years later I flew with him again for several sectors intended to prepare him for command. At the end of these he paid me a great compliment. 'I don't mind flying with you,' he said. 'You're a bad-tempered b****** but at least I learn something.'

Being back in Europe meant flying in European weather again. Most jet airliners, the 737 included, have very effective hot-air de-icing systems on the leading edges of the wing and engine intakes. This, coupled with a good rate of climb and descent so that they spend less time in the icing levels, means that they rarely accumulate large amounts of ice. On the other hand, their wing sections are more highly refined than the previous, slower types and it takes less accumulation to ruin the performance. There is a particular danger after the aircraft has spent several hours cruising in the stratosphere where the outside temperature is around –56°C. The airframe becomes 'cold-soaked' and if it then descends through cloud holding water droplets at just above freezing, they freeze rapidly onto the aircraft surface. Pilots have to anticipate this situation. Held at 10,000ft for a few minutes after just such a descent on a mild spring day, I saw over two inches of ice build up in less than three minutes.

On another occasion I took over an aircraft that had landed from a long night flight two hours earlier, while it was still dark. Rush hour was developing at the airport, with passengers queuing to board at the gates and aircraft roaring into the sky every minute or so. It was one of those fine, bright, blustery days when everyone is busy and the system is stretched but working well. I had to disrupt it all with a call for the de-icing crew because, unnoticed by anyone else, there was a quarter of an inch of hard, knobbly rime ice on all the leading edges of the aircraft. The machine must have passed through a thin sheet of cloud on its descent without its pilots noticing the ice. No other aircraft had needed de-icing that morning so there was a delay. First the handlers did not believe me, then they had to round up a crew, get the truck loaded, heat the fluid and get everything out to the aircraft before they could set to work.

Generally, the de-icing crews do a good job. When they are needed, the weather is usually foul and always cold. Often it is dark and they have to work round the chaos of vehicles and people surrounding an aircraft before departure: baggage handlers; refuellers; engineers; and caterers. They work long hours and, of course, everyone is in a hurry.

It is tempting in such circumstances for the captain to delegate the whole process to the experienced team leader, but not wise. One such fellow pushed through the throng on to our warm flight deck at a UK airfield one morning with a chit for me to sign. 'All cleared, Captain,' he said, 'and your baggage doors are closed. You can go right away.' I signed the chit automatically, but struggled out of my seat and started to dress up for the cold walk round the aircraft. 'No need, Cap,' he assured me. 'It's OK.'

'Yeah,' I said, 'but …'. And I set off in the freezing cold wind, splashing through the puddles round the dripping aircraft. He was right, of course. They had done a wonderful job. Not a trace of ice anywhere, fluid sprayed over every surface and in every crack and orifice – on the port side of the aircraft. They hadn't touched the starboard side! The poor chap didn't believe me. He was distraught and I felt sorry for him.

In the inclusive tour holiday business, we uplifted our passengers in the cold and wet of the UK and transported them swiftly to the sunshine of the Mediterranean. They came on board tense and stressed, white-faced in their best clothes and ready to argue about anything. We picked them up a week or two later, bronzed in their bright beachwear, laughing and relaxed. Well, sometimes. Unfortunately the first busy period of the season, the school Easter holidays, often saw warm sunshine in Britain after a long, hard winter. Worse, the Mediterranean resorts were often experiencing high winds, rain and thunderstorms over the Easter period. On one occasion, after a five-hour flight from the balmy spring sunshine of central England, I found myself doing a procedural NDB approach to minima at the cloud-covered island of Rhodes. I had actually opened my mouth to say 'Go-around!' and started to move the thrust levers forward for full power when we broke out of cloud and caught sight of the runway through a heavy snowstorm. Welcome to the Greek Islands!

From time to time a number of airports on some list made up by the Air Line Pilots' Associations or some other agency find their way onto the pages of the popular press, where they are described in lurid terms as 'dangerous'. In fact, there is no such thing as a dangerous airport. The airport, whatever its location or terrain or situation, just sits there and doesn't threaten anyone. Any danger associated with it is generated entirely by those trying to fly into it. Every part of the world has its challenging airfields, but providing there is adequate runway length for the intended operation and the weather is acceptable, there should be no problem. It is a combination of commercial pressure and the pilots' over-confidence or vanity that causes difficulty.

The trick is for the airline to set realistic weather minima and operational restrictions and to ensure that the pilots stick to them. If that results in too many diversions or an unacceptable level of service, it is up to the airport authority to provide improvements in runway length or slope or better radio navigation aids to improve reliability. But since we live in the real world, the result is often a compromise. Pilots could be heard to sigh when they had to fly into Corfu at night, or Leeds–Bradford in the winter.

Only very rarely have I encountered turbulence on the approach to land that has been violent enough to make me consider diverting to another airfield. At Hurn, Bournemouth, and again at Bristol the limiting factor was passenger comfort rather than any control problem and in fact I landed on both of those occasions. I had to make two attempts at Heraklion on the Greek island of Crete, however, and the passengers were subjected to an uncomfortable experience.

When a strong wind blows over the island from the south, the turbulent air sweeps off the mountains down over the airfield, which is situated on the northern coast. The navigational charts warn pilots of the turbulence to be expected and caution against attempting to land in certain combinations of wind speed and direction. Conditions were just marginally acceptable when we arrived. It was night, but the Boeing 737 is an ideal machine to have in those conditions. With an excellent power to weight ratio and superbly effective controls it inspires confidence.

We passed over the VOR by the airfield and let down over the sea, experiencing increasing turbulence as we descended. I had started the turn inbound early so that we would not drift too far out to sea and prolong the approach and was pleased to see the approach lights just about where I wanted them. With the aircraft yawing and rolling in heavy gusts I reduced speed, lowered the flap and gear and set a power that should have held the speed as we descended on final approach. But we didn't descend. The 737 flew stubbornly level. I pushed the nose forward and reduced the power and still we flew level. The instruments showed we should be descending normally, but the altimeter confirmed that we were not losing any height at all. We were getting closer to the field and the angle of the approach lights showed me that if I did not descend steeply, and do it quickly, we would not be in a position to land. Eventually I found myself in a steep nose-down attitude with full flap and throttles closed. These conditions would normally have the 50-ton aircraft dropping like a brick at 2,000ft per minute, but we were still far too high and actually descending very slowly.

It crossed my mind that, should the enormous updraught we were experiencing suddenly stop, or, worse, turn into a downdraught in the last few hundred feet of the approach, it might be very difficult to arrest the subsequent rate of descent. So, reluctant as I was to subject the passengers to any more of this turbulence than was absolutely necessary, I nevertheless opened up the power and went around for another try.

Now the decision was whether to try again or to divert. The nearest alternative airfield was just along the coast and the weather conditions there must be similar. The next possible destination was a long way away. I reasoned that the passengers would prefer to get on the ground as soon as possible and that we would be unlikely to encounter such freak conditions again.

The turbulence was worse if anything on the second attempt. This time I went further out and started the descent earlier. It was very difficult to hold anything like a constant attitude. The airspeed indicator was fluctuating wildly and I was hitting the stops on the control column in roll, quite a feat on a 737, which has enormously powerful ailerons and spoilers, but we did not find the giant uplift again and somehow the aircraft remained reasonably close to the glide path.

Normally, turbulence melts away in the last 300ft or so because the ground damps out the vertical movement of the air. Not this time. I was working hard, right up to the moment when the wheels touched the ground. I taxied in and shut down quickly so that the passengers would be able to get out into the fresh air as soon as possible. Our very experienced senior cabin crewmember was wide-eyed when she came onto the flight deck to report that many of the passengers had been sick and were upset. I sympathized with them, but there was nothing more I could have done. Some of them turned and shook their fists at me as they walked the few yards from the aircraft to the terminal building. Not a good day for the company; people are supposed to enjoy their holiday.

I got cold and got my boots wet in Goose Bay in Canada while delivering the 737th production Boeing 737 from Boeing Field in Seattle to East Midlands in the UK. I was supposed to be sharing the flying with the company's Flight Operations Director, but I soon learnt that his idea of sharing was for me to do all the donkey work. He stayed in the warm chatting to the senior managers and their wives who were our passengers. After organizing the refuelling process, I trudged through deep snow-drifts to study the weather reports and to file a flight plan. The office was warm but the welcome was restrained. No one seemed interested in me; everyone was gathered round a TV set mounted high on the wall. I joined the throng, staring up at the screen and asked a chap with his hands in his pockets what was going on.

'They shot Reagan,' he said without turning round.

'Oh, yeah?' I replied. 'Got the weather for UK and the North Atlantic?'

Reluctantly he tore himself away from the TV and provided the paper-work I needed. I dropped the flight plan in his tray and made my way to the door.

'Thanks! See you,' I called, but nobody answered and I trudged back through the snow to sign for the fuel and make my external check of the machine.

Such was the extent to which major world events impinged on our flying world. I was more concerned about whether my shoes and trousers would dry out during the five-hour flight through the night and whether I would get to land the aircraft at the end of it.

Airlines had for some years expressed a strong preference for recruits who had completed a full-time residential course at recognized train-ing establishments. Several Chief Pilots held the view that pilots trained in this way were of a higher standard, followed company SOPs more closely and were more likely to stay with the airline. There might have been some merit in this view if the long established and highly respected schools in the UK such as the British Airways School at Hamble or Air Service Training in Perth had been used. But the airlines were reluctant to contribute towards such training and very few private individuals could afford to pay for it themselves. Most went to the USA, South Africa or Australia, where flying training was cheaper and they could build up their hours with lower aircraft hire costs. When they returned to the UK the CAA decreed, on the merit of individual cases, what further train-ing and tests they must undertake to convert their licences into a Brit-ish ATPL. Not all were scrupulously honest about the flying hours they claimed and the result was an even greater variety in standard than there had been in 1967.

Even original academic research was beginning to find its way into the airline pilot training syllabus. Crew Resource Management (CRM) and various other techniques devised by psychologists were supposed to improve communication and decision-making on the flight deck, but their application has not been an unqualified success. Somewhere between the original research and development of the philosophy and its introduction on the line, the message has been distorted. Those trainers who cham-pioned CRM the most seemed to understand it the least. The idea was to avoid accidents caused by captains acting autocratically as one-man bands; Atlantic Barons, they used to be called. There are two pilots, both trained to a high standard, and a professional cabin crew. All of these people should now function as a team. In addition, air traffic controllers, company engineers and operations staff are available for consultation over the radio; the commander should make full use of these resources.

Like many good ideas, it triggered change in the manner of a pendulum. Some of those who adopted the philosophy wholeheartedly swung too far away from the notions of command, authority and responsibility. Someone, the individual in charge, has to make the decision and take responsibility for its outcome. Committees just don't work on flight decks. You can have discussion, exchange ideas or ask for help, but the decision must always be down to the captain.

Unfortunately, I saw an increasing number of incidents, on the aircraft and in the simulator, where that situation was being eroded. The relationship between the captain and the co-pilot has been described as the 'cross-cockpit authority gradient', depicting the captain's authority as a straight-line graph. A positive, steeply sloping line, high on the captain's side, low on the co-pilot's side, shows the Atlantic Baron who operates autocratically; communication is in one direction with orders issued from the captain to the co-pilot and only acknowledgements flow in return. A shallower angle represents a more approachable captain who is prepared to discuss decisions, listen to suggestions and perhaps modify his opinions. All good stuff so far. But the line must remain positive. If it should go negative, that is, if the co-pilot is allowed to assume greater authority than the captain so that he now starts to make the decisions, anarchy and chaos ensue.

CRM was desperately needed fifty years ago. Today, technology and changes in society have reduced the need for it, to the point where the cross-cockpit gradient can easily tilt too far. Radio communications have improved so that crews can speak to their airlines' operations centres easily and quickly. Managers on the ground at base (and anyone else who overhears the exchange) welcome the opportunity to influence decisions as the captains are making them, rather than leaving authority and responsibility with the man on the spot. And there is generally less formality in our society today. People are well aware of the need to be 'approachable' in supervisory positions. They are fearful of appearing to be dogmatic and there is reluctance among a significant number of potential captains to accept the 'loneliness of command'.

There were still some captains around who could show us how it should be done. One such joined the line and it fell to me do his final line check into Verona in Northern Italy. Van probably had more flying experience than anyone I had flown with before. He had fled Holland to join the

Royal Air Force early in the war and had been piloting aeroplanes ever since. And I was supposed to be checking him!

I kept my head down and watched the master at work. It was a foul night. The air mass was filling the Po Valley with thick cloud and pushing it up against the mountains, triggering violent thunderstorms. When we arrived overhead, we learnt that the VHF radio navigation aids were out of service. The ILS and the VOR/DME were both off, leaving us with two weak NDBs.

Van's briefing was a model of brevity: 'ADF approach, then!' And he checked that the approach charts we were using had the same issue number and date, and that we were using the same figures for safety heights and minima. Then he disconnected the autopilot and began the descent.

Initially, the scene outside was dramatic. Frequent flashes of lightning momentarily illuminated heaped masses of stratus and cumulonimbus clouds towering higher than the snow-capped mountains and seemed to intensify the complete blackness in the intervals. It was smooth until we entered the cloud. Then the turbulence began and it was no longer possible to determine where the lightning flashes came from. Our windscreens were opaque.

Van was impassive and his flying supremely accurate, even though the ADF needles were quivering indecisively and occasionally swinging wildly, 90 or 180 degrees in error for several seconds at a time. I was watching him and the needles and frequently consulting the chart, so I knew we were following exactly the correct path at the correct heights, as far as it was possible to tell. But as we got lower and ground clearance became more critical, tension began to mount. The turbulence got worse and hail lashed against the screens. Had we passed the first beacon or was the needle just swinging to point at a thunderstorm? The aircraft rolled and bucked and my eyes were racing over the instruments when Van, who had been silently concentrating until now, spoke.

'I've retired from flying twice, you know,' he said conversationally. Then, after another particularly violent thump, while the needles went their separate ways and the outside grew even darker, added: 'Can't remember why I came back.'

There is a better chance of getting a direct command in a new airline, but then, as it expands, the old race for promotion by those who didn't quite make it resumes. It can get bitter. Hard decisions have to be made. Co-pilots can get passed over for making apparently trivial errors. They may be justifiably aggrieved. Even if in their hearts they know they failed, they sometimes find it hard to admit such a thing to their nearest and dearest.

I developed the technique of getting the candidates to evaluate their own performance. Often they were harder on themselves than I would have been when they were asked for an honest assessment during the debriefing. If I had already decided a candidate was not yet ready for command, I found it easier if they agreed. More importantly, I could let them go back to co-pilot duties knowing that they recognized their faults and might therefore be able to do something about them. If they were in denial, they would never correct their deficiencies. But they often changed their minds within twenty-four hours. After a few beers and a night's sleep, fired by the disbelief and indignation of their friends and family, they would besiege the Chief Pilot in his office. They would thump his table, claim that they had been unfairly treated and demand to be given another chance.

The Chief Pilot has an unenviable task in these situations. He must trust the judgement of his trainers, but he must also be seen to be fair. A second chance with another trainer was often provided and sometimes the candidate passed. If he didn't, resentment could turn to bitterness, though on rare occasions this was mitigated by humour.

Our new Chief Pilot determined to meet all of his pilots to discuss his policies face to face and to listen to suggestions for improving the operation. A series of meetings was arranged over the winter when we were not so busy. In order to keep the numbers at each meeting small and to fit in with scheduling, he would meet a group of captains on one day, then a group of co-pilots on another.

I took my place in a warm classroom one frosty morning to take part in one of these meetings along with a dozen or so of my colleagues. The new Chief Pilot was taking his position seriously; he had on a new suit, a sober tie and he had had his hair cut. A table had been set up at the front of the room and he took his place facing us with his lieutenants on either side. He was impressively businesslike when he stood up to call the meeting to order, asked for the door to be closed and cleared his throat to make his opening address. 'Gentlemen,' he began, but he got no further.

The door burst open again and in strode one of our co-pilots who had recently failed his command check. We were all surprised to see him. Not only was this meeting for captains, rather than co-pilots, but he too was unusually smart and businesslike. In fact, his power dressing outshone that of the Chief Pilot himself. In a smart, pin-striped city suit, carrying a new, very smart briefcase, he strode confidently towards the front of the room, smiling at us all and wishing everyone a very good morning.

'Er ... I, er ... I think you've got the wrong meeting, Chris,' the Chief Pilot stammered. But by this time Chris had reached him. Facing the Chief Pilot across the table, he put his briefcase down, opened it and took out a large water pistol.

'No, no mistake,' he said gaily and fired his toy gun repeatedly, hosing the Chief Pilot from the top of his recently coiffured head down his tie and onto his brand new suit, saying, 'I hope you will take this in the spirit in which it is intended.'

To his everlasting credit, the new Chief Pilot retained his control. 'I'm trying to, Chris,' he spluttered. 'I'm trying to.'

Chris dropped the gun back into his briefcase, snapped it shut with a flourish and smartly walked from the room, waving at the rest of us and expressing the wish that we might enjoy a productive meeting.

Needless to say, the meeting was not a great success. It was nearly lunchtime before the laughter had died down. Chris hadn't enhanced his prospects for a command in this company, but he had ensured he would be a legend in the airline industry.

CHAPTER 10

Flight Management Computers

When the new Boeing 737-300 came it was much more advanced than we had been expecting. Boeing, then still a rather conservative company run exclusively by managers with aircraft engineering experience, had originally intended simply to stretch the airframe slightly and to fit the new higher-bypass turbofans to improve field performance and range. Their customers, however, were pushing for the latest avionics and they won the day. The airline I flew with took delivery of the first example in Europe and we had to learn about Flight Management Systems (FMS) from scratch. Boeing was not much help.

Apart from the engineering simulator, Boeing had no training equipment to offer us in Seattle, save for a personal computer running a modified version of the 'Microsoft Flight Simulator' software, which was supposed to help us understand how the Flight Management Computer (FMC) worked. It didn't. It might have helped a little if we had been already familiar with computer games, but we were not. In retrospect it is easy to see this as the first indication that I no longer belonged to the coming generation in airline flying. During World War I, potential pilots were asked 'Do you ride?'; now they are asked, 'Which video game consoles are you familiar with?' Our skills and attitudes were honed in the generations between.

When the aircraft finally arrived, the Instructor Pilot Boeing sent with it had never flown the type. He had watched from the jump seat on one flight while the test pilots flew it. Our own Training Captains were charged with designing a programme of instruction for the company's line pilots, while accepting and validating the new simulator. Given management insistence that the aircraft would go into service on a specific date, we concentrated on trying to learn from our own mistakes as we went along and to create a list of traps to avoid, rather than recommending any particular procedures.

And traps there were. This was a whole new way of operating an aircraft. The central computer gathered information automatically from whatever radio navigation signals it could receive and compared them with an inertial platform 'memory' to calculate its final position. The crew typed the route into the database, told the system where it was on start-up and, at any time after take-off, engaged the autopilot, which could then be set to follow the route.

The opportunities for inventing new ways to make mistakes seemed unlimited. The official position was that the pilot could always revert to conventional, manual flight and the quick, instinctive way to do this was to disconnect the autopilot. But if the aircraft was not doing what it was meant to do, the autopilot must have been following incorrect instructions, so the pilot would be left with incorrect information on his instruments. We did not yet have what are now known as 'glass cockpits', where all the navigational information, in the form of a map, along with system status, is displayed together on flat panel displays. Instead, we had old-fashioned instruments with round-faced dials. We could switch the display between the conventional VOR radial deviations and an indication of the deviation from the FMS-derived track, but it was easy to get confused. What was to become an infamous question on the flight deck began to be heard for the first time as pilots strove to understand what was happening: 'What's it doing now?'

Our task as trainers was to try to maintain the line pilots' normal competence and confidence in command. The answer proved to be fully in accordance with the traditional attitudes that airline pilots had developed over the years; if you are reacting to a situation, you are already too late. You have to be thinking well ahead of the aircraft at all times, to be planning and anticipating at every stage. For example, at a simple waypoint over which there was to be a change of heading, the pilot had to know exactly what should happen and what heading the aircraft should turn on to. If that did not appear to be happening, he must intervene immediately to make sure that it did. But that was not easy. The system was so accurate and so reliable when it had been programmed correctly, that pilots doubted their own interpretation. The new technology, imperfectly understood, induced a passive attitude with a slow response. So the idea that the pilot could always resort to traditional, manual control was flawed. Intervention by disconnecting the autopilot would simply provide the pilot who suspected a navigational issue with an additional handling problem. We had to learn to monitor in a new way, and to intervene if it became necessary, through the automatic system. Gradually we learnt that the Control and Display Unit – a computer-like screen and keyboard which provided an interface with the FMC – was best for inputting long-term navigational requirements, while short-term variations were best made through the autopilot controls.

At the other extreme, particularly prevalent among the younger pilots who were familiar with computers, was an obsessive fascination with the new technology. Pilots would spend half the flight with their heads down, typing complex instructions into the computer, often to the detriment of lookout or even interest in the current progress of the aircraft.

It would take time to develop new working practices and to learn the best ways of using equipment that offered undoubted benefits in accuracy. We were all willing to learn, but none of us then quite realized the extent to which flying had changed. The designers and engineers had done a magnificent job in producing the new systems. No doubt they had carried out a great deal of research, talked to and flown with many pilots and felt that they had anticipated all our requirements. The big omission, as so often with new technology, was in communicating what they had done to the people who were going to use the stuff. People can't make full use of new technology unless they understand both it and the philosophy behind it. Training is not really expensive and I don't believe the cost of training was a significant factor in this major omission. I think it had something to do with the way that new technology is promoted and our belief in its efficacy. It is new, therefore it must be better and people will love it. The people providing this equipment simply could not foresee the problems it might generate for the end users.

This dichotomy between those who understand and produce the technology and the people who are going to have to use it was to reappear during the introduction of aircraft with fly-by-wire Control Laws and we see it today on the high street. Stand in my local bank branch and watch two distinct types of customer: those who embrace the automated teller machines, tapping enthusiastically at the keyboards to complete the transactions; and those lost souls hesitating, searching for a friendly face to explain what they must do. The help provided by smart but patronizing young ladies who can't understand the problem is woefully inadequate and serves only to alienate a significant proportion of the bank's customers.

The day to day business of line flying continued as we struggled to come to terms with material change. Realization of how much technology was insulating us from our environment came slowly. At times, we were so wrapped up in the demands of the day that we hardly noticed it. At other times, it was highlighted by sudden contrast. I was pleased to find, when taxiing onto stand at London Gatwick after a long night flight that the next crew were ready and waiting to take over from us. It meant that the operations department was on the ball and the next flight would depart on schedule.

I was still putting on my coat when the new captain came onto the flight deck and started stowing his gear. He would, as usual, have a warm seat to slide into and he brought good news. The light aircraft that had positioned them to Gatwick was waiting to take us back to base, so we would not have to endure several hours in a taxi or bus.

Our crew piled into the light piston twin as dawn started to creep across a clear sky and the pilot told us that, because of the early hour, he had been offered a clearance due north, at 1,500ft, over the centre of London. We were all tired, but the spectacular views woke us up. There were shrieks of delight as we identified all the famous landmarks and pointed them out to each other excitedly. At such a low level, even more than from the windows of a circling airliner, it was a privilege to view the capital from such a vantage point and a reminder once again of the unique advantages of flight. When we reached the crew room back at base, the other crews preparing for morning departures must have wondered how we could be so buoyant and animated after a long night flight.

CHAPTER 11

Wide-Body

First impressions of the Airbus A300-B4 were dominated by its size. This first aircraft from Europe's Airbus Industries had a maximum take-off weight similar to the Boeing 707-320C, but it had been designed to carry a greater number of passengers more efficiently over shorter distances. It set a new record for me. Should he have to declare an emergency, one of the first questions an airline pilot can expect from Air Traffic Control is, 'How many souls on board?' For years I had been in the habit of writing the total figure of passengers and crew on the top right of the notepad that I kept clipped on my side window ledge. The A300 was a quantum leap; never before above 200, the figure now sometimes exceeded 340.

Airbus had been the big story in aviation since its inception. Much was expected from this new, international manufacturer and though the A300 did not break much new ground in terms of technology, it was the first wide-body aircraft to rely on just two engines. The press might question the wisdom of this, but the industry was gaining confidence in the big fan engines. Boeing, Lockheed and McDonnell Douglas quietly encouraged any disquiet, gently reminding the public that their products had three or four engines, but they were concerned that their sales would be hit.

On a visit to Seattle to pick up a new 737 a few months before my company bought the A300, I was surprised to notice an odd silhouette on an enormous Boeing wall chart. The chart showed full-colour outlines of all Boeing types positioned on a graph of payload against range. Such was the corporate confidence and conviction in Boeing that I had never heard any other manufacturer's name mentioned by any Boeing employee, yet here was a plain white outline which surely looked like …

'What's that?' I asked.

'Oh, er,' the engineer accompanying us took a deep breath, 'That's the European Airbus,' he said. And in response to my questioning smile added, 'It's keeping us honest.'

The most critical performance point in the test schedule of a new civil airliner is what is known as the 'second segment climb'. This is the angle of climb the aircraft can achieve once the gear is retracted after an engine has failed on take-off. The result confirms or disproves the designer's promised payload and runway requirements; sales depend on it and it drives many other design parameters. Since the failure of one power plant is assumed and the minimum climb-out angle required is the same for all types, twin-engined aircraft are assumed to lose half of the power available, whereas four-engined machines lose only 25 per cent and tri-jets 33.3 per cent. So the climb performance available when all engines are performing normally is much greater for the twin. The Boeing 737-300 had raised eyebrows with its climb performance when it first arrived, but the sight of the enormous A300 climbing steeply after take-off was truly spectacular.

I liked the aircraft. It was what pilots call an 'honest aeroplane'; it was straightforward to operate and always achieved the figures published in the manuals. It was also nice to fly with flight engineers again. But somehow the A300-B4 didn't have the character of other aircraft. It had no soul, some said. Many pilots will react to a statement like that with incredulity; what on earth does he mean by it? I can offer no objective evidence, but I believe my lack of empathy with this aircraft had something to do with its hard-worked wing. The wing was undoubtedly highly efficient and, as I have said, delivered everything that was required of it, but it achieved its performance through sophisticated design and clever retractable high-lift devices. The actual wing area was considerably less for the weight it had to carry than types I had flown previously and, despite the aircraft's enormous power, it just did not seem as enthusiastic in its element as they had.

Designers, engineers and pilots will snort at this nonsense, but I ask indulgence for an old pilot's reminiscences. Perhaps if I had flown more hours on the aircraft I would have felt differently. As it is, I remember it as sound, but without particular affection. The biggest distinctive feature remains its size. The pilots sat a long way above the tarmac and on approach the aircraft had a slightly nose-up attitude, so judging the height at which to commence the flare for landing was not easy at first. The trainer in charge of my conversion to type explained the answer to this difficulty. He was of mid-European origin, highly intelligent and a strict scientific disciplinarian. His rimless glasses glinted and hid his eyes as he delivered his instructions, his closely cropped head motionless.

'All instinctive power adjustments are wrong power adjustments,' he intoned. 'Calculate the new power setting you need, move the throttles to initiate the acceleration and then, when the correct speed is indicated, set the power precisely. I will monitor the radio altitude. When I call fifty feet, smoothly close the throttles and start the flare.'

We took off and flew a couple of ILS approaches, going around at 200ft and then a visual approach for my first landing. The aeroplane handling provided no surprises and I had no problem with the inertia, easily achieving a stable approach.

But when the expressionless voice called, 'Fifty feet!' I was sure he was wrong. It seemed to me that we were much higher, so I closed the throttles very slowly and delayed the flare. We struck the ground with an almighty bang. The enormous machine, still descending at several hundred feet per minute, dissipated its energy in noise and a bone-jarring crash. I could do nothing but hang on, try to minimize the bounce and bring the machine to rest in a state of shock. Shaking, I taxied clear of the runway and stopped on the taxiway.

'When I called fifty feet,' said the rimless glasses, 'you did not flare. Why?'

'I just ... didn't believe it,' I answered, crestfallen.

'Ah!' The shaven head nodded slowly. 'But now you believe?'

'Yes,' I answered meekly. During the rest of the session I did as I was told and the landings were fine.

The sheer size of the aeroplane introduced other new problems. Instead of three or four cabin crew, we now carried twelve. That put a lot more responsibility on the senior cabin crew member and changed the working relationship with the captain. We had to rely a great deal on the professionalism of the 'Number One' or 'Purser', as she or he was now known. We also had to make more of an effort to introduce ourselves to the other crew members. It was becoming impossible to know them all, yet it was important that they did not see the flight-deck crew as remote or aloof. We wanted to maintain the crew spirit so that they would have no hesitation in reporting anything they were not happy about during the flight.

The engineers were a constant source of amusement. Just as most of our pilots had never flown with a flight engineer before, most of the engineers had little experience of pilots from two-crew aircraft. Misunderstandings and rash judgements had the potential to spark personality clashes and I worked hard to encourage mutual respect. One aspect of the three-crew flight deck that can cause problems if it is not adequately addressed is the isolation of the co-pilot. Whether a new boy or an experienced old hand, the pilot in the right-hand seat simply isn't provided with the same information as the other two. All the main systems status is indicated on the engineer's panel behind his seat. The captain in the left-hand seat can see it quite well by turning to look across the cockpit, but the co-pilot would have to be a contortionist to acquire any useful information from that source.

Inevitably, most of the communication about fuel state or malfunctions and the resultant decisions to be made occurs between the captain and the engineer. Given that the right-hand-seat pilot is usually engaged in making the radio calls during these exchanges it is not surprising that he sometimes feels left out. If he happens to be young and inexperienced, while the engineer has been flying since before the co-pilot was born, ill-considered or dismissive comments can generate fierce resentment.

Humour helps. Nearing the end of a routine trip, we settled onto final approach with some relief. Our engineer on that day was highly experienced and capable, but was nearing retirement age and had little inclination to consider his relationship with the rest of the crew. He had a tendency to leave his microphone open on the intercom, so we had been treated to frequent amplified sounds of his coughing and belching, provoking the co-pilot to snap at him several times.

When I called for the undercarriage to be lowered, the co-pilot made the selection, but a warning light indicated that the nose wheel might not have locked down. My call for the engineer to run the checklist was answered with silence. I tried again and, when I found the time, looked back to see what the problem was.

The engineer had clearly assumed that his duty was over for the day. He had packed his slippers away in his briefcase, put on his uniform shoes, raincoat and hat, stowed his log and all the paperwork and was all ready to go. His headset was hung neatly on its hook and he was busily engaged in eating what remained of the cheese and biscuits provided for all of us on a tray by the cabin crew.

His alarm and discomfiture when I was able to get him to hear my shouts and set to work were a great source of amusement. He cursed and thrashed around and had to raise the hatch and disappear under the flight-deck floor in his full uniform while we flew a go-around and lined up for a second approach. The co-pilot was smiling for a week afterwards.

For a number of reasons, maintenance of these aircraft fell below a standard any of us were comfortable with. Everyone in an airline goes through a learning period when operating a new type and we were using the aircraft in a way that was quite different to that of previous operators. On scheduled services, the aircraft tends to operate on fixed routes, frequently passing through a main maintenance base and it is cared for by a limited number of ground and flight crews. On inclusive tour charters the operation is more intensive. The aircraft was configured to carry more passengers and it was frequently detached to outstations for long periods. Many agencies were involved in maintenance of the machines and getting spare parts in the right place at the right time was difficult.

The situation came to a head when I took over one of the A300s from a previous crew at Manchester for an overnight flight. There were a few 'B' defects recorded in the technical log. These were equipment malfunctions that could not be fixed at the current station, but were acceptable to defer until the next scheduled maintenance activity. They were minor items, the only significant one of which concerned the autopilot.

The aircraft had two autopilots; one was completely unserviceable, while the other had caused some uncommanded pitch movements during climb and descent. Nowadays most airlines would ground the aircraft until at least one autopilot was fully serviceable, but hand-flying was still considered perfectly acceptable then. I wasn't too pleased. We had a long

night ahead of us – four hours or more to Rhodes in the Eastern Mediterranean and five on the return, but I accepted the aircraft. The passengers,
over 300 of them, boarded and we took off into the darkening sky.

It was a pleasant task to hand-fly the aircraft to the top of the climb.
The big machine handled well and it was satisfying to practise the old
skills. At 29,000ft I stroked her into the cruise, set the power and adjusted
the trim. When I was sure everything was stable, I engaged the serviceable autopilot and monitored its operation closely for a while. Satisfied at
last, I slid my seat back and turned to talk to the co-pilot and flight engineer, only to see their mouths and eyes open wide as we were all thrown
violently upwards against our straps.

I spun round to grab the control wheel, but the co-pilot had been quicker
and was already arresting the dive. I took control and eased the aircraft
back to its assigned cruising level. The three of us discussed the event and
agreed that, although the height loss had been only a few hundred feet,
we had seen a descent rate of 6,000ft a minute, far too violent to risk a
repeat performance. The senior steward confirmed that everything had
been secure in the cabin and no one was hurt. So, with some rueful grins
all round, we settled down to a long night of hand-flying.

It requires delicacy and concentration to fly a large aircraft accurately
at high altitude and the non-handling pilot needs to monitor the situation
in case the handler's attention wanders. We took turns of about forty
minutes each and, while we were still fresh on the outbound leg, it was
not too onerous.

The engineer discovered a few more malfunctions on the way, but
nothing to stop us continuing. As part of the airworthiness process, a
master list of allowable deficiencies is agreed between the aircraft manufacturer and the regulatory authority, in this case the UK Civil Aviation
Authority. These lists are prepared for each system on the aircraft: fuel;
electrics; hydraulics; navigation; and so on. The engineers are the best
people to calculate what penalty any particular system failure carries and
what are the risks of taking off or continuing a flight with an unserviceable item. They do this for combinations of failures too, but only in the
same system. By law, the person responsible for deciding what is acceptable and what is not when failures in more than one system occur, is the
pilot in command.

We turned round at Rhodes and set off on the return journey with a
fresh load of passengers. We did try re-engaging the autopilot, while ready
this time to resume control in an instant and, sure enough, after a minute
or two, the aircraft tried to pitch violently down again. Once again, we
settled into the routine of forty minutes' flying and forty minutes' monitoring. The engineer was watching us carefully, too. But now it was that
dread time in the early hours of the morning when fatigue steals up on
us. As one old friend put it, your eyes hurt, your tongue is cracked in

your mouth, your teeth are loose and you can hear your beard growing. Headwinds slowed our progress as we crawled westward over Europe.

Then a hydraulic pump failed and something else, I forget what. But to the task of hand-flying was added a nice command problem – are we safe to continue the flight, or should we divert to land at an en-route airfield? We considered the situation and discussed it until something else failed and we had to start over again, reconsidering our options. When this had happened a few times we began to giggle. The situation was getting ridiculous. It was like a mad simulator exercise driven by some demented check captain determined to break us if he could. Weary and perhaps a little hysterical, we greeted each new problem with shrieks of laughter. Yet careful analysis of the situation convinced us that nothing prevented us continuing to our destination. All thoughts of fatigue were banished. Dawn saw us descending on Manchester in high spirits. I felt like John Wayne leading the US Cavalry through ferocious Indian attacks to relieve the fort at last. All we needed were bugles to accompany the landing.

On stand at last, our oblivious passengers disembarking, the engineer read out his list and we wrote up twenty-eight defects in the technical log while the ground engineer looked on in mounting disbelief and horror. He could fix some of them in a short time, but by no means all of them. Walking to our transport, we met the outgoing crew who were intending to take over the aircraft. Briefly I explained the state of the machine to my colleague. He wasn't very interested. He was fresh from a good night's sleep and eager to get the job done. It was starting to rain and, just as I would have done in his place, he accepted the aircraft and did his flight. Later I heard that on his return he had entered thirty-two defects into the log, a new company record.

At another stage in my career I was to observe pilots placing a faith in the autopilot and other automatic equipment that I was simply unable to share. I would have liked to be able to take them on a trip like that. They might have learnt a little scepticism. It was a different aircraft and the equipment had improved, but it had not changed all that much. The reliability of any system is only as good as its maintenance and operational environment allows.

CHAPTER 12

Starting Again

I was waiting for my crew to board our transport outside the old terminal building at Birmingham one day when a big articulated truck stopped beside me with a jerk and a great hiss of air brakes. The driver's window was open and I walked towards him, expecting him to ask for directions to the freight area. Instead he gazed ahead in silence for a moment, towards the line of stewardesses crossing the road. He watched as, one by one, they put their bags in the back of the bus and stepped aboard. Then he turned to me and said, 'I wish I had a job like yours.'

It made me look at them in a different light. They did, I had to admit, look good. The airline had selected a traditional uniform: a navy blue suit with a white blouse, small hat, neat black shoes and gloves. It was morning and we were starting the day on schedule. They might not look quite so smart when we returned in twelve hours' time, but I was always amazed at how hard airline cabin crew worked and how cheerfully they did the job. The passengers could be fun, or a nightmare, but they handled them professionally and well, even when they were tired and their feet ached.

The new airline had got many things right; in addition to the uniforms, it had chosen to operate the best aeroplane for the job. After the first year's operation with the Boeing 737-200, the airline switched to the 737-300 with the B2 engines that gave excellent field performance, good range and were supremely reliable. The crews were enthusiastic and a pleasure to work with. Unfortunately, we were to learn before too long that the company had based its business model on new European legislation that would not come into force for several years. By the time the conditions for which the airline had been created came into being, the airline would be long gone. I was to hear that the airline had gone bust while I was lying in a hospital bed, immobilized by a prolapsed disc. But I knew by then that it is only the first time you are thrown out of work that is traumatic. Age and experience soften later blows; one becomes philosophical.

Events had already begun to suggest that I was no longer the youngest captain around. After arriving in Humberside – a wartime airfield reopened as a commercial venture – as dawn was breaking over England, I was intrigued to be told by the driver of our crew transport that he was taking us to a hotel that had been booked for us in Grimsby. What, I wondered, was an international airline pilot, approaching his fifties and in his prime, doing in Grimsby? I had an image of the town as a once bustling commercial fishing port that was now without its fish and seriously run down. But I was too tired to care much. All I needed was a clean bed and silence. We were, again, on minimum rest. The regulations allowed us twelve hours from leaving the airport to reporting again for the next night flight. We had lived like this, it seemed, forever.

The hotel was fine and only a few moments after checking in, I was sinking gratefully into a soft bed. Two hours later, as so often happens, I was awake again and feeling pretty rough. It was clear I was not going to sleep any more for a while so I resolved to go out for a walk, to get some fresh air and exercise and perhaps something to eat before I tried again to sleep, in the afternoon.

Fresh air Grimsby had in plenty. My spirits raised a little as I explored the town and saw evidence of energetic revival. The inhabitants had suffered real hardship from the decline of the fishing industry, but it was uplifting to see the efforts being made towards rebuilding and revitalizing the town. Constructive human energy is always impressive, anywhere. I found a smart building containing a National Fishing Heritage Centre and decided to spend an hour investigating that.

The young woman in the ticket kiosk was pretty, with a quick smile and a twinkle in her eyes. My spirits rose further. Not just a nice town with an interesting museum, Grimsby was offering a chance of some playful banter, a light flirtatious exchange that might brighten my day considerably. I asked about the price of admission and, quick and efficient, she explained the options. Then, without a second's hesitation, she asked, 'Do you qualify for a senior citizen concession?'

It was like being hit over the head with one of the boxes of herring they used to land here. My face, in addition to exaggerating my age, must have registered my dismay. The poor girl realized her mistake and was embarrassed. It was a painful moment that we spent staring at each other. Flirtatious banter was obviously out of the question. In that moment I felt as old as a pensioner and was conscious of the full weight of fatigue resting upon me. The museum was actually good; make an effort to visit it if ever you find yourself in Grimsby. And if you are an airline pilot on minimum rest, see if you can get a concession.

We were flying charters again, both ad hoc and inclusive tour holidays, so the destinations were generally familiar. Changes to our way of life were minor, but I was becoming nostalgic for the old ways. We no longer carried topographical charts. It is true that we never used them seriously; they used to be kept in a fat brown envelope that got in the way and was ripped and scruffy by the end of the season. But sometimes, in good weather, when we ventured into Eastern Europe, we would dig out the appropriate chart and follow our progress over the unfamiliar territory. Those maps were the culmination of centuries of development in the cartographer's art. They were beautiful, providing a wealth of information clearly and concisely from a rich palette of colours and symbols. We didn't need them, but reading them was entertaining and instructive. I wish I had a set now. Studying them in an armchair would be far better than watching television and as good as reading many a classical novel.

But they had gone – no longer required under the provisions of the Air Navigation Order, presumably – and we were left with our modern radio navigation charts, which told us what we needed to know with functional minimalism. The scale was too small. Printed in a blue-grey monochrome that was supposed to work best under cockpit lighting, I found that I could not read them without my glasses and they did nothing to inspire the imagination.

The meteorological forecasters had gone, too, or at least our interaction with them had been seriously curtailed. The formatted reports were now produced by computer and delivered to us anonymously. I missed the long, instructive chats I used to have with the professionals, full of character, in Amsterdam, Birmingham, Taipei, Faro and elsewhere. The last real example I found of the sort of met-office Ernest Gann wrote about in his novel, *The Trouble with Lazy Ethel*,[8] was in Malta. The airfield there had been built by the RAF and manned by them for many years, but had long ago been repopulated by local civilian forecasters. Unfortunately it was situated on the opposite side of the airfield to where we parked our aircraft and we rarely had time to go there. Occasionally, if our departure was delayed for some reason, I would ask the agent for the loan of his van and drive round to visit this temple to the old-fashioned notion of scientific observation and prediction. It smelled, as it should, of floor polish and dust. A few of the metal-framed windows were usually open to allow a cooling breeze to waft in the scents of the island and sometimes to lift the edges of papers resting on the large wooden desks. Those desks, the wooden furniture and the metal filing cabinets, shone with a deep patina gleaned from a thousand workers' elbows. The forecasters were mild, studious types, beloved of unhurried precision and careful routine. Their dress, the worldwide uniform of their profession, was 1950s-style academic casual. They always made us welcome, sometimes even offering us tea, and they were touchingly grateful for any first-hand reports we could provide of conditions further north. It was as if they too missed the days when each crew would report to them before and after every flight. I'm sure they felt isolated by technology. Their work and their surroundings had stayed the same and it was difficult to reconcile the comfortable atmosphere of that office with the Brave New World of the modern airliner's flight deck.

The weather itself could still spring surprises. Settling on a long final approach at Venice after an uneventful flight in good weather, we were handed over to the tower controller early. He cleared us to land and read out to us the wind speed and direction as usual. He said something else too, but we didn't catch it. We asked him to repeat the information, but we still couldn't understand it. Eventually we got the message. He was reporting the airfield visibility reduced to 2,000m by flying insects. That was a first.

I was still learning about flying. For some people airline flying is boring. 'All you do is paperwork and all you see is sky,' as a flight dispatcher in Borneo had once told me. But the very remoteness of the upper air, its detachment and its vastness, can provide a contrast to reality that challenges the emotions. The view can change suddenly.

Sandy, under training in the left-hand seat, drew my attention to a rising indication on the exhaust gas temperature of one of our engines. He was progressively moving the thrust lever back to reduce power, but the rpm remained constant and the temperature continued to rise. He was ready to shut the engine down and really only seeking confirmation of this action as a matter of form. But I hesitated. Trouble with Pratt and Whitney's engines was so unusual that it was difficult to believe at first. Sandy was absolutely right; we had no alternative and probably, by the time I nodded, the temperature had exceeded its limit, doing more damage than necessary. But the discipline of the checklist brought me back from my reverie into active consideration of our predicament.

We were over the North Sea, having just crossed the Belgian coast. The nearest airfield was Ostend, but that was behind us and the passengers had paid to get to Birmingham. There were a thousand reasons why it would be much more convenient for everyone if we landed in England and from 33,000ft and Mach .73, in good weather with London and the whole of the south-east in view, it seemed sensible to continue at least as far as Stansted.

Not long afterwards, on one engine at 10,000ft and 210 knots, the earth looked a lot closer and Stansted seemed to be getting further away. In a few minutes, the view and the emotions had changed. There was never any danger. The 737 flew perfectly well on one engine and Sandy had the handling well under control while I was busy with the radio, letting everyone know of our intentions and getting clearances. But in the long few minutes that we flew level over the green fields on one engine, before we could begin our final descent on the ILS, I vowed that, faced with a similar decision in the future, I would need a very good reason indeed to land anywhere other than the nearest airfield.

The company was too small to have its own simulator. We used one belonging to Aer Lingus and I found myself commuting so regularly between Birmingham and Dublin that the Special Branch officers manning the security check began to greet me by name. Our simulator slots were never booked far enough in advance to secure the most favourable times, so we wandered between the Airport Hotel and the simulator building at odd hours of the day or night. Dry after a session through the small hours, I asked the hotel porter if we might get a drink. 'Oh no, Sir,' he replied in shocked tones. 'That's quite impossible. The bar won't be open until 10am.' Then, by that wonderful logic unique to the Irish, he added, 'But if you'll just take a seat here I'll get you each a pint of Guinness while you're waiting.'

On another occasion, after a late evening session in the simulator, we discussed our arrangements for returning to Birmingham. Two of us were for a late breakfast and catching the lunchtime flight, but the third member of our group wanted to get back as quickly as possible and was prepared to sacrifice some sleep. When the night porter took his booking for an early morning call he was most apologetic. He agreed the time of the call and assured him it would not be a problem, but he was very sorry to have to tell us all that the management had now insisted on a charge for early calls. My colleague tried to reassure him that he would not argue about an extra ten pence on his bill, but the porter was clearly distressed that a charge should be levied for such a small service.

When the two of us who had decided to travel later strolled into the dining room for our late breakfast on the following day, we were surprised to be joined by the early bird.

'Change your mind?' I asked him.

'No,' he replied. 'When I answered my phone the porter seemed overjoyed to speak to me. He said, "Good morning, Sir. This is your six o'clock call and it won't cost you a penny!" When I managed to mutter my thanks and ask why, he said, "Because it is ten past eight."'

The simulator exercises could become a bit of a chore and it was sometimes difficult to maintain our motivation through the long hours of the night. I was not blessed with the bizarre eccentricity of some of the simulator instructors whose pranks I had suffered myself, but I felt the need for a bit of levity sometimes. So I dug out the little cassette recorder I had bought in Singapore and prepared some tapes to play at suitable moments during the sessions. If, during the early stages, a pilot on check was nervous and tense and overcontrolling, so that the simulator swayed and hissed and clanked alarmingly, I would play Wagner's 'Ride of the Valkyries' at ever increasing volume. Later, when he had relaxed and was demonstrating just how smooth and complete his mastery of the machine could be, I would play the theme song from the Tom Cruise film, *Top Gun*, 'Take My Breath Away', although the accompaniment was not always appreciated.

There was not to be much more flying with that company, which was a pity because in spite of its faults, or perhaps because of them, the crews were happy and there was a great camaraderie. I drove to Manchester one afternoon and checked into a hotel intending to take out an early flight on the following morning. I had a beer with some other pilots in the bar, but my enjoyment of their company was marred by a wretched backache and shooting pains down my leg, so I retired early. The following morning I could not get out of bed.

So it was that I came to be lying in a hospital bed when I learnt of the company's demise. In addition to my medical problems, I now had no job and could look forward only to an uncertain future. I knew lots of pilots who had suffered serious back problems. The ex-RAF fast-jet types liked to put it down to having used an ejector seat in some spectacular fashion, but that did not apply to me. It was likely to be the result of long hours slumped in a worn-out seat on the flight deck of an airliner. Most pilots are able to resume flying after treatment, but trying to find a new employer at the same time would add a new twist to the problem.

For once I had time to reflect and take an interest in the world around me. Change was everywhere. I had watched the television footage in amazement while the Berliners tore down the wall that had been a central feature of life in their city for so long. Now I was watching the collapse of communism itself.

I had always tried consciously to savour every moment of my flying career and yet suddenly, before I had grown used to the privilege, nearly twenty-five years had flown. More than at any other time in history, it seemed, lives were changing. There is nothing new in having to hand over control to the next generation and we are not the first to think that they want to assume responsibility before they are ready for it, but now there was a more serious threat. Farmers, who in previous centuries could expect their occupation to vary little over a thousand years, were being forced to diversify into other businesses. There were no more stevedores and precious few shipbuilders. My father, a seven-year apprenticeship, hot-metal printer, had seen his craft made redundant in the digital age. Bank clerks, draughtsmen and artisans of all types were finding their skills superseded by technology. Where once men could acquire patiently the knowledge, skills and attitudes that differentiated them from their fellows and enhanced their value to society, the trend now was towards deskilling jobs and dumbing people down into unthinking machine-minders. Oh, the products are of excellent quality, health and safety statistics improve and the companies' profits increase, but the individual is diminished.

I resolved that I would fly again and squeeze the last drop of fun I could from the occupation I loved. Little did I realize how much it had yet to change.

CHAPTER 13

And Again

There were to be other interesting aeroplanes before I got back to my beloved Boeings. One came in the form of the McDonnell Douglas MD-83. Douglas had been building airliners since the earliest days of the airlines. The DC-1 first flew in July 1933, leading to the DC-2 and the ubiquitous DC-3, known in the UK as the Dakota. There were more DC-3 military transports in World War II than any other type and they formed the bedrock of airlines around the world thereafter. Some are still flying. When you get acquainted with a modern Douglas you can see why. They are built to last, like the Forth Bridge.

The commercial success of any airliner depends, in large part, on its weight. The higher the payload it can lift in relation to its empty weight, the higher the return on investment. So all manufacturers build their airframe structures as light as possible. McDonnell Douglas achieved this and by clever precision engineering managed to combine it with great strength. The small twinjet DC-9 had never sold in quite such prodigious numbers as the Boeing 737, but the companies that did buy them enjoyed efficient, long-lasting service with minimal maintenance costs.

The MD-83 was one of the last developments of this iconic machine. Pratt and Whitney had grown a much larger engine from its original power plant and MD had stretched the fuselage to such an amazing extent that the wings just did not seem big enough anymore. In fact, the wing loading was the highest I was ever to fly and during the conversion course there were signs that performance was going to be marginal in certain circumstances. It is normal practice on most commercial jets to take off with reduced thrust if possible, but the MD-83 incorporated a system that automatically restored full power if it detected any further reduction of thrust during the take-off. Well, that was nice, but there was more. If the system continued to detect a variation in thrust, indicating that one engine had failed, it would provide additional power, over and above the normal maximum thrust, to the good engine. I was not so happy with this. Is this the time, when you are reduced to a single power unit, to demand extra effort from it? Oh, I know, there should be plenty of reserve power in a modern turbofan engine, but it went against my ingrained airmanship attitudes to push my luck in those circumstances. I would have preferred to retain that option for myself.

To find another automatic system later, that retracted the landing lights in the event of an engine failure, increased my concern. If they were worried about the drag from the landing lights, just how much margin were we looking at? Not much, I surmised.

But in practice everything was fine. To my surprise the aircraft was a joy to fly with beautifully harmonized controls and I never had a moment's doubt about its performance. It was permitted to lower flap at ridiculously high speed and pilots did so, frequently, using them like air brakes to fit in easily with Air Traffic requirements without any apparent penalty in the form of wear and tear on the flap mechanism. The flight deck was small and old fashioned, more of a cockpit really, but it was comfortable and we came to feel very much at home in it.

I found that converting to a new type got harder. I had always enjoyed conversion courses – the technical information, the simulator exercises and then actually flying the new type and learning to exploit its idiosyncrasies. But several factors affect our learning abilities as we get older. A trawl through research published on the Internet suggests that only motivation can be isolated as the relevant factor. But how do you define motivation? And how do the things that motivate us change as we get older? I found I was less tolerant of poorly designed manuals, instruction packages and examination requirements. It was difficult to motivate myself to remember facts and figures that, I knew from experience, I would never need again when I was operating the aircraft on the line. The problem was to become more acute a few years later while learning about the A320 in Toulouse. After years of flying Boeing aircraft on which the engine instruments were colour-coded (green, yellow or red to indicate safe, caution or prohibited operating ranges), it seemed ridiculous that Airbus expected me to remember the exact figures of engine temperature and pressure limits. Why? Their gauges were colour-coded too!

Perhaps we just get irascible as we get older; that certainly would not help the learning process. Age creeps up on us without our noticing, though we get plenty of warning. I remember drinking with Dickie, one of those wonderful World War II veterans, in the old Luton Flying Club. He was the centre of attention as always and happy to be surrounded by half a dozen lovely young stewardesses. He charmed them as no doubt he had always charmed the girls. They adored him. They hung on his every word, while, wreathed in smoke from his pipe, he beguiled them with stories. We younger pilots were ignored. His eyes twinkled and his smile broadened until one of the pretty young things cried out, 'Oh, I do love you, Dickie.' Then his smile collapsed when she added, 'You're just like my granddad.' The pub dissolved into laughter. Eventually, Dickie ruefully joined in, but I should have learnt the lesson.

Age and experience can have their advantages occasionally, though. Flying the MD-83 level at 29,000ft over Belgium one beautiful morning we hit an entirely unexpected patch of turbulence. There was first a tremor, then a more substantial shaking and the aircraft rolled a little. Phil, co-pilot for the day and an experienced pilot who was new to airline flying, reached up to flick on the seat-belt signs to warn the cabin crew. But the turbulence vanished as quickly as it had appeared. Then with remarkable speed the aircraft started shaking violently again. It rolled left wing low to 45 degrees and the nose pitched sharply down.

I had the autopilot out and was smoothly applying corrective controls in an instant, but mentally I was back in San Juan on a similarly fine day in the Caribbean. I had plenty of time to reflect that here, this time, there was a lot more height to play with, so I glanced across at Phil. I was going to tell him that we had almost certainly hit the slipstream of a large, heavy aircraft, but I burst out laughing instead. We have all heard the cliché of 'eyes like saucers' and seen the cartoons, but you don't see it for real very often.

De-icing before take-off took on an even more important role in our pre-flight preparations on the McDonnell Douglas MD-83. Investigations into an accident in Scandinavia uncovered a previously unexpected phenomenon that could bring the aircraft down. In certain circumstances, where the aircraft spent time on the ground in drizzle after being cold-soaked, with cold fuel in its tanks, a thick, continuous sheet of clear ice could form over the inboard portion of the wings, close to the fuselage. Being clear ice, it simply could not be seen, however closely you looked. When the wings took the weight of the aircraft on take-off, they flexed upwards slightly, breaking the sheets of ice free so that they could fly back into the engines and flame them out.

The Scandinavian pilots who discovered this phenomenon did a magnificent job of putting the aircraft down in a snowfield, but the rest of us had no wish to demonstrate similar skills. It was decided that, before every cold-weather take-off, the captain would personally place his ungloved hand on the inboard upper surface of the wing, to make sure there was no clear ice there.

In an ideal world, a mature, well-travelled airline pilot would encounter ice only in his gin and tonic. But the MD-83 had another trick with the stuff. The servicing point for the forward toilet was located below the nose on the left-hand side of the aircraft where the truck was clear to back up to it and at a convenient height so that the operator did not need a ladder. He could open the outer panel, release the pressure cover and connect the evacuation hose easily. When the tank was empty, he disconnected the hose, charged the system with the blue chemical fluid and fastened everything up securely again.

Unfortunately, when the pressure seal became worn, or did not seat properly, and, after a long flight with a full passenger load when the toilet was filled to capacity, the valve sometimes leaked. This allowed the liquid contents of the tank, now a very dirty blue colour, to seep past the pressure cover and fill up the void between it and the outer panel. This panel simply preserved the smooth aerodynamic profile of the aircraft's skin and was not designed to contain liquid. So the liquid seeped out of there too, on to the skin of the fuselage. Now all this happened at cruising altitude where, as we know, it is very cold, so the fluid froze. Blue ice formed in the void and outside and expanded until the outer cover gave way and a great mass of the stuff broke free. Aerodynamics took up the story and conveyed the great lump of ice smoothly, in the twinkling of an eye, up over the wing and into the port engine.

Pratt and Whitney build tough engines, but treatment like this was unfair. No engine failed, as far as I know, but the compressor blades got knocked about a bit. Often the pilots did not notice anything amiss. One of the cabin crew would call the flight deck and say, 'We've got that funny buzzing noise in the rear galley again.' If we walked back to check we'd notice a slight vibration, shrug our shoulders and enter it into the technical log for the engineers to investigate on the ground.

Repairs were expensive, but the temporary operational fix was worse. Captains were instructed to close the forward toilet hatches personally to ensure that the pressure valve was properly seated before every sector. We were issued with latex gloves, but the expressions on our faces as we performed this smelly task at arm's length provided priceless entertainment for everyone else.

The MD-83 even boasted autoland. Flying down route during my first annual line check, Rex, the Check Captain, asked me what I thought of the system. He said they had been getting complaints that it sometimes gave hard landings. I was able to reply that I had not had any problems like that; on the few occasions I had used it, it had worked like a charm.

On landing back at base I elected for a manual landing, but it wasn't one of my best. At the debriefing, when Rex signed the paperwork, he said, 'Well, I haven't really got much to say. But I can see why you never complain about the autoland!'

Pilots are expected to report anything unusual or significant that happens in the course of their flights. For certain categories of events, where they are related to the safety of the operation, the regulatory authorities make a written report compulsory and lay down conditions in which this Mandatory Occurrence Report (MOR) must be submitted. One incident, which certainly qualified for an MOR, went unreported at this time because the vehicle I was operating was my own Volkswagen Golf.

I had woken after a normal night's sleep and felt fine. My roster showed that I was on standby from 11am, so I decided to drive into the nearby town to get a newspaper. I had plenty of time; it took only a few minutes. On the way back, in light drizzle, a vehicle I could see in my mirror seemed to be very close. I continued to drive in the traffic stream at about

40mph, but allowed a greater than normal gap to the car in front of me in case we had to stop suddenly. After a few minutes, I glanced in the mirror and was pleased to see him turn off. Then, when I looked forward again, I realized things had changed. The car in front had stopped. He had pulled slightly to the right of the lane, signalling right, and his brake lights were on. I braked hard. The front tyres lost grip and I crashed into the back of him.

No one was hurt and the chap I hit was very calm about it all, even asking me into his home and inviting me to use his telephone. But I was in severe shock, not from the accident itself, but at how slow my reactions had been. Now, I have always maintained that only incompetent pilots need quick reactions, but this was ridiculous. What was going on? My wife picked me up and I phoned the airline to report sick – if I couldn't control my car, it would probably not be wise to go flying an airliner.

It took the rest of that day and another good night's sleep before I began to understand exactly what had happened. Then it was obvious – fatigue. The pilot's old enemy that I had defeated time and again in the air had caught up with me on the ground. I had felt fine, it was mid-morning, half an hour before I was due to be available for duty after the minimum rest period required by the regulations. Yet I was clearly not fit even to drive on the roads.

I should have submitted that MOR, but I was sure it would be laughed out as irrelevant. My boss would say I was making an excuse for my bad driving. But it was a classic example of the effects of fatigue. By their very nature, aeroplanes operate at odd hours. They have great range and cross time zones. They also cost a great deal of money, so, to achieve a commercial return, they must be used intensively. But should the crews be used intensively, too? The old questions were still not answered.

The Flight Time Limitation regulations worked reasonably well, most of the time, but they were by no means perfect. Pilots were sometimes put under considerable commercial pressure to 'bend' the regulations and some did. But the real problem was, and I'm sure still is, in recognizing the symptoms. It is such an insidious condition that the pilot suffering most severely from fatigue is, by the very nature of the condition, quite unqualified to recognize it. And guess who, in law, is responsible for making the decision on whether a pilot is sufficiently rested to fly safely? Yes, it is the pilot himself.

I'm not complaining. I wouldn't have had it any other way. But it does mean that pilots must be constantly alert for signs of fatigue and allow for its effects on their decision-making. It is possible to achieve a state of numbness, where all sensations are dulled, and one carries on doing the job almost automatically. The pilot doesn't feel tired because he doesn't feel anything and when he is put under pressure to fly a couple more sectors, it is easier to do it than to argue.

One of the skills an airline pilot develops in order to cope with all this is the ability to pace himself over his duty period and over the course of his flying life. It is an odd life. The lifestyle of long-haul crews is often described in the newspapers and comes in for the bulk of research into fatigue, but the problem can be just as acute for short-haul crews. It is easy for people who have never done it to imagine that very long flights, overnight and crossing several time zones, can disrupt sleeping patterns. It requires a little more imagination to see how a random short-haul roster can have exactly the same effect.

Pilots must adapt to the life in their own way. In the long term, they must learn to enjoy it and to appreciate the advantages more than they rue the disadvantages. If they don't manage to do this, they will set up conflicts that make their lives miserable and they will ultimately leave the industry. I noticed an increasing trend over the last few years of my career for certain pilots simply to report sick, frequently giving trivial reasons and never mentioning fatigue. Some just ignored standby duties. They turned off their mobile phones or went out, so that, if the company needed them, they could not be reached. Of course, this is a symptom of bad management. Such selfish behaviour is indefensible. Not only does it put an unfair burden on the conscientious pilots in the fleet, it is a flagrant abuse of contract. In well-run companies such pilots are given one warning, then sacked for the second offence. But if the management is failing in its responsibilities, operating with too few crews and encouraging pilots to flout the flight-time regulations, enforcement becomes impossible.

In the early days I had worked hard, but, being young and enthusiastic, had hardly noticed it. Later, flying became more intense and commercial pressures imposed more control on my way of life. At first, that didn't matter. Even after five night flights in a row, playing hard and sleeping little in-between, three days off allowed enough time to recover and to bounce back full of vigour for the next five. The summers were hectic and even young enthusiasts like me began to look tired. By September, towards the end of the season, I noticed my colleagues had a grey complexion, the lines on their faces were deeply etched and their shoulders were hunched as if they couldn't stand up straight. It was a shock to look in the mirror and find that I looked the same.

We accepted without question the disruptive, antisocial life of the airline pilot. There was never any thought of going off sick. None of us liked standby duty, but we accepted that it was necessary. We would rather be scheduled for a flight than sit at home waiting for a possible phone call. If the call came, it was usually right at the start of the duty, before we could use any of the free time we had anticipated, or right at the end so that our roster for the rest of the week was disrupted. Still, we reckoned we were paid well for standby duties; the flying we did for free.

We learnt to pace ourselves on the job, too. Flying often involves concentrating hard for long periods when tired, so it is essential to learn to relax whenever possible. The trick is to adopt an appropriate arousal level for each particular phase of flight.

Fortunately, the lifestyle of the airline pilot offers distinct advantages over other ways of earning a living. You get to fly aeroplanes, for a start. You work with a great bunch of people, you get to see different parts of the world and the pay is usually good. Even working antisocial hours has its plus points. When driving to the airport to start an evening duty I confess I often envied the people relaxing with their friends in the pubs I passed. I would have liked to have joined them, but the knowledge that when I had time off there would be less traffic on the roads and fewer people at the places I might want to go, was compensation enough. And I could sometimes watch cricket when people with normal jobs were at work.

CHAPTER 14

Beauty and Two Boeings

Seattle was a familiar town now and I always looked forward to my next visit, but this was special. The Boeing 767-300 promised to be everything an airline pilot could wish for in his aircraft and it didn't disappoint. Carrying as much as the Airbus A300, but with the range of the Boeing 707 it was another big machine. Boeing had accepted the two-engined philosophy for a wide-body and had brought all the company's experience and expertise to the project. In many ways, it was the pinnacle of traditional aircraft manufacture. It had fully powered flight controls with artificial feel for the elevators and its handling was ideal, providing exactly the right balance of crisp response and solid stability. It had a sophisticated autopilot with autoland capability and a Flight Management System, but it was easy to hand-fly in any configuration, especially on one engine.

The flight deck layout was simple and logical. The primary instruments were replaced by flat panel displays providing the pilots with all the information and navigation equipment they could want in a readily accessible form. The seats were comfortable, there was space to move around and the first time I sat in it I thought, 'This is damn near perfect.' I heard several pilots on the course comment: 'This is just the level of automation we need. Don't go further.' I never discovered anything about the aeroplane that made me change my mind. With both engines operating, it had so much power available that thrust was normally reduced during the early climb. When the reduction was cancelled at 10,000ft and full power automatically restored, the surge upwards was exhilarating. It could remind even the most jaded old airline captain why he had first taken up flying all those years ago.

That enormous smooth power produces some fine sounds. Stand near the runway when any jet takes off and you cannot fail to be impressed by the solid, roaring blast of superheated air that is thrown backwards. Even better, position yourself towards the other end of the runway and listen to the fan noise as a big jet takes off. Most modern aircraft use a flexible-thrust technique for take-off below maximum weight, reducing the power to conserve engine life, but on those occasions where full power is used the big fans are pushed to their maximum revolutions and the tips of their blades reach the speed of sound. The distinctive, chainsaw buzz this gives a big fan engine at full take-off power is a celebration of extreme physical science, turning the thin vapour of the air into a solid, hardworking medium.

Those vortices shed from the wings and flaps that had been visible as condensed moisture and gave rise to accusations of fuel dumping had got stronger with the increased size and weight of the aircraft. They contributed more to the overall noise on the approach and gave rise to another, perhaps more legitimate, concern. Stand near the threshold of an active runway on a calm day and, after the landing aircraft has passed, you will hear the whistling of these vortices as they snake through the air around you. They sound weird and can be powerful, doing occasional minor damage to buildings in the area.

Size cannot be divorced from complexity and the larger the aircraft, the further the pilot is removed from physical interaction with the elements. Even an aircraft as well designed and thoughtfully produced as the 767 could not entirely compensate for that. Its effortless performance over great distances diminished the travellers' experience. In the golden age of airline travel in the 1930s, when passengers flew only during the day and stayed at the best hotels every evening, there must have been a few who missed the leisurely progress of ships and long overland rail journeys. Sitting in their wicker chairs and watching strange lands slide past below through picture windows, they must have wished sometimes that they could stop for an hour to soak up the atmosphere of the place and talk to the inhabitants.

Today, in a jet, we fly so high, so far and so fast, that we rarely see enough even to whet our appetite for foreign adventure. The stratosphere is much the same the world over. Unless there are mountains or other unusual ground features, it is often difficult to tell where you are visually. We might be flying over Vietnam, Albania or Cuba; it makes no difference. We board the aluminium tube at one airfield and alight, a few hours later, at another. Often even the hotels we stay at are indistinguishable. We can't get to grips with the countries over which we travel. Today's air travellers, in many ways so much more privileged than their predecessors in the 1930s, are even more impoverished by the experience. The writer Milan Kundera draws attention to a related phenomenon in his novel, *Slowness*.[9] We hurry, increase our pace when we wish to forget; to remember, we slow down.

And yet flight still fascinates. As the raw adventure faded, other concerns claimed my attention. Flying came to be all about rules, complex training schedules (Have I covered everything? Can I sign it off?), Air Traffic requirements, NOTAMS, SOPs and special instructions. Everything I needed to master was artificial, composed of layers of an administrative and technical fabric that insulated me from the air and its mystery. But the people I worked with were real. Their unique comradeship survived the changed circumstances. I never failed to be amazed by the speed and completeness at which a disparate collection of individuals melded into a crew. Some of those assigned to a particular flight may never have met each other before. They might be of widely different ages and backgrounds, but they come together for a single purpose and are instantly united in that purpose. Night-stopping down route, firm friends who perhaps shared a house back at base or who normally socialized together, would, if they were on different crews, stay with their crew.

A good 'Number One' cabin crewmember can make or break a trip. They set the tone, form the main communication link among the crewmembers and often provide a viewpoint on problems that the pilots might not have thought of for themselves. It is the senior cabin crewmember, male or female, who really turns the crew from a collection of well-trained individuals into a team. They tend to be reliable, resourceful, wise, articulate and funny. They start off with a formal, respectful relationship with the pilots, but it soon mellows on the basis of mutual respect.

In terms of people, the airline world was still a very small place. Personal contacts were brief and occurred in strange places. Flying east to west, I was contemplating the awesome vista of the Greenland ice cap from the comfort of a Boeing 767 flight deck and fell to discussing the region's range of extreme weather conditions with the co-pilot, Simon. Many aircraft had come to grief here before they had the power, altitude capability and range to cross it safely. Even today, flying there in smaller aircraft is a hazardous business and stories abound of near misses and real tragedy. I recalled a pilot I had met and befriended some years before. We met only for a few days, but he had impressed me with his knowledge, professionalism and warm good humour. I explained to Simon how this chap and his colleague had died attempting to cross the mountains in a light turbine aircraft. They had engine problems and encountered icing to such an extent that they were unable to maintain a safe altitude. 'I know,' said Simon. 'That was my father.'

On a two-day slip in Barbados, I was sipping my rum punch at a poolside bar when a British Airways crew showed up. I watched the skipper order the drinks, then spoke to him.

'Hello, Barry.'

He turned towards me. 'Oh, hello Keith.' It was an unremarkable exchange leading to a natural, relaxed conversation. Yet we hadn't seen each other for thirty years, since we were both impoverished hopefuls desperately struggling to get our licences. Such encounters are typical, though that was perhaps an extreme example. There is nothing predictable about the life of the airline pilot. Friendships are made, strong bonds sometimes formed, but paths diverge and cross again unexpectedly. We hear about old colleagues from time to time. We often just miss meeting up and sometimes we realize that one has disappeared without a trace.

There are far more airline pilots now, but, for much of my time, if a British pilot got his name in the papers, I would know him, or know someone who did.

No matter what the size of the aircraft, or the routes flown, or the age and experience of the crew, spectacular sights still bring delight and surprise. Early mornings are the best, after a good night's rest, before weariness of the daily task dulls the senses. After my first visit to the Caribbean for many years, we took off from Barbados to the east and turned left to fly up the coastline. We climbed rapidly on track with no restrictions to demand our attention and I had time to study the effect of the sun's low angle on the scene below. The sparkling sea, the golden sands, the dark green waving palms and the colourful roofs of the houses were spread out beneath me in incredible clarity and detail. I was filled with a great feeling of warmth towards the islands, the people and their music. It was as if I had been visiting home.

A friend who had built his own aeroplane tried to explain something he'd seen from the biplane's open cockpit when he was positioning between two airfields in England. 'I wish I could paint,' he said. 'I had been skirting some heavy cloud build-ups, negotiating the dark valleys between heavy showers of rain, in turbulence with black tendrils reaching down towards me. Then suddenly I burst out into glorious sunshine. Through the struts and wires the view was transformed into sparkling green fields and trees, wet from the rain, and the visibility was crystal clear to the far horizon.'

I knew well what he meant. It is impossible to express the beauty of such scenes in words. The view from a biplane is even more significant because it is framed by the wings and the wires. It is a viewpoint that, once enjoyed, is forever implanted on the retina of the pilot like a complementary colour image. The cones of the eye are ever-after waiting, primed for that picture. But you would have to be something of a genius to express it in paint. The problem is the emotion. The view itself, the scene that would have been captured by a camera, is only a small part of the experience. The rest comes from within the observer. It is a complex reaction between personality and environment.

Large cities are particularly impressive from the air. Another image that persists in my memory came about when we received a revised clearance while flying south over the eastern seaboard of the United States. It necessitated a prolonged left turn and as our aircraft banked, I found myself looking vertically down on New York, the skyscrapers reaching up towards me in stark clarity. From contemplating the high and lonely desert of the upper air, I was suddenly peering into the centre of downtown Manhattan.

Why does the view from the air provide such memorable scenes? Philosophers have tried for centuries to define beauty, but they always fail. They talk about symmetry, economy, elegance and truth, and they are right, but we are never quite convinced they have got the essence of it. Poets get closer. They capture accidental coincidences of features ('a certain turn of neck or knee') and they understand that surprise is one of the ways in which our emotions are touched.

So flying can provide the different perspectives that help to reveal beauty, while the speed that is inseparable from flight can deliver the surprise. The sights are certainly transient, which is another feature of exceptional beauty. But in modern machines these remain purely visual experiences that we see without physical involvement. Flying now is too easy and too comfortable to let us feel the cold of the Arctic wastes, or taste the salt of the sea spray while we watch a pitching trawler take green waves over her whole length. It is unreal, like watching a film. We would have to go back to open cockpits to change that. But then again we still have the underlying beauty of flight and of the aeroplane itself, what the poet Rupert Brooke referred to as the, 'unpassioned beauty of a great machine', though he wasn't thinking of jet airliners. It's another sort of beauty, a more familiar, workaday beauty that we shouldn't ignore.

People the world over recognize the magic of aeroplanes, especially children. No doubt boys climbed fences to wave at sailing ships setting out from the world's ports hundreds of years ago, just as they wave at taxiing aircraft today. I always felt it was important to wave back. Whether at Manchester or Madras, it connected us for a moment and, I hope, gave their dreams some link with real life. Even the shepherd who kept a flock of sheep on the airfield at Tempelhof in Berlin used to wave to us as we taxied out in the morning, the timeless saluting the new, yet already obsolete, technology. Only the weather was actually timeless in our world.

Once, returning to the UK at night from the Middle East, we flew for hundreds of miles across Hungary, Austria and Germany between layers of cloud. A thin, continuous sheet of cirrostratus lay just above our flight level, while a dense blanket of nimbostratus lay far beneath. Embedded in the lower cloud were active thunderstorms producing a spectacularly extensive display of lightning. Frequent, irregular flashes lit up the cloud below and as far as we could see in all directions to the distant horizon. Each flash reflected off the cloud above us. In our darkened cockpit, devoid at this late hour of the usual radio chatter, we watched, entranced, in silence. The effect was eerie, ghostly, like walking across the floor of an enormous, deserted disco dance hall. The lighting effects were on, but the dancers had gone.

There was something supernatural about the tornadoes in the Caribbean; sinister black snakes moving out on the horizon, sometimes half hidden by rain showers. They oozed an aura of evil power and we gave them a wide berth. Not like the thing I found unexpectedly at Tenerife in the Canary Islands. I was supervising a captain new to the Boeing 757 and he had a high workload because the runway in use changed after we had started our descent. Instead of the expected and familiar routing to the west of the island to land to the east using the ILS-equipped runway, we were routed to the east for a VOR approach to land to the west. It was necessary to maintain a higher than usual rate of descent in solid cloud that got quite turbulent in the lee of Mount Teide. The weather broadcast on the Automatic Information System was benign: just a little drizzle reducing visibility slightly, a light westerly wind and a 2,000ft cloud base. On the final approach track the turbulence was stronger and we encountered heavy rain. I asked the controller for the latest weather conditions and he repeated the observation on the broadcast. It didn't match up with what we were experiencing and I began to think we might not see the runway at our decision point.

At about 1,500ft we broke out of cloud into quite good visibility. In light drizzle, the runway came into sight a few miles ahead, but that was not what attracted my attention. Just off our port wing tip was the biggest waterspout I had ever seen. A great, solid-looking column of water nearly half a mile in diameter appeared to reach up from the storm-tossed waves to the billowing cloud base like some apocalyptic symbol.

We landed and taxied in. The passengers disembarked and we went down onto the tarmac to join pilots from the other aircraft on the ramp who were staring at the phenomenon. We watched it in awe. It held its position for several minutes, just off the coast to the south-east of the airfield. Then it slowly thinned and weakened, before finally fading into a general mist of rain and drizzle. Few spoke. There was the odd exclamation of, 'Gee, look at that!' But mostly we were preoccupied and humbled, trying to imagine what it would have been like to fly into the centre of a solid shaft of water on the approach. The automatic weather reports for the airfield never mentioned it.

The weather colours every aspect of a pilot's day. It influences everything he does and every decision he makes. Technology has reduced the impact of extreme weather and distanced the pilots from the most intimate involvement with it, but still it cannot be ignored. The first information a pilot reaches for when he checks into the crew room (after he has checked his pay slip) is the weather forecast. It will influence how much fuel he takes, the route he follows, the altitude at which he flies, what sort of approach he will make at his destination, the alternative airfields he chooses and even the information he provides for the passengers over the PA system. In this respect he is like a farmer, the only passengers in my experience who could be relied upon not to complain if weather delayed their flight.

When I leave my home in the morning, even now, I glance up at the sky and search for clues to explain the nature of the air mass and how it might impinge upon whatever it is I have planned to do. I check the wind strength and direction, the visibility and the cloud type and height and I feel the temperature. I use all the knowledge and experience I have accumulated during a lifetime in aviation and, spurning the BBC and the Meteorological Office, I make my own forecast. Sadly, its accuracy has not improved.

Boeing had been developing the 757, another twin-engined aircraft, at the same time as the 767. It was intended to be a replacement for the 727 and was narrow-bodied with a big wing to give exceptional take-off performance. At a late stage in the development of the two aircraft, someone suggested that pilots should be able to operate both the 757 and 767 on a common type rating. It was a novel idea. Until then commercial pilots had been rated to fly only one type at a time. If their pilots could fly two types, the airlines would benefit from greater flexibility and reduced costs.

Of course, there were safety concerns and the Federal Aviation Agency (FAA), the American regulatory authority, needed to be convinced. The Boeing design department proved equal to the task and modified the 757 so that the flight decks were nearly identical as far as the pilots were concerned. The windscreens were enlarged to give exactly the same field of view, but the cleverest trick was to write the manuals and the checklists so that it was difficult to tell them apart. Many of the systems were different, especially the hydraulics, but if you read the checklist carefully and did what it said, the correct drill would be achieved every time.

It was best not to delve too deeply into the technicalities and idiosyncrasies of the systems. Some pilots have criticized Boeing over the years for the lack of detail provided on technical conversion courses, saying that the Boeing training school operates on a 'need-to-know' basis. Curious pilots, asking to know more about how the undercarriage retraction system works, might be frustrated to receive the answer: 'Works real fine; lasts a long time!' But just as Apple Computers promised people engaged in word-processing and desktop publishing a 'transparent' means of working that did not interfere with the real job in hand, so Boeing provided a 'transparent' operating system to the pilots of its 757 and 767.

Boeing had accepted that turbofans were now reliable enough to justify designing large, longer-range aircraft with only two engines. The larger engines were also highly efficient, offering significant operating economies, but to get full benefit from the configuration they had to be able to operate over the world's oceans. Airbus had come to the same conclusion and the regulatory authorities were coming under pressure to re-examine the rules that had been framed in the piston era. All public transport aircraft were required to demonstrate that they could fly safely after the failure of one engine, but twins, in recognition that they would be left 'hanging by the thread' of a single engine after such a failure, were required to remain within one hour's flying time of a suitable diversion airfield at all times. There was a vigorous debate over the proposals to extend this distance. On the one hand, the statistics existed to show that the chances of the second engine failing on a twin, given the first failure, were remote – far less than many other risks accepted routinely in many different transport systems. On the other hand, the passengers and crew of a twin with an engine failure would still be 'hanging by a thread', possibly for a long time. It was a classic conflict of facts versus feelings, of science versus emotion.

Initially, I had been firmly in the emotional camp, but the statisticians and the engineers did a great deal of work to convince people like me that it could be done safely. In addition to proving the reliability of the engines, it was necessary to improve maintenance procedures and to amend the allowable deficiency lists. Items that had previously been allowed to be unserviceable for several sectors now had to be fully serviceable before every despatch. The diversion airfields had to be accessible too, which meant improved weather information and communications.

In the course of all this work the authorities realized that existing regulations allowing virtually unrestricted operation of three- and four-engined aircraft might not be as robust as they should be, particularly those concerned with fire suppression in the aircrafts' holds. The result of all this research was a general revision and updating of the regulations governing all long-distance flying, leading to improved safety levels worldwide.

The new regulations had been in force for a year or two before I started to fly twins across the North Atlantic and I found I was able to do so without a qualm. Modern engines fail very rarely and if they are going to fail it is most likely to happen during take-off or initial climb, when full power is being demanded of them. That part of the flight takes place close to alternate airfields anyway, as does most of the cruising flight. On the North Atlantic, only small portions of the route lie outside the one-hour diversion radius.

Today, twins fly routinely over the Pacific Ocean, at times more than three hours from a diversion airfield, with a remarkable safety record. Once again, technology and experience together have demonstrated what is possible. The difficulty now is to guard against complacency.

Our crews flew both the 757 and the 767 on transatlantic routes and switching between the types proved easier than flying different models of the same type in some airlines' fleets. The 757 handled slightly differently to the 767: the controls were not quite so crisp and the whole airframe was less rigid, flexing like a 707 in turbulence. But apart from the different figures involved – weights, speeds and so on – and the raised seat rails on the flight deck floor, which we all tripped over – flying one was much the same as the other. Again, the advice was, just don't try to remember the figures!

The words of my old mentor in Berlin, Alex, came back to me. When a Check Captain asked him a question he would shake his head solemnly, reach for the manual and say slowly, exaggerating his rich Scottish brogue, 'These things are far too important to commit to memory.'

CHAPTER 15

Fly-By-Wire

Toulouse is very different from Seattle, but they are both attractive cities. Apart from their individual character and history, and the profusion of good eating places, there is a buzz, a vibrant feel to both places. Perhaps that stems from people working at the cutting edge of technology or, more probably, enjoying what they do and being proud of it.

For its new A320, competitor to the phenomenally successful Boeing 737, Airbus pulled out all the technological stops. The company had the advantage of a clean sheet of paper and it had confidence. The initial model used similar engines to the latest 737 and the airframe was a conventional aluminium structure, so the difference came from attention to detail and bold technical innovation. Airbus was not just designing a new aircraft; it was planning to create a whole range of new-generation aircraft that would raise the art of airliner production to a new level of excellence. It produced a superbly engineered airframe with a highly efficient wing. The fuselage diameter was increased to give passengers more room and the flight deck was a model of modern ergonomic design.

The press made much of Airbus's decision to opt for a side-stick controller instead of a conventional control column. Designers had struggled with that control column for years. No matter how it was shaped – half wheels, handlebars or ram's horns – it got in the way. It tended to obscure some of the instruments and it made getting in and out of the pilots' seats awkward. Airbus would be free of these problems forever and could use the space to provide a retractable tray for charts, an additional computer keyboard, or lunch. All this was made possible because the control inputs made by the pilots would not operate cables, pulleys, pushrods and bell cranks as they had since the days of the Wright brothers. They would, instead, send electrical signals to computers that would compare these inputs with the aircraft attitude, speed and configuration, take into consideration the pressure and temperature of the air mass in which the aircraft was flying, and signal hydraulic power units to move the aerodynamic controls exactly enough to produce the desired response.

Many advantages were claimed for this method of control, which was dubbed 'fly-by-wire'. It would reduce weight over a conventional system and would make flying easier. Safety limits could be built in. It would be impossible to stall the aircraft: close the throttles, point the nose of the aircraft to the sky and keep pulling back on the side stick, and the angle of attack of the wing would increase as it does on any other aircraft. But just before the airflow broke away from the wing and destroyed the lift in the normal way, the computers would sense a limit, move the controls to hold but not exceed that limit, and command the engines to full thrust as a bonus. But the side stick would not move. All these corrections would occur while the pilot continued to hold the stick hard back on the stop. In a similar way, maximum speed limits would be protected and even the angle of bank would be limited. Trim and stability were automated. All the pilot had to do was to direct the aircraft to the pitch and bank angle he needed and release the side stick; the aircraft would then maintain that attitude precisely, until he wanted to change it.

Computers featured throughout the aircraft. Computers now controlled all of the systems such as pressurization and air-conditioning, which had previously been controlled by manual selectors and electromechanical actuators. Even the warning systems were computerized, with details of failures being displayed on a central screen along with the appropriate checklist, the actions required disappearing as they were completed.

Airbus had introduced a brave new world in which the engineers had taken over. Skill, knowledge and experience would no longer be needed by the pilot – the engineers had done it all for him. Except of course, they hadn't. Oh, they had improved many things; I liked the spacious, comfortable flight deck with its clean, convenient layout and the excellent displays. I found no difficulty accustoming myself to using the side stick and I particularly liked the ability to call up clear diagrams of any of the aircraft's systems on a screen – fuel, hydraulics, pneumatics, for example – with the positions of all the valves and accurate quantities displayed in real time. There was more information available, in a better format, than ever before. But ... though the Airbus philosophy promised many things, it was far from perfect. The FMC calculation of the descent profile was not flexible enough to be relied upon routinely and the automated electronic checklists had just as many traps for the unwary as had the old paper ones.

I fully appreciated the many improvements to the aircraft control that the Airbus system introduced. The safety protections it provided sounded sensible. The designers had done a great job and, if pilots were machines, it would be ideal. Unfortunately, they are still the old human model: essentially lazy, frequently bored and easily distracted.

I had misgivings from the start about how Airbus incorporated fly-by-wire into its products, but I seemed to be alone in this. I still encounter fierce opposition from pilots who are completely won over to the Airbus philosophy, but I remain unconvinced. The problems that fly-by-wire produces for pilots are, in my view, threefold. First, there is the problem of reversion to Alternate or Direct Control Laws in certain failure cases. While everything is working as it should, the system operates in Normal

Law and provides whatever handling characteristics are deemed appropriate. It also provides those protections against many of the undesirable conditions in which an aircraft may find itself: stalls; overbanking; high or low speeds; wind shear; and so on. When other aircraft systems fail, however, as they will from time to time, the Flight Control Laws revert to secondary modes where the protections are not available and, worse, the handling characteristics are different. Thus the pilots, who don't get enough handling practice anyway, may find that while they are running the checklists to deal with malfunctions and facing crucial operational decisions, they are simultaneously confronted with an aircraft that handles differently and still has most of the limitations of conventional aeroplanes.

The second problem is a direct result of human nature. If you provide humans operating a machine with safety devices designed to protect them from undesirable situations, they will use them. Instead of operating carefully within their envelope as they have been trained to do, safe in the knowledge that, even if they didn't, the system would protect them, they will get sloppy and inattentive and rely on the system all the time. So the safety protections are not protections any more, they are the new envelope limits.

Third, there is the reduction in physical feedback. The side-stick controller gives no aerodynamic feedback, as it is simply centred by a spring, like a video-gamer's joystick, and the throttles remain in their detent regardless of the power delivered by the engines. These may seem to be small things, but they contribute significantly to the distancing of the pilot from his environment. The way they operate removes two more of the means by which the pilot can be informed of exactly what is happening to his aircraft. Airbus pilots rely entirely on visual clues. Everyone can agree that effective control is enhanced by a high level of situational awareness, yet, without the sensual feedback given by control feel and throttle position, two important ways in which the pilot is made situationally aware are removed.

Airbus will produce the safety statistics and point out that the A320 ushered in a new era of safe flying. So it did, but it introduced a new type of accident, too. Three or four early accidents to the type gave warning of this. Experienced pilots who had hitherto been considered of above average ability came to grief because they did not fully understand the technology they had been given. The Air France crash in Mulhouse, the Indian Airline in Bangalore (now Bengaluru), Air Inter near Strasbourg and Lufthansa in Warsaw were investigated in detail. Differences and similarities were analysed, causes were attributed and lessons were learnt. But the response was largely technical. Where pilots were thought to have shown a lack of 'situational awareness', new instruments or improved ergonomics were developed to solve the problem. It seemed to me that the engineers had solved some of aviation's traditional problems and introduced another, big one. They had taken another step on the road to full automation, that is, towards a pilot-less aircraft, rather than giving the pilots the tools they needed to develop and improve their expertise. With every technological advance, the pilots were being moved further and further from personal engagement and responsibility.

While navigational accuracy and display have been revolutionized, all the new information is presented visually. Pilots don't need the wind in their hair or their feet frozen, but it seems negative to deny tactile information on the position of the aircraft's flight controls and throttles. Modern pilots are taught to trust the machine – the autopilot – more than they do themselves. They are taught to believe that they cannot fly as accurately as the autopilot, so they don't try and they don't achieve the same rapport with the machine and its environment.

This is not just a fanciful impression. Many of the traditional clues that provided the pilot with information were missing on the A320. In an older aircraft, approaching the stall was a sensual experience. The throttles were probably retarded from their normal position, giving visual, tactile and muscular clues; the airframe began to shake, the controls felt slack and ineffective and the wind noise died away to a whisper. On the A320 fly-by-wire airliner, the throttles stay in position when the power is reduced and the side-stick feel is governed by a spring, which never varies. The aircraft cannot stall, we're told, the computers won't allow it, but under certain conditions it still can. Approaching the stall, none of the natural sounds or feel of the controls would be there to warn the pilots. They would hear only a synthetic 'stall warning', another of the many electronic noises that annoy them, and the roar of the air-conditioning system that drowns out everything else.

The pilots and engineers who champion this approach, and there are plenty of them, will say that natural clues are no longer needed. And perhaps for 99.9 per cent of the time they are correct. But human beings come to rely on artificial systems to the detriment of their natural ability and skill. If you produce an automatic system that protects the pilot from errors, he will use it and he will come to rely on it. That is not the designer's or the regulatory authority's intention, but it is human nature. It was not long before we heard another notorious expression on the flight deck: 'The aircraft will look after you.'

I was quite prepared to adapt; enough people were saying there are no longer any jobs for life and that we must get used to lifetime career development. Well, I had retrained every time I changed aircraft types and every time I changed companies, as well as being checked two or three times a year. But people are not machines. We can increase our knowledge fairly easily. It is quite possible to learn new skills, but most firmly entrenched are attitudes, possibly because they are acquired more slowly and less consciously. Our attitudes – our personalities – are resistant to change. And it is just possible that there might be good evolutionary reasons for that.

The rapid technological development that has characterized the last couple of hundred years is accelerating. Farm labourers, miners, stevedores and countless other trades, which people expected to exist forever, or at least for beyond their lifetimes, have vanished. Printers, draughtsmen, bank clerks; all have been made redundant by technology. The airline pilot is not immune. His job has changed out of all recognition and there are lessons to be learnt for all of us. It is surely time to ask some questions. Is technology inevitable? Is it always beneficial? Are we allowing technology to rule our lives? Do we employ new technology because we can, before considering what we really need? How should we organize our future? Should we not think very carefully before throwing away skills that have taken a long time and a lot of sacrifice to obtain?

Management's approach to operating aircraft in the technological age changed. Pilots received little consideration and recruitment procedures deteriorated. I was frustrated by a lack of planning. In an earlier age, airlines would expand carefully. They would rejoice when their aircraft were full and be pleased that they were actually turning work away. It meant that they could charge higher prices and know exactly what they were doing when they did eventually commit to more aircraft. But greed and fear had come to replace cautious optimism. As the start of the season loomed, the accountants would discover that there was still some business they hadn't grabbed. They would suddenly acquire another aircraft and expect it to be crewed for service in a few weeks. At one meeting I was able to claim with some accuracy that we had time now for only two questions at pilot interviews: 'Have you got a licence?' and 'When can you start?'

The pilots coming into airline flying were from varied backgrounds and there were some excellent characters amongst them. The number of pilots leaving the RAF had declined, but they still formed a large percentage of our recruits. We even took a number of helicopter pilots directly onto the Airbus A320. Despite their limited fixed-wing experience, they made the transition without problems.

On the line, however high the technology, weather still caused problems. Snow tends to make more trouble in the United Kingdom than it does elsewhere. The Scandinavian runways are often snow-covered for several months of the year and it rarely seems to cause any inconvenience. Icing in cloud above those countries is more of a problem. The Germans cope well by being highly organized. It is an impressive sight when landings and take-offs at Munich are suspended for fifteen minutes while the formation of snowploughs move into action, swinging off the runway just in time for the next aircraft to land.

But it is more difficult in Britain. The snow is unpredictable – some winters see heavy falls, others none at all, so that the airport authorities find it difficult to plan and to train their staff. The snow is often wet, melting within hours of falling, then freezing to give treacherous surface conditions. Taxiing out at Manchester on one of my first flights in the Airbus A320, I was happy to oblige when the ground movements controller asked us if we could possibly alter our routing to make a left turn of more than 90 degrees onto a different taxiway. Snow had been cleared, leaving snow banks 2ft high on either side of the taxiways, and there were patches of ice on the tarmac. Even so, I thought the controller was being overly diffident about making his request. I positioned the aircraft so as to increase the radius of the turn required as much as possible and adjusted the speed so that, while moving no faster than was necessary, we had enough inertia to complete the turn without having to increase power from the engines, which might have blown snow and ice onto other aircraft. The ground steering tiller on the Airbus is fly-by-wire like everything else, but it works fine when you get used to it. All seemed to be going well until we passed the apex of the turn and the slight slope of the taxiways became apparent. There was a juddering noise from the nose wheel and the tiller felt dead in my hand. The lack of feedback in the system left me feeling helpless. Sixty-odd tons of aircraft started to slide towards the snow banks. We didn't slide far, a few yards only, until the wheels gripped again. No damage was done, but in those few seconds my warm, beating heart sank into my boots, which were already soaked in melting snow, and I confronted the prospect of an ignominious end to my career.

Crosswinds were still fun. Even a fly-by-wire machine with its software-determined Control Laws requires a pilot's skill and judgement for a good landing under these conditions, though it demands a slightly different technique. The fact that a fly-by-wire side stick provides no aerodynamic feedback takes some getting used to. If correcting for the turbulence means you are hitting the aileron stops on a conventional aeroplane, it is merely an indication that you have reached the limit of effectiveness of that control and it is time perhaps to supplement it with gentle rudder pressure. The first time it happened to me on a fly-by-wire aircraft I felt instinctively that the roll control had failed completely. Without feel, there is no increase in force as you approach the limit and when the stop is reached it feels dead, useless. Most disconcerting.

Nevertheless, taxiing in after a demanding crosswind landing, the pilot can bask in the knowledge that he has done something the autopilot can't do for him. There is still a need for his special skills. But this will be a silent, personal triumph and short-lived, because no doubt the engineers are working on ways of making it unnecessary.

On the A320's successors, the combination of very long-range flights with the provision of fully automatic Flight Management Systems presents new problems. There is an increasing tendency for pilots to rely on the automatic monitoring of systems. There is less for them to do and less need for them to stay alert. Air Traffic Control will keep them separated from other aircraft and if they don't, their aircraft's collision avoidance system will alert them in time to take action. How else can the emergency landing of an Airbus A340 aircraft in February 2005 be explained? En route from Hong Kong to London with a known fuel system fault, the tanks feeding the outboard engines were allowed to run dry. The crew had available to them a wonderful diagrammatic display of the fuel system. Dial up the relevant page on their screens and they would see how much fuel was available in each tank, the total fuel figure and the real-time position of every valve in the system. I would have expected them to check that page every hour of the flight, yet they were surprised when the engines flamed out over Brussels.

The investigation by the internationally respected UK Air Accidents Investigation Branch inspectors[10] completely exonerated the pilots. The safety measures they recommended all involved technical modifications. They noted that the pilots had not checked to see how the automatic fuel management system was operating during the long flight, but pointed out that they were not required to do so. No one, it seems, expected them to browse the wonderfully detailed pages of real-time system status diagrams provided for them in their electronic displays. If something was not operating correctly, a clear warning should have been provided to alert them to the fact. Airmanship is clearly dead. Creative intervention by imaginative aviators is not now considered necessary or desirable.

Whatever the technology, many of the problems and pleasures of airline flying remain the same. The descent and approach phases of a flight are still the most demanding, so the pilots must try to ensure that they are fully alert and concentrating at the top of the descent. During the cruise there is less to do. The routine tasks of monitoring and position reporting are rarely very demanding and the pilots can, to some extent, relax. Yet the busiest period, perhaps surprisingly, has become the first hour and a half or so of the duty day. The time between reaching the crew room to sign on duty and climbing through 10,000ft on departure generated, I reckoned, 80 per cent of my day's workload. I had to assimilate more information and make more decisions in that short period than at any other time during the flight. If I could do it well, avoid all the pitfalls and distractions and not encounter any insurmountable obstacles, we might get away on schedule. That was the key. Depart on time and the rest of the day is pleasant and easy. Take off late and the job becomes much more difficult. It is a perverse fact of nature that, if you are late and trying to make up time, you will encounter more problems that will make you later still.

For all the changes, time spent in-flight is different to time spent on the ground. We may have moved on from Gann's image of airline flying as the ultimate adventure, a game of chance with Fate itself, but the concept of the pilot as the operator of an automatic train or a push-button elevator is wide of the mark, too. There is still a tension in the unnatural business of being aloft. Perhaps it is an evolutionary thing; it is not that long since we worried about falling out of trees, so no wonder so many people feel apprehensive in the air. Or perhaps the knowledge that continued existence can only be guaranteed while there is fuel in the tanks exerts a degree of stress on those so engaged. Speculation on cause may be fanciful, but the effect is real. Perhaps it is simply linked to the level of technology. In the West Indies, my old friend Pete, a jet enthusiast if ever there was one, had been asked to investigate the pilots' claim that six sectors in the day was too much on the BAC 1-11, though they regularly accepted six or more on the turboprop Avro 748. A knowledgeable expert on both types, Pete enjoyed a hectic spell of flying them on a wide variety of inter-island services and was surprised to find the local pilots' concerns confirmed. I remember him shaking his head in baffled frustration. 'There's no reason I can think of why it should make any difference which type you fly,' he said. 'But it does; the jet is more tiring.' And the company settled on a compromise scheduling agreement for the jet: normally a maximum of four sectors per duty day, occasionally five, never six.

Some days were still sheer joy. If the roster had not been too frantic in the previous weeks and I had managed a good night's sleep before departure, I really looked forward to a long day's flying. A departure just before 8am local time was good. A gentleman's hour we called it. It was the best possible start. All the crew would feel it; the atmosphere on board would reflect the happiness of a well-trained team doing a job they all loved and doing it well. We could relax and enjoy the flight. It was easy to stay ahead of events. We had time to plan the next sector, to radio ahead and give fuel figures and any special requests to our agents at any intermediate stops and the turn-rounds would go like clockwork. And it is an undeniable truth known to all navigators that, when you are on or ahead of schedule, you have a much better chance of picking up a tailwind. The day would fly by in such a pleasant and satisfying fashion that we were surprised when, eventually, it was time for our final approach and landing. With the paperwork almost completed before descent we might be on the ground, through the terminal and out of the crew room by the scheduled time of arrival. If there was a pub nearby where we could have a beer together before going home, it rounded off a perfect day.

I enjoyed many days and nights like that. But then there were the other sort; the sort people might call stressful. There is a lot of talk about 'stress' nowadays, but it is a lazy, blanket term, often used by people who can't be bothered to find a more descriptive word. Stress is used instead of anxiety, frustration, ignorance, a lack of time or nervousness. The problem is that if we can't describe a condition we are suffering from accurately, we will find it very difficult to devise a strategy for dealing with it. A complete absence of any form of stress can surely coincide only with death. We know that human beings often achieve their finest performances under what most people would recognize as considerable stress. For this reason, people often put themselves under stress deliberately: the journalist who delays submitting his copy until the deadline is upon him; the athlete who trains for months for the big race; the businessman who 'psychs himself up' for the crucial meeting.

My own definitions of stress were evolved during quiet times in the cruise, or during walks or while sipping a quiet pint. They are not very scientific and the experts would probably ridicule them, but they work for me. They help me to recognize what is happening and to do something about it. They revolve around the difference between what I want or need, and what is. I recognize two sorts of stress: physical and mental. I identify physical stress when conditions are in any way less than the optimum for what I am doing. If it is too hot or too cold, if I am desperately hungry or bursting for a pee, or it is too noisy or I have a raging toothache, or if I can hardly keep awake; that is physical stress. It is usually easy to reduce that sort of stress: cool off; turn up the heating; have something to eat; and so on. But sometimes the condition just has to be endured for a short period until it is convenient to do something about it. Planning can help to avoid situations in which physical stress might arise.

The other sort of stress is mental stress. All mental stress is self-inflicted. That is a sweeping statement, but I am not talking about mental illness, I am considering the effects of doubt, anguish, insecurity and other mental conditions that put extra pressure on healthy, robust personalities. The most common stress we put on ourselves is the fear of failure. We are brought up to do our best, to compete, never to let anyone down and while these attitudes make us reliable and good at our jobs, they sometimes distort our priorities and cause us to get things out of proportion. It helps to take a step back mentally from what we are doing, to relax and reconsider the priorities. Often it is possible to see a complex job as a combination of simple tasks that we know we can do well, then to do them one at a time.

The stress resulting from time pressure is difficult to classify as physical or mental because it is a subjective concept; as I get older the years fly past, but waiting a few seconds for a page to change on the Internet seems like an age. In the air, keeping to the schedule is usually important, but it is easily overruled by the more fundamental constraint imposed by the fuel remaining on board.

I reflected on the scientific research done on stress one day after climbing out of a newly opened airport in Bodrum, Turkey. It was daylight, the weather fine in hazy sunshine. The airport had been well equipped, but the procedures were new and untried. Traffic was heavy and both controllers and pilots were learning how things worked. We were late. I had already exercised my discretion to extend our permitted duty period in order to get the passengers where they wanted to go and the aircraft back where it was needed for the next operation. We had a deadline by which we had to be airborne again. If we didn't make it, the crew would have to night-stop and the operation would grind to a halt for twelve hours. Just for fun, our Auxiliary Power Unit – the small turbine engine in the tail that provided electrics and air-conditioning on the ground when the main engines were shut down – had failed.

If a research scientist wanted to study the effects of stress on people, he might want to include as many stressors as he could in one scenario. He would surely prepare his subjects by fatiguing them with a high workload over a long period. He might ensure that they had suffered sleep deprivation and would also disorientate them with random shift patterns or time-zone changes. He would then confine them in a small, claustrophobic cell, preferably restricting their movement further by strapping them into their chairs. The temperature would then need to be increased, say to 38°C, and they should be forced to face bright lights or to stare into the sun. Loud, distorted noise could then be played into their headsets, containing important instructions in a heavy accent that was difficult to understand. The subjects should be given a tight time frame in which to complete a complex task that required prompt cooperation from a number of people, who were themselves overworked and did not understand the urgency of the situation.

No, of course, I reflected as eventually we took off and climbed away from the airport and the air-conditioning started working again, no self-respecting scientist would impose such conditions on his subjects. Professional ethics would not allow it. But if he did, I can assure him he would notice, at the very least, some thinning of patience.

At jet cruising altitudes, it never really gets completely dark over Europe in the summer; the sun sets well north of due west, then its glow travels across the northern horizon to the north-east and threatens forever to rise properly again until at last, when you had given up hope, it pierces the skyline and its brilliant light slices painfully into your eyes.

Cruising up from North Africa after a long night the radio is filled with voices as pilots and controllers clamour for attention. The airspace over Italy's west coast gets very busy during the morning rush hour. The short-haul jets linking the Italian cities are shouting for climb or descent clearances, overflying traffic needs to make position reports and get frequency changes for handover to the next sector, while the overnight transatlantic traffic is arriving from the west.

Wearily negotiating this Babel, I became aware of an American voice patiently repeating his call. I can't now remember his call sign – I'll call him United 46 – but he must have been approaching the Rome Flight Information Region Boundary and he sounded as if he too had been up all night.

'Roma! Roma! This is United 46,' he called. And again, 'Roma! Roma! This is United 46,' over and over again at intervals of a minute or two. Either the controller couldn't hear him, or he was just too busy to reply.

We were all relieved when at long last the harassed controller answered. 'United 46 this is Roma. Go ahead with your message!' he shouted. For a long second there was complete silence as every other pilot waited for the American to have his say.

'Aw ...' drawled the American, 'no message, Roma. I just wanted to say, have a nice day!'

Such moments cannot be contrived; they just happen, spontaneously. Tension spills over into laughter and life goes on at a more relaxed and reasonable pace.

On another level, technology has changed everything. Jeanette Winterson put it better than I can in a piece she wrote for the *Sunday Times* 'Books' supplement in November 2006, though she was talking about poetry, not flying. 'Our modern life shies away from real experience, preferring the virtual and the mediated to the immediate and intense,' she wrote. She's right and the poetry has been driven out of flying. Whatever the reason, I never warmed to the Airbus A320 or its bigger brother, the A321. Oh, it was clever, well built and a comfortable place in which to work, but it was not flying.

These are very personal feelings. When I gently suggested, in a trade magazine, that the Airbus designers might be going down the wrong track, only a few pilots expressed agreement with me. Far more disagreed. This did not surprise me as much as the manner in which they disagreed. They defended Airbus with a ferocity that bordered on the fanatical. They produced no rational arguments, only blind prejudice. Clearly there were many pilots who saw the fly-by-wire, nearly fully automatic airliner as the answer to their dreams.

However clever, the machine was still subject to failures. On the occasion of the first revenue flight of our company's brand-new Airbus A321 aircraft the failure was banal. Apart from a change of engines, this machine differed little from the A320 we had been flying previously other than in its length and weight. A short classroom course served to acquaint us with all the details we needed to know. Nevertheless, it was decided that each captain should be supervised by a Training Captain on his first flight. Such decisions inevitably create a problem. Who is going to supervise the Training Captains' first flights?

Thus I boarded the pristine new aircraft with the Fleet Captain and another senior Training Captain, Mike. A flight deck crew of senior pilots like this is always courting disaster: all chiefs and no Indians. The cabin crew and engineers made the usual jokes about there being so much gold braid on the flight deck that perhaps the compass should be reswung. But the trip went remarkably well. We took a passenger load of holidaymakers out to Fuerteventura and brought another, bronzed load, back.

It was not until we actually touched down at Manchester that anything untoward happened. Even then, I didn't notice any problem save for a slight directional instability during the landing run causing us to weave slightly. But in the fading light of evening, the tower controller had seen a sheet of flame from our undercarriage and had pressed his alarm button. He calmly informed us of what he had seen as we slowed and we acknowledged, bringing the aircraft to a stop on the runway.

I was quite busy for the next few minutes. I had to say something to the passengers. I told them we might have burst a tyre and were waiting for the Fire Service to check if there was any other damage. Then I discussed the incident with the other two captains and briefed the cabin crew on how we saw the situation at that point. The crash tenders arrived and we were speaking by radio to the crew chief in his vehicle and advising our company of what was going on.

There was a moment of bizarre comedy when one of the firemen who had gone to inspect the wheel appeared at the nose below my side window and appeared to be suffering some sort of fit. The universal signal given when anyone wants an engine stopped is to draw the hand, held flat like a knife, across the throat. It is so common that it is usually reduced to a casual gesture made with one finger. But the pantomime performance the fireman delivered was so elaborate I couldn't recognize it at first.

When at last I did, I quickly closed the fuel cocks to cut both engines and, because the auxiliary power unit was not running, plunged us into darkness. That meant another explanation to the passengers and the cabin crew. By then the crew chief had got the fireman's report and told us that there was no sign of fire, but they could not be sure the gear leg was safe. He had asked our company engineers to come and make a further examination. I confirmed that everyone was prepared for a passenger evacuation, if it should become necessary, but there was no reason to start that potentially dangerous procedure yet.

All this time the Fleet Captain, who was on the flight deck to check out Mike and myself, seemed most concerned about whether we had checked the braking system on final approach as a recent notice required. What he meant, of course, is that I might not have checked it and he might subsequently be criticized for failing to notice that I had not checked it. His twittering was beginning to get on my nerves and I was grateful when Mike, who obviously felt the same, began to wind him up even more by asking him whether we had passed our check yet. It put things back into perspective.

When at last I had time to look outside I was amazed at the scene that stretched before me. It was now full night and the whole of the runway in front of us, and much of the rest of the airfield, was a sea of flashing lights: amber, blue and red. In addition to the airport's own rescue services, the full resources of the local area had responded. There were fire appliances and ambulances as far as the eye could see. From being the centre of a minor problem with our aircraft, I suddenly realized I was but a small cog in the vast machinery that nowadays swung into action in response to the slightest possibility of an aviation accident. It was reassuring in a way, of course, but I couldn't help but feel I was no longer really in control; greater forces were at work.

In time everything was declared safe. It appeared that some valve had malfunctioned in the braking system, preventing the port outer wheel from rotating so that the tyre had burnt down to the rim with no further consequences. It was a fault already known to Airbus that had occurred on other aircraft.

The passengers disembarked in the normal way by steps brought out to the runway and we, the crew, followed them, leaving the aircraft to the care of the engineers. I made my report and the rest of the paperwork was completed. The Fleet Captain confirmed that Mike and I had passed our check and were now free to check out other captains on the type.

We parted and I drove home. It occurred to me that a full alert status at Manchester Airport would not escape media attention, so I stopped at a pub on the way and phoned my wife to remind her not to believe everything she heard on the *Nine O'Clock News*.

Sipping my pint, I reflected that the whole incident left a rather flat taste in my mouth. When I had started in this business, anyone who described even a major flying incident he had been involved with in anything other than dismissive, matter-of-fact terms would be ridiculed as a 'line shooter'. Now it seemed that the most trivial incident was afforded sensationalist coverage. I know that precautions must be taken and that it is far better to err on the side of caution, but it seems to be done in an exaggerated manner. The concern of the Fleet Captain for his position, for his reputation and his job rather than for the specific problem we had encountered, was perhaps symptomatic of this change of attitude. Airline flying has become so safe, so boringly routine that people had to find other ways of stimulating their interest.

The newspaper headlines the following day did nothing to dispel my mood. We were relegated to the inside pages – no one had been hurt after all – but the subeditors still found room for headlines like: 'Passenger Jet in Crash Landing at Manchester'.

CHAPTER 16

Culture Shock

I drove out of the gate and down the lane as the sun rose to bring some colour into the day. The sight of a hare loping over the field was a good omen. I was looking forward to this; a day simply of flying the aeroplane, just as I had always dreamt.

Being a Senior Line Training Captain does not allow much actual flying. The more experience one has, the greater one's store of knowledge and skill, it seems the less flying one does. There is the paperwork, there are meetings and there is the simulator. God, I've had enough of simulators! Then, when I do get to fly, it is usually training, supervising or checking, so that one's concentration is on the subject pilot, watching his every move. Oh, I'm not saying that can't have its compensations. Most of the pilots are very capable and when you can help them take the next step, see them learn something new, you are rewarded with a sense of satisfaction few other jobs can offer. With some of them, though, I sit in silent torment, squirming, tense, willing him or her to wake up and do what to me is obvious. If only pilots under check would realize that it is far easier for the examiner to record a pass than a fail, they might be a little less tense themselves.

Given a day free from those responsibilities and starting at a gentleman's hour after a refreshing night's sleep, my old enthusiasm is back. I feel as I did in Berlin thirty years ago. Alicante, a simple out and back in good weather. The aircraft is already on the ground, serviceable and waiting. True, it's an Airbus, not the most poetic flying machine with its fly-by-wire and its computers, but I'm in command with a simple job to do. One of the great advantages of an airline pilot's life is that each day starts afresh; nothing is carried over from yesterday.

There is not much traffic at this time of day and I use the quieter roads anyway for a swift, easy drive. I grin at the security guards at the car park, but their response is muted. They're wary, still sensitive about the ribbing they got when their fine new guard dog was stolen.

In the crew room there is the usual friendly banter. I recognize old friends and new ones as I search for my pay slip in my locker and scan the latest roster. I'm aware of changing my mental outlook as I prepare to start work. Time for professionalism now. I must avoid all distractions and concentrate fully on the flight ahead. If my years of flying have taught me anything, it is never to assume things will happen as everyone

expects. One should be relaxed; it is a good thing to be outwardly uncon-
cerned, but a pilot's mind should be working all the time: Is the …? What
if …? And will …? This frame of mind was almost automatic now and
I assumed it like a comfortable old coat as I went to introduce myself to
the first officer.

I knew only that he had recently passed his final line check. This would
be one of his first trips on the line without supervision. He was a smart
young man in a new uniform, already sorting out the paperwork for the
flight at one of the expensive, sloping desks a thoughtful company had
provided for us. His fingers flew without hesitation over the computer
keys to print out the flight plan from the terminal. I approached him with
a smile, but our first meeting did not start auspiciously.

'Oh, hello,' he said. 'It's Keith, isn't it? Which leg would you like to fly?'

Now, I've never made a big thing about being called 'Captain'. It's a
courtesy title after all and it is only when a member of the crew speaks
to me in the presence of passengers or employees of other companies
that it is really appropriate. But meeting a Senior Captain for the first
time? I ruefully recalled my own generation's rebellion when we refused
to call the captains 'Sir'. No, it was the assumption that he would fly one
of the legs that rankled. It was company policy that pilots would share
the flying where possible, but the decision was the captain's and a first
officer had no right to expect it. Thirty years ago the response would
have been delivered with some force: 'It's Captain to you, sonny, and you
can assume I fly every leg until I say otherwise.'

I nearly answered, 'I'll fly both legs, thank you.' I would have been
fully justified since I hadn't handled the controls myself for weeks. But
that would have introduced an element of conflict that I wanted to avoid.
Nothing should mar my day of freedom. Instead I examined the flight
documents he had prepared and told him he would operate as handling
pilot on the outbound leg. I'll call him Joe. We introduced ourselves to
the rest of the crew and made our way out to the aircraft.

Refuelling had already started, cleaning was finished and the catering
was well under way. I looked through the technical log and watched Joe
start his checks before I did my walk around the aircraft. I enjoyed this
part of the day as much as any. The cabin crew were flirting with the
caterers, the engineer had everything under control, the passengers were
at the gate, ready to board and my optimistic mood was preserved.

The briefing Joe gave me for the departure was, I thought, rather
brusque. He recited it formulaically, as if he had learnt it by rote, rather
than really ensuring I knew what he was going to do. But, hey! It's a lovely
day and this is not a training flight. A colleague of mine used to wait until
they had lined up on the runway before inviting the first officer to fly the
leg. Then, if the hapless pilot moved to adjust his seat, would say, 'Oh,
but if you're not ready …' and do the take-off himself. That wouldn't do

today. The tenets of our new religion – Crew Resource Management – made it obligatory to maintain cordial relations at all times, lest someone be offended and sulk, and fail to do their job properly.

I was determined to enjoy a relaxing day. Joe probably didn't know I was a Training Captain and I didn't want to tell him. I longed for a straightforward, uncomplicated trip. It would also be an opportunity to see how our training department was working and to observe a final product in which, on this occasion, I myself had no part in shaping.

We were easily on time and the departure was textbook, with a direct clearance after passing 10,000ft that shaved a couple of minutes from our flight time. The weather was perfect and the air was silky smooth. We settled into the cruise before reaching the coast and Joe spoke to the passengers, pointing out the sights as we crossed the Channel. I would have waited until we changed frequency so that we could both listen to the clearance given by the French controller, but no matter. His technique on the PA was better than mine and he seemed to be operating the aircraft in the approved company manner.

The Flight Management Computer system on this aircraft was an advanced piece of equipment, but it had its traps just the same. There is always the possibility of errors going unnoticed. Joe used it fluently, casually perhaps, but as far as I could see, accurately.

We didn't talk. The familiar route unfolded below us. The purser brought us coffee and I savoured the flight. When everything is going well and the weather is fine, it always seemed incredible that I was being paid to do this. When we crossed the Pyrenees I could see the eastern coastline of Spain down as far as Valencia and the curve of the cape that pointed towards the Balearic Islands and I began to calculate how I would plan the descent, if I were flying the leg myself.

I got the latest weather report and passed it to Joe so that he could select the details of the appropriate runway and instrument approach procedure from the database, though it was unlikely we would need it today. Even if we couldn't make a continuous visual descent to the west of the airfield with a sweeping turn onto finals for runway 11, we would surely be cleared overhead to make a visual, right-handed, descending turn to final approach. I made the usual mental calculation to determine exactly when I would want to start descent: three point three times the flight level, minus a bit for a tailwind, plus a bit for the weight, and aim for a compromise between a straight-in route and the normal one that passed overhead the field at the procedural safety height of 7,000ft. I decided that if I could disconnect the autopilot and ease the aircraft into a descent at 78 miles, I would be able to manage our existing energy – whichever route was approved – so that the engines could stay at idle power until 1,000ft on finals. We should achieve maximum efficiency: minimum noise; near minimum time; and minimum fuel burn.

I waited to see what figure Joe would come up with. He had had his head down over the centre console, tapping keys for some time. The Multifunction Control and Display Unit, affectionately known as the MacDoo, was our interface with the FMC and it was a well-worn joke that young co-pilots could type on it at 200 words a minute, while us older pilots stabbed at it slowly with thick fingers. So what was he doing all this time?

Leaning forward slightly, I could see. The screen showed he had created a series of waypoints before and after the field, each with speed and height constraints. To my amused disbelief, I realized that he was constructing a detailed profile that would enable the aircraft to fly a complete visual circuit automatically. Why? Pilot-constructed waypoints below safety height were not Standard Operating Procedure – expressly forbidden in fact, because of the high possibility of error – but everyone used them occasionally. A judiciously inserted waypoint could make the electronic route match up more closely with what might actually happen, making the distance to run and the crossing altitudes at other points more realistic. Provided you did not rely on them for navigation below safety height, or were fully visual when you did so, and that the position of the aircraft was accurately monitored at all times, there was no danger. But to build a complete circuit into the machine? Perhaps he felt he needed to practise entering data into the MacDoo? I reckon it took him about thirty minutes, during which time he hadn't once looked out of the window. Eventually he sat back and folded his arms, looking rather pleased with himself.

The controller passed our descent clearance. We warned the cabin crew and did our checks. Joe sat motionless. My calculated descent point came and went. I said nothing. I toyed with the idea of asking the controller for a direct route to join left hand for the runway, which might have saved us two or three minutes and would certainly have rendered Joe's programming useless. It would have been amusing to see how he would react to that. But no, let him do it his way.

The sudden pitch down of the nose and reduction in power when the aircraft responded to the computer's command to descend startled me even though I was waiting for it. I don't know what the passengers made of it. A friend, when he first encountered this phenomenon, had remarked that the aeroplane seemed to 'fall out of his arse'.

Still, the Airbus followed the profile faithfully. Since we hadn't asked for anything else, the controller cleared us to pass overhead the field at 7,000ft and to descend visually thereafter in a right-hand pattern for runway 11. The Airbus did as it had been programmed, reducing the speed to 250 knots at 10,000ft and again towards 210 knots as we neared the field.

Joe called for the first stage of flap at the appropriate time and the speed continued to reduce, so that, directly overhead the field, he was able to call for the next stage of flap and for the gear to be lowered. We could see forever. There was no other traffic and we were free to position ourselves as we liked from here. It was a perfect opportunity for Joe to hand-fly the aeroplane and polish up his handling skills. Even the Airbus could deliver some satisfaction for good judgement in these circumstances.

But Joe sat motionless. The power fluctuated once or twice with the configuration change, then abruptly fell to idle as the aircraft started to turn and pitched steeply down in descent to the circuit height of 1,500ft. It was all reasonably accurate, if not very smooth. My attention was divided among the changing view outside, the instruments and Joe, who, with checks complete, had now crossed his legs as well as his arms and pressed his nose to his side window, looking down at the airfield like some matron on a coach tour. He didn't move as the rate of descent increased and we plunged towards the arid landscape.

With 500ft to go to level off and a descent rate approaching 2,000ft a minute I was moved, at last, to speak. 'Er … Would you mind just placing your hands and feet on the controls,' I asked mildly.

Joe turned and looked at me with an expression of absolutely horrified incomprehension. 'What for?' he demanded.

The aircraft pitched up again and, after a delay, the power was restored, so that we levelled at circuit height and the speed settled at the correct value. It was technically impressive, but what machines can't do is anticipate; they can only react to information as it is provided, so they are never as smooth as a human pilot would be and one can never be sure they are going to do exactly what is required until it is too late to achieve the original intention. It made me nervous, but clearly Joe had greater faith.

He had reluctantly assumed a position from which he could at least reach the controls and he watched smugly, clearly regarding the idea that something might go wrong as absurd, as the aircraft flew round the circuit and positioned itself on finals. He called for more flap until we were settled on the glide path in landing configuration. We were cleared to land. At 500ft Joe clicked the autopilot disconnect button and, since the aircraft was stabilized, had only to initiate the flare to achieve a smooth landing.

We taxied in, shut down the engines and the passengers disembarked. We didn't speak. The gulf was too wide. I was in a state of shock. I didn't criticize Joe. I didn't try to influence the way in which he operated the aircraft at all, which was not like me. I couldn't think of anything to say to this young man who clearly was so different in temperament, ambition and values to me. And it was not just him. He had only recently completed the company's conversion and line training course and passed all of his competency checks, so perhaps they all flew like this now. Perhaps they were right? The answer now was just to trust the machine and all would be well. Yet if that were true, all the lore and cunning and experience I had accumulated, everything I had ever learnt about flying, was a waste of time.

I flew the aircraft back to Manchester, hand-flying the approach and landing there. I didn't do it particularly well and there was little satisfaction to be won from the fly-by-wire side stick that communicated only the strength of its centring spring. So during the drive home and when I stopped for a pint at 'The Flying Horse', I did not enjoy the satisfying tiredness of a job well done. Instead, I felt unsettled and old and out of touch. I brooded on the possibility that the knowledge, skill and attitudes by which airline pilots had for years kept themselves, and therefore their passengers, safe were now obsolete. I had no wish to go back to propellers, poor performance or primitive navigation, but if we assumed that the automation was infallible, that it would always do exactly what we expected it to do, then what were we there for?

The evening light was taking on that dreamy golden quality as I relaxed and I began to hear birdsong above the noise of the traffic on the road outside. I was wise enough to know that I would feel differently the next day. By then, I would have put today's experience into context and I would regain confidence in my priorities. But I also recognized the possibility of some fundamental cultural change. Until now, everyone I had ever flown with had been in love with flying. Every pilot, whatever their personality, ability or background, was dedicated to learning everything they could about the business – the art – of flying. If Joe was an outlier, a one-off, we could deal with him. But if his attitudes were typical of a new generation, then flying – and training – would never be quite the same again.

CHAPTER 17

Concerned Observer

In the early hours of 1 June 2009, Air France Flight 447 was crossing the South Atlantic. The flight from Rio de Janeiro to Paris is a long one. The pilots had enjoyed a few days' rest, but they would have been conscious of the insidious effects of fatigue. Each would have had his own strategy for coping with being awake and working for a long stint. The over-water stretch should be dark and quiet, easy, even dull. The captain went aft to sleep.

The two pilots left in charge were well qualified and had completed the relevant training courses provided by the airline. The only challenge was an old and well-known one. Over this particular stretch of water a conflict of air masses has taken place for thousands of years. It is known to sailors and flyers the world over as the Inter-Tropical Convergence Zone (ITCZ). It is a region of cloud, thunderstorms and turbulence, but Flight 447 was a fine example of modern technology. The A330 is a long-range wide-body airliner incorporating all the automatic systems that have propelled the European consortium into the forefront of international aerospace constructors. What could possibly go wrong? Yet nothing was heard from them again. The aircraft disappeared and the public was intrigued by press speculation until, after two years of searching and research, the answers started to appear.

The change in technology during my airline flying career was impressive. Whilst only about twenty years old, the Viking freighter was already obsolete in 1967. Compared to the Airbus A320 I flew twenty-eight years later, it was primitive, archaic even. This rapid development of the airliner changed the job. We still came together as a crew, we still tried to get the passengers or the freight where it was supposed to be, on schedule, safely and efficiently, we still competed with the weather and we still fought fatigue, but the equipment with which we did it was dramatically different.

The introduction of this technology coincided with the rapid expansion of the airline business. The number of passengers carried worldwide grew, and continues to grow, steadily at between 4 and 6 per cent per annum. Thus, in my time, from 1967 to 1998, airlines grew by a factor of more than four, yet the accident rate – the number of fatal crashes per million departures – fell by 60 per cent. Knowledge and the adoption of best practice played their part, but the preferred weapon in the fight against accidents was technology and it was highly successful.

If we look at the accident statistics today, we find not only that the rate of improvement is slowing, but that the type of accidents that occur has changed. Aircraft used to crash because their crews did not know where they were, or because they flew into weather beyond the capabilities of their equipment. Military or terrorist action appears to be more common now, but, as with the disturbing phenomenon of deliberate crashes by pilots committing suicide and mass murder, they may just be more readily identifiable with improved investigation techniques. More surprising, and of more interest to me, are events where the technology designed to make flying safer contributes itself to a new type of accident.

The 'technology-induced accident' first came to prominence after the introduction of the Airbus A320 aircraft. An Air France Airbus A320 crashed in Mulhouse in 1988, followed by an Indian Airlines A320 in Bangalore (now Bengaluru) in 1990 and an Air Inter A320 near Strasbourg in 1992. These three crashes in less than four years occurred in very different circumstances, but there was a disturbing link. In each case, experienced, competent, well-trained crew members had failed to understand the full implications of the systems they were using. The selections they made on their control panels produced results very different from what they expected.

The response of the regulatory authorities and manufacturer was rapid by historical standards. Control panels were redesigned and procedures modified, but again, the primary reaction was technological. Terrain warning systems were enhanced and a culture grew that emphasized the use of the autopilot in all circumstances. Crews were learning more about the use of automation too, and the chances of a catastrophic result following a simple error receded. But the danger had not gone away. Accidents in the last twenty years or so have revealed a related but more subtle pattern.

The loss of AF 447 over the South Atlantic in June 2009 caught everyone's attention. Interest was intensified by mystery because it took two years to locate the wreckage and retrieve the flight recorders. Ice had blocked the pitot tubes that measure the airspeed, even though they are heated and, recognizing that it was not receiving reliable information, the autopilot disconnected. This is not a new problem. It has happened before and the pilots read a notice warning them of the phenomenon before they left their base in Paris, a week before. It is annoying, it should not happen, but neither should it constitute a great difficulty. There are other ways of measuring the speed of the aircraft. True speed can be read from the GPS and anyway, the aircraft is trimmed for a particular airspeed and if the attitude and power setting are unchanged, the aircraft will continue its flight with only minor excursions from the previous flight level and heading.

But that is not what happened. It will never be possible to be certain. We cannot know, for instance, exactly what the pilots saw on their instruments – the displays are not recorded – but the investigators' conclusions were shocking.[11] It appears that, had the pilots done nothing, just sat on their hands until the aircraft emerged from cloud, it is likely that its natural stability would have kept them safe. Instead, a nose-up input was applied to one of the control sticks and the aircraft climbed until it stalled and then fell vertically into the ocean.

There had been and would be other strange accidents. In August 2000, a Gulf Air A320 crashed while trying to land at Bahrain. In January 2004, a Boeing 737 belonging to Flash Airlines crashed into the Red Sea near Sharm el-Sheikh. In May 2003, an Armavia Airbus A320 crashed into the Black Sea near Sochi. In February 2009, a Turkish Boeing 737 crashed on the approach to Amsterdam. Then there were the Ethiopian Airlines Boeing 737 on take-off from Beirut in January 2010, an Afriqiyah Airways Airbus 330 in Tripoli in May of the same year, an Asian Airlines Boeing 777 at San Francisco in 2013, and an AirAsia A320 flying over the Java sea in December 2014.

Each of these tragedies was unique with its own distinctive chain of causal factors, but they shared some common features. In each case it appears that the pilots were disorientated. Either they misused their automatic control systems, or, having taken manual control, they lacked the capacity to recover from the situation in which they found themselves.

Aircraft accident investigators are not in the blame game. They seek understanding of what happened so that a recurrence can be avoided. So, did the problems in these tragic events arise as a result of the failure of the pilots, or of the aeroplane, or of some procedural anomaly? Let's be clear; this is an airworthiness issue. All of the automatic equipment fitted to aircraft is certified on the assumption that, should it fail, the pilots will be able to take over and fly the aircraft to a safe landing. If they are not able to do that for any reason, then the aircraft is not airworthy.

People far better qualified than me are working hard to address these problems. Engineers, academics, journalists, safety and training specialists recognize that, as automation on the flight deck has increased, some areas of pilot competence and skill have proved to be inadequate. At the same time, the automotive industry is financing research into phenomena associated with the automation in cars. Some of their findings reinforce the idea that there are particular dangers in partial automation and in the switch from fully automatic to manual control. These are modes of operation where weaknesses in human performance have been exposed.

It is important to keep things in perspective: the large majority of pilots are dedicated to their profession and are highly competent. The low accident rate confirms this. But it is also clear that all is not well. The problem is one that will impinge on other industries as the use of automatic systems increases. It is time to take stock, to reflect on the historical trends and to challenge our philosophy for the design of such equipment in the future.

Two obvious answers spring to mind. We could either do away with pilots altogether – make the airliner (or the car) fully automatic and autonomous – or we could extend and improve pilot training. The first is attractive economically and, I believe, will come to pass, initially in cargo aircraft, in the near future. We have the technology. I believe the oft-quoted objection to pilotless airliners – that the travelling public would not accept it – to be erroneous. In the days when passengers were encouraged to visit the flight deck, young, tech-savvy students, born to calculators and video games, were horrified to learn that we could disconnect the autopilot and hand-fly the aeroplane. If the flight is reliable and cheaper, people will want it. The accident rate would almost certainly improve, given that many researchers find that human error is a causal factor in 60 per cent or more of all airline accidents. Full automation will not be applicable to all airline operations, however. There are problems too, not least with legal considerations of liability. Someone would still have to be in control. If there is a medical emergency on board, who decides whether the aircraft should divert to another airfield? Can decisions such as this be handled by the cabin crew, or should they be handed to ground controllers? Wouldn't it be better to have a highly trained and experienced aviator actually on board, on the spot, to make that sort of call?

The second obvious option, keeping the pilots but spending much more on their initial and continuation training, has the appeal of continuity. Costs would increase, but safety always comes at a price. It's a judgement call where, it would seem, the investment so far has been insufficient. As the old saying goes: if you think safety is expensive, try having an accident.

Before we take sides in this argument, it would be wise to do some more fundamental research. However we configure the control systems of air travel, it is going to involve some combination of human and technological input. Let's forget how we got here for a moment and figure out how we would address the issues now, if we were starting from scratch. Surely we would want to assess the benefits and drawbacks of the various types of technology available to us. It would also make sense to evaluate situations in which the trained human can offer benefits that the machines can't replicate.

We have enough experience of computers in every walk of life to understand that they can be more reliable, more accurate and more cost-effective for almost any simple, repetitive function. They don't get bored, they don't get tired and they don't need holidays or sick pay. The 'Simple and Repetitive' description covers most of the physical actions required to operate a flying machine. Humans, on the other hand, can contribute something extra. Humans are good at anticipation. They can assess a developing situation and quickly design a flexible response that may be outside the normal operating parameters. The difficulty lies in maintaining their interest, motivation and skill at a level that inspires their ingenuity. We know that humans are poor at monitoring automatic systems; they should not be expected to do it, but that is what they do now.

While training and assessing pilots in the simulator and in the air, I have noticed that the best captains or potential captains are the ones who are smooth and accurate when hand-flying on instruments. It is about situational awareness, about making decisions, constructing a plan and monitoring the plan in operation. Good captains are the ones who are most aware of everything that happens to their aircraft. Not only are they conscious of every change in its movement through space, they are aware of the changing environment and even what is going on in the cabin behind them. In short, they have the mental capacity to observe, plan and anticipate even while they are hand-flying under challenging conditions. They can think AND fly at the same time.

Another crucial task on the flight deck is monitoring. To do it well, the pilot monitoring the progress of the flight, whether hand-flown by the other pilot or under the control of the computers, must himself be good at instrument flying. Ideally, he too must be thinking ahead, anticipating, at least as fully engaged and conscientious as if he himself were flying.

The process of learning to hand-fly a large aircraft accurately, on instruments, with enough spare mental capacity to be able to consider a multitude of other things and also to make rational decisions, does not come easily. At the moment, Commercial Pilot courses consist of about one year of full-time academic studies to cover the theory and up to 200 or 250 total flying hours, some of which are in a simulator. It is not enough. The performance standard of the graduates may be high on completion of the course, but the skill is recently acquired and will need to be reinforced over time before it is second nature, that is, before it becomes a reliable long-term part of the pilot's skill set. On the line, there is nowadays no opportunity to develop and reinforce that skill. The only hand-flying the new pilot will do in the vital two or three years after his initial training will consist of an hour or so every six months in the simulator. That again is nowhere near enough.

There is no substitute for flying a real aeroplane either. Simulators today are good and will get better, but there are aspects of real flying that they can never reproduce. The new class of accidents has prompted researchers to identify phenomena such as the 'Somatogravic Illusion', an acceleration-induced form of spacial disorientation, which we older pilots used to call 'the leans'. The effect cannot be reproduced in simulators and today's pilots will probably only learn about it the classroom. Until they experience it for themselves, in the air, they can have no real appreciation of its power or its insidious nature, nor can they train themselves to combat it.

The more enlightened airlines are trying to address such shortcomings by putting pilots through a course of training to recover an aircraft from unusual attitudes. That is to be commended, but it is not the real answer. Going on a short course that involves a couple of hours' flying in a manoeuvrable aircraft with an instructor will be good fun, but what the pilot really needs is to learn basic aerobatics at an early stage in his career and to go off solo to practise them. The researchers also identify something they call the 'Startle Factor'. They suggest that some pilots encountering unexpected failures or upsets do not respond according to their training because they are shocked into immobility. The first time a student pilot falls off the top of a solo loop into a spin will not only provide him with a memorable introduction to the 'Startle Factor', it will also introduce that well-known motivation-enhancer: fear, another thing the simulator can't reproduce.

Since I stopped flying, I've studied these problems and reflected at length on possible answers. I believe the contribution that well-trained pilots can make to the safety of airline flying over the near- and medium-term future is too valuable to be lost. Their skills, anticipation and resourcefulness are invaluable during unplanned events and emergencies. The most recent high-profile example of this was provided by Captain Sullenberger, who was in charge of the US Airways Airbus Flight 1549 out of LaGuardia, New York, in January 2009 when both engines failed. It was his experience, skill, courage and decisiveness, along with the professionalism of his crew, that led to the survival of all on board. Pilots are certainly not all Sullenbergers, but, properly prepared, they remain the best resource available when everything else has failed. They act as the team's goalkeeper. Furthermore they are traditionally and legally seen as the ultimate authority on the aircraft. They are uniquely positioned to provide leadership focus and decision-making.

Yes, pilots are expensive and they are fallible. To reduce that fallibility even a little bit is going to cost a lot of money and a lot of effort, but do we want to improve safety or not? Initial training should be extended to include much more actual hands-on instrument flying. It should include basic aerobatics and plenty of solo flying. Of even more importance is the way they fly the aircraft on the line – they should hand-fly most departures and arrivals. Only when the skills they have learnt in basic training are reinforced by constant repetition over a substantial period of time will most pilots develop the reliable skill set that the aircraft airworthiness standards demand of them.

Modern autopilots, FMS and automatic systems are better suited to the monitoring task. Why not reconfigure the operating procedures so that the human pilots do the flying – the interesting bits, anyway, the bits they need to be good at – and the machines and computers do the monitoring? Wouldn't that be putting each in the roles for which they are best suited? This approach might be applied to cars too. Provide a choice between fully automatic operation and manual control, monitored by the automatic systems.

I see the flight being planned and entered into the Flight Management Computer in exactly the same way it is now. The aircraft could still be operated as it is now, but, for a substantial number of departures and arrivals, the pilot would hand-fly the aircraft while the FMS operated the autopilot in a reserve mode and monitored his performance. The computers would be programmed to intervene if the aircraft were to go outside acceptable parameters. That intervention might involve a visual or audio warning for short-term exceedances. More serious excursions would trigger detailed recovery prompts, or, if the situation became dangerous, the computers could assume control – as they do now to limit speed and attitude on fly-by-wire aircraft.

This would keep the pilots current in hand-flying the real aircraft safely, without the need for lengthy, unproductive simulator time. The pilots' performances could be monitored and recorded so that any errors or undesirable tendencies they developed would be noted and could be addressed at the six-monthly competency check. It would become a matter of pride to complete a series of flights without any intervention of the automatic monitoring system and make redundant many of the repetitive exercises currently done in the simulator. Simulator sessions would become more relevant, more beneficial and more interesting.

Used in its monitoring function, the Flight Management Computer could be an ideal development ground for the application of Artificial Intelligence. If computers can learn to predict reliably, they may one day do the job of a really good co-pilot, on a really good day, all day, every day and night.

The pilots would be flying a machine equipped with advanced head-up displays to show infra-red and computer-generated images of the outside world, as well as instrument information on an expanded scale enabling very accurate hand-flying. The future airliner would be a pilot's dream. With aerodynamic 'feel' applied to the flight controls, trimming done manually rather than automatically and throttles that move when the power alters, the machine would display classical handling characteristics. Perhaps the air-conditioning noise could be suppressed and aerodynamic and engine sounds enhanced so that the crew are provided with the full range of relevant natural audio, visual and tactile sensations. Pilots could yet find themselves regularly hand-flying nicely handling aeroplanes with sensual feedback on approaches to touchdown in zero-visibility conditions while being monitored closely by unsleeping automatics. That should improve the pilots' skill and their motivation. It would raise their game. It might even be fun.

CHAPTER 18

Post-Flight

Suddenly, it was all over. After three years on the Airbus A320, I was back on my beloved Boeing for a short stint that was to end, though I didn't know it then, with my last flight. I gave away my last leg and as I went 'ashore' for the final time, I was still trying to pass on my thoughts on how best to fly the Boeing 757 to a new co-pilot.

The first question people ask when they learn that I have retired from airline flying is: 'Do you miss it?' The second, rather tactless question, considering that an airline pilot's job is to avoid such things, is: 'Did you have any dangerous moments?' I usually reply to both in the negative, muttering about irregular, unsocial hours, impersonal hotel rooms and airline food.

There were things I expected to miss. There were the training moments: the times when someone learnt a new lesson or understood a new truth and moved on to the next stage of his or her flying development; when 'the penny dropped', as we used to say. It was a privilege to be present and to share in such moments. There was the sense of adventure when we set off over new routes to different places and other times when I caught a glimpse of the earth or its atmosphere in full, unexpected beauty. There were the times, descending in smooth air at the end of a successful day, when, against the odds, we had completed the trip on schedule and pleased everybody and could enjoy the satisfaction of a job well done. There was the banter over a pint with like-minded people and, most of all, the company of those people. There were the moments when a group of very different characters with different backgrounds and circumstances had come together, bleary-eyed at some unreasonable time of day or night, started the routines for which they had been highly trained and within minutes had formed themselves into a disciplined, effective crew. These moments held a special resonance for me.

But did I miss these things? No. There is no question that I was remarkably fortunate in my career, but I had known that all along. I had been fully conscious of my luck, of what a privilege I had been granted to earn my living – a good living – doing the job I loved. We tend to miss things, to wish for their return, when we feel we have not fully appreciated them. I can honestly say I was always conscious of my luck and fully appreciated every moment of my flying career. I made mistakes, of course, and there are many things I would have done differently, given the opportunity. But I know that, presented with the same information in the same situation, I would inevitably react in the same way again. I can move on without regret.

For the next generation of airline pilots, many of the things that I remember with special pleasure will still exist, as they must have existed in previous times for Captain Olley or Ernest Gann. But I sometimes wonder how much of it is the love of flying and how much the joy of simply being alive and active in the world. Wonderful experiences are not exclusive to airline flying. The great pleasure of making a large, heavy airliner do exactly what you want it to do is perhaps unique, but I know myself that landing a biplane on grass or drifting out into the centre of a lake in the early morning to take off in a small float plane can be magical experiences. So can waking up in a sailing cruiser at dawn in an English south coast anchorage, or an early morning ride on a motorbike, or even just a walk after dinner beside a lake in Cumbria. Other people get satisfaction from climbing mountains, running a large company or teaching children.

It is difficult to identify what it is that is special about flying and about aeroplanes. A large number of people are interested in, or fascinated by, aviation in its various forms and there is something special too about the people who engage in it. There is a large market in flying memorabilia and history, which gives rise to museums, books and films, although most of it is concerned with military aviation.

The curious lack of literature surrounding airline flying helps to ensure that there can be no lasting legacy for an airline pilot. The work appears to be transient and without an end product. Ultimately, skill is measured in the ability to avoid trouble. But at least I can answer truthfully, if anyone asks me what job satisfaction I was able to draw from my career. I can sum it up as: Fun! Unfortunately, when I consider what the experience will be like for the next generation, that concept appears to be under threat. There is something of the killjoy about technology, something serious and grown-up that cannot admit to fun.

Hope lies in uncertainty. One thing history should have taught the human race is that we are hopeless at predicting the future. Technology has a habit of misbehaving; it never does quite what it was intended to do. Surprise is a feature of life. The original pioneers of flying – the Wrights, Blériot, A.V. Roe and the others – thought of many applications for their revolutionary form of transport, but none would have predicted that in the future, over half of all the passengers carried the world over would be holidaymakers.

Even when the vast market for carrying northern European holidaymakers to the south was recognized and developed, a new generation of entrepreneurs was devising a new business model, matching the power of the Internet with the increasing sophistication and independence of the customer and offering a better deal. The regular, scheduled service they offered was basic even in comparison with the inclusive tour specialists: no in-flight meals and no guarantees. All of the customer care that the passengers no longer felt they needed was stripped out. The entrepreneurs cut operating costs by increasing productivity still further. Employment contracts were pruned hard. Pilots, cabin crew, engineers and operations staff were offered good basic salaries, but without extras such as pensions, expenses and insurance. Some employees even had to pay for their own uniforms and the low-cost airline was born.

The philosophy that spawned the low-cost airline relies heavily on the technical transformation of the business of airline flying. For this ruthless, customer-orientated approach to work, airliners must operate reliably and predictably. There is no room at all for individual flair or interpretation.

Many traditional airlines were caught out by the change. The trauma of the attack on the World Trade Center in New York sparked a recession that felled more. I remember hearing with a shock that one of the icons of the world airline system had crumbled: if Swissair has gone bust, no one is safe.

It is easy to look back now and identify three crucial points at which technology transformed the job of the airline pilot. I don't mean the incremental changes that made things safer, things like improved performance, better de-icing or improved navigation, though they certainly changed things. I discussed FMS and GPS navigation once with Alex, who, like me, had progressed from the Viking to the Herald, the BAC 1-11 and Boeing 737 before retiring, and he acknowledged, 'Ay, it must be amazing: to know where you are … all the time.'

No, I refer to innovations that demonstrated a change in attitude towards the pilot and a readjustment of the philosophy that justified his existence. The first was mechanical: the autopilot. Simple affairs at first, like the Sperry device we had on the Viking, they quickly developed into sophisticated ways of steering aeroplanes more accurately and more reliably than human pilots could. The next was an idea adopted to satisfy the regulatory authorities: autoland. The human pilot can't land in fog, the scientists said. Lack of peripheral vision means that the job has to be done by the autopilot. (Try telling Speedy that; he would have curled his lip and dismissed you with an oath.) It was decreed that, for reliable operations in low visibility, the autopilot must land the aircraft. So we learnt to watch it happen, ready to intervene and to 'go-around' if anything went wrong. And ready to take the blame.

The third crucial innovation was procedural and is still not universal. It came without fanfare and the public hardly heard of it. Air traffic density is too high for pilots to cope with while flying manually, safety experts said; they make too many mistakes. Some airline managers agreed and orders were issued. The autopilot must be used at all times and pilots are forbidden to hand-fly the aircraft on the line.

We did not comprehend the full significance of these changes when they arrived. One needs some time, a little distance and some leisure to see the bigger picture. The lesson to be learnt from reflecting on all this now is how technology tends to be focused on the specifics and often ignores the overall culture. Remember, as noted earlier, ALL of the technical advances incorporated into commercial aircraft have been certified on the understanding that, should they fail, professional pilots will be there to take over and land the aircraft safely. If the pilots are not capable of doing that, it must follow that the aircraft is not airworthy.

In the practical application of this technology, the contribution of the pilots has been neglected. Not enough thought has been given to the knowledge, skills and attitudes that they need to develop and need in particular to maintain. Consequently, some of the aircraft flying today cannot be considered airworthy.

There was one last incident during my short final stint on the Boeing 757 that illustrated some of the changes I had seen in thirty-one years of airline flying. We carried a relatively new piece of equipment known as Traffic Collision Avoidance System (TCAS), which is designed to give warning of conflicting traffic. It provides visual indications on the aircraft instruments and computer-generated voice warnings and commands to help pilots avoid collisions. Like any other technological answer, it has its limitations, but on the whole it seemed to work well.

Southbound over Faro on Portugal's south coast, en route for the Canary Islands, we were relaxed and enjoying the delightful weather. This was a favourite trip. It was usually preceded by a sensible rest period, had a civilized departure time and, though a long day, was generally operated on schedule without hassle. The Portuguese controllers in Lisbon were clear and professional with a friendly, co-operative attitude.

Three things suddenly happened at exactly the same time: I noticed the contrail just above the horizon ahead of us; the computer-generated voice of the TCAS sounded 'Traffic! Traffic!'; and the controller's voice spoke urgently in my earphones: 'Descend immediately! Descend immediately to flight level three two zero!'

It took only a second for me to select a descent on the autopilot and to drift down the thousand feet required. The other pilot on the flight deck responded to the controller's call and acknowledged the urgency, reassuring him that we were already descending.

Before our aircraft began to level, the traffic, a DC-8 jet freighter, passed directly overhead our flight deck. There was a short silence before the controller called us again.

'Very sorry, gentlemen,' he said, clearly shaken. 'That was a late handover from Casablanca and he was at a non-standard level. How far off your track was he?'

I smiled as I replied: 'He passed exactly overhead,' I said.

And there was another, longer silence until he transmitted the one, drawn-out and rather unprofessional word: 'Jeeeezus!'

The incident had obviously alarmed the controller more than us. After all, the systems had worked perfectly. An error had been made, but our lookout, the TCAS and the controller's action had all acted exactly as they should to avoid a disaster. We thanked him for his help and cruised serenely on our way. It was a curiously uplifting experience and raised our spirits. We felt it had been a job well done, another day and another dollar.

For some reason it made me think of other encounters in bygone times. Once, in the Viking with Alex as handling pilot but engrossed in writing his book, I spotted an unusual object in the distance. It appeared to be about the same height as us, 5,000ft, but I couldn't identify it at first and risked his sarcasm by drawing his attention to it.

'Balloon!' he announced confidently and, to my amazement, stowed his writing gear and moved the great lever that disconnected the autopilot. Without any thought of notifying Air Traffic Control, he turned out of the airway and flew towards the apparition. Sure enough, the wonderful sight of a near-spherical gasbag with two figures in the suspended basket soon filled our windscreen. We circled it twice and waved. One of the aeronauts waved back with what looked like a bottle of Champagne, before we rejoined the airway and continued our flight to Berlin.

Just like Captain Olley, all of us think we are witnessing the peak of technological achievement, only to discover we haven't seen the half of it. I hope pilots of today and tomorrow will look back and say, as I do: 'I had the best of it!'

References

[1] Olley, Captain Gordon P. (1934), *A Million Miles in the Air* (London: Hodder & Stoughton).

[2] Gann, E.K. (1961), *Fate is the Hunter* (New York: Simon & Schuster).

[3] *Ibid.*

[4] Gann, *op. cit.* in note 2.

[5] Cobham, Sir Alan J. (1978) (ed. by Christopher Derrick), *A Time to Fly* (London: Shepheard-Walwyn).

[6] Golding, W. (1989), *Fire Down Below* (London: Faber and Faber).

[7] Olley, *op cit.* in note 1.

[8] Gann, E.K. (1958), *The Trouble with Lazy Ethel* (New York: W. Sloan Associates).

[9] Kundera, Milan (1996) *Slowness*, translated by Linda Asher (New York: HarperCollins).

[10] UK Air Accidents Investigation Branch (2007) *Formal Report on Airbus A340-642, G-VATL en-route from Hong Kong to London Heathrow on 8th February 2005* (London: Department for Transport).

[11] Bureau d'Enquêtes et d'Analyses pour la sécurité de l'aviation civile (2012), *Final Report on the accident on 1 June 2009 to the Airbus A330-203 registered F-GZCP* (Paris: BEA).

Glossary

ADF   Automatic Direction Finder (aka Radio Compass). An MF radio receiver providing bearings to the station relative to the centre line of the aircraft or to magnetic north.

ATPL   Airline Transport Pilot's Licence.

Autothrottle Automatic thrust regulation slaved to selected airspeed.

CAA   Civil Aviation Authority, the regulatory authority for aviation in the UK.

CRM   Crew Resource Management.

Dead Reckoning Deduced Navigation. Position calculation by applying assumed wind to the heading and airspeed vector.

DME   Distance Measuring Equipment. A VHF radio transponder reading in miles from the station.

Doppler   The change in frequency of a radar signal when reflected from a target moving relative to the source.

FAA   Federal Aviation Agency, the regulatory authority for aviation in the USA.

Flight Director An instrument, usually incorporated into the artificial horizon, providing computed commands to achieve the selected flight path.

FLIR   Forward Looking Infra-Red imaging device.

FMS   Flight Management System. A computer system that integrates navigation, performance and flight-planning information for presentation to the pilots or direct to the autopilot.

GPS   Global Positioning System.

ILS   Instrument Landing System. A VHF approach aid using a horizontal radial beam aligned with the runway and a vertical beam to provide glide-path guidance.

INS   Inertial Navigation System. Gyro and accelerometer based navigation system comparing accelerations and attitude against time to measure displacement from the departure point.

Link Trainer An early electro-mechanical flight simulator.

MOR   Mandatory Occurrence Report. Civil aviation scheme to provide for the analysis of safety-related incidents.

NDB   Non-Directional Beacon. A ground-based medium-frequency radio transmitter provided to enable navigation by the use of a radio compass or ADF equipment in the aircraft.

NOTAMS   Notices To Airmen containing information on the availability and serviceability of airfields and other aviation resources.

Phugoid   An oscillation of an aircraft in pitch. If an aircraft is disturbed from level flight, it will follow a wave-like motion, nose up, nose down, nose up again. These excursions may be stable, so that the motion decays back to the original condition, or (rarely) unstable, where the excursions increase, potentially to a dangerous level.

Radio Compass   *See* ADF.

Slip   A rest period at an intermediate station on a long-haul route. The aircraft continues the flight with a new crew while the resting crew takes over the next aircraft to be operated through that station.

SOPs   Standard Operating Procedures.

TCAS   Traffic Collision Avoidance System. Computerized transponder system that provides visual and aural warnings of similarly equipped aircraft in the vicinity of the receiver.

VOR   VHF radio navigation beacon radiating 360-degree tracks. An instrument in the aircraft gives direction to or from the station and indicates left/right deviations from the selected track.

Index